Secret[illegible] Energy

Achieving Health, Happiness, and Success
By Increasing, Focusing, Directing and Fully Self-Empowering
Your Physical, Mental, Emotional and Spiritual Energies

Barbara Gray

Author

Energy Management, How To Increase Your Positive Energy Levels

Copyright

Publishing information

First Trade Paperback Edition, 2004

Starlight Productions

First published 2004

Disclaimer

This book is not intended to be a substitute for the services of health care professionals. Neither the author nor publisher is responsible for any consequences incurred by those employing the remedies or treatments reported herein. Any application of the material set forth in the following pages is at the reader's discretion and his/her sole responsibility.

Printed in the United States of America

Contents

Preface
Acknowledgements
Principles of Energy

1. What Is Energy 1-22
2. Subtle Energy 23-34
3. Properties Of Subtle Energy 35-42
4. We Are Pure Energy 43-58
5. Energy Is Moveable And Transferable 59-80
6. History of Subtle Energies And Human Energy Research 81-84
7. What Is "Mind"? Where Is "Mind"? 85-104
8. Subtle Energy Called The Aura 105-121
9. Meridians And Acupressure Points 135-154
10. Health And Energy 155-174
11. The Living Matrix And Posture 175-192
12. Human Performance And Energy 193-232

Appendix 233

Glossary 234-235

Suggested Reading, Institutes, Organizations 236-238

Index 239-242

Preface

A mind stretched by a new idea can never go back to its original dimensions. Oliver Wendell Holmes

Why You Should Put Your Time And Energy Into Reading/Studying This Book

For most of us learning about subtle energy will be a totally new idea, though subtle energy was created in the beginning of time. Or more specifically, it was from subtle energy that all physical reality and matter was created. Why haven't you heard about subtle energy? Because scientists couldn't measure it; therefore, they couldn't name it. With this kind of reasoning we can see that scientists believe in gravity only because they can measure it. Don't you think they have felt being out of energy or having high energy? We measure energy with our bodies and the new technological devices. You, on the other hand, know that energy moves through your body. Some days you say, "all my energy is spent." Others days you say, "I'm high energy." You know that your energy can travel to other places and to other people's energy fields. We may also define subtle energy as our Spirit, that which enlightens us. Most of us believe that this subtle energy called Spirit is eternal–with no beginning and no end. There is a lot of disagreement about what happens to this Spirit. This book, however, is only going to be concerned with how to use our physical and subtle energies best in this lifetime.

What are the benefits of being aware of your own energy and other people's energies? It is important that we are aware of when our emotions are out of balance or in negative states because if we hang on to these emotions, we will be lowering our vibrations. If you tune into their energetic level you know the level of their thoughts, how free they are to express their feelings, what memories and traumas they are holding on to, and the beliefs held in their sub-conscious...absolutely everything there is to know about them.

Most people are so unaware that they do not discern their own level of thinking and feeling. They are not living an "Integrious Life" so they are not speaking honestly or expressing their feelings honestly. They are unaware that the memories and traumas they are holding on to are keeping them from experiencing what they want in life. Finally, their perception of life is filled with untruths so that they see everything as distorted and limited. Integrious people learn to look at people with discernment, not judgment, because when you place a judgment on someone you are placing a value on them. They simply are where they are. Your discernment is the ability to make the right choice–not a judgment–to decide if you want to be affected by that person's energy.

A quote from Dr. Samuel Berne says, *"In the process of seeing old unconscious patterns we may re-awaken memories, emotions, or experiences that were too painful for us to look at. In terms of our awareness there is an outer vision, how we see the world, and an inner vision, how we see ourselves. The clearer we can see inside ourselves, without denial, the clearer our outer vision will become. Light seems to be able to cut through the roadblocks and resistances we have set up, such as, ego, personality, and the rational mind and helps us discover unconscious patterns about ourselves. It is as though light fills up all the dark places of the inner vision. When we look at light, what we see is a clear mirror of ourselves."*

Before you start reading this book, I invite you to stand outside and look at the magnificent stars in the cosmos. Pick out one star and visualize the streams of white light that star is sending to you. Remember, white light contains all the colors, so see all of the rainbow colors flowing into your body. Now see the same colors flowing out of your body. See yourself as pure energy with an energy field that extends all the way to the stars and out into infinity.

How does that make you feel? If you don't feel powerful, energetic, and loved, some things are blocking the stars' light, energy, and love. If you can feel your spirit and energy connecting to the star, then all your receiving channels are open. You can live magically, miraculously, and majestically. In the same way you feel love, light, and energy from the star, you can receive the same from the universe–they are free and in abundance just for the connecting.

For it's only the illusion of individuality that is the origin of all suffering-when one realizes that one is the universe, complete and at one with all that is, forever without end, then no further suffering is possible.

David Hawkins *Power vs. Force*

Your spirit entered the physical plane as pure energy. You agreed to come to earth to experience and grow from the challenges being a human creates. When we leave the physical body, a larger stream of energy can be seen or felt as it moves into a higher plane of existence.

This book is for anyone who wants more energy...to be more alive and active, healthier, inspired, and more transcendent mentally, physically, spiritually, and emotionally. Energy heals diseases, lifts depression, and ignites our creativity. It is the only force that pervades all living and non-living matter. It is the only force that enlivens us. It is the glue that holds everything together.

It is time to be enlightened about energy. Energy is mind. It knows what hormones, chemicals and fluids to send to the precisely needed place in the body. Atoms and molecules that make up cells are held together by energy. Cells are held together with other cells by energy. We must begin to understand the relationship between energy, matter, and consciousness. You already feel it. You know when you have a lot and when you don't. You know that the energy in a room is good or bad. You know if a person has positive energy (high vibrations) or negative (low vibrations). ***Secrets of Energy*** gives the scientific information healing practitioners are looking for to help them work with the healing energies of the body. It proves that energy medicine, also called vibrational medicine, works.

Secrets of Energy gives scientific and measurable proof of the existence of electromagnetic energy fields around all matter. Understanding how the HEF or human electro-magnetic field works gives us great insight into how we operate or how we can choose to operate. You have to wonder how the ancient Egyptians, Assyrians, and other ancient cultures knew more about the HEF than the average person today. The effect is obvious, however. Lack of knowledge about the HEF, portraying it as evil and mystical, keeps people in the "dark" about abundant health and how to self-heal spiritually, mentally, emotionally, and physically.

What a difference it would have made if we had been taught that we are pure energy beings!

- We would have learned how to increase our energy through awareness.
- We would understand the effect of our thoughts, words, and actions on all of our energetic levels.
- We would have learned how to increase our creative and intuitive abilities, and how to stay emotionally healthy.
- We would have been taught techniques to stay calm and relaxed.

We would be whole and healthier, and live more powerful lives. Diseases caused by a weak immune system like cancer, chronic fatigue and rheumatoid arthritis would be reduced. Depression and heart disease wouldn't be a national dilemma. When we act as spiritual energy beings we become responsible and mindful of our thinking and our physical and emotional health.

You will receive the instructions on how to remove the traumas that are stopping your flow of energy by teaching you how to open and balance your chakras, how to move blocked energy in your meridians, muscles, organs, and in the cells of your body. You can learn how to have strong, vibrating, and pulsating energy fields. Finally, you will feel more connected to the universe, nature, and all of the people on the planet, beginning with yourself. I hope you will keep these main ideas foremost in your mind as you read *Secrets Of Energy.*

All of this is to say that I am blessed to be able to express my ideas and beliefs without having to worry about repercussion from an institution or company. I don't have to worry about being judged by my peers. I feel totally free.

Acknowledgements

My sincerest appreciation goes to Bill Phillips and Larry Daniel for all their help explaining the complexities of subtle energy to me. Both have amazing minds that are constantly in search of knowledge and truth.

Thanks to Sarah VanDeusen for all the hours spent editing the book. Also, special thanks to Kevin Hutchinson for doing the illustrations.

I would like to thank the following authors

Dr. James Oschman, author of *Energy Medicine: The Scientific Basis* and *Energy Medicine in Therapeutics and Human Performance* has written two excellent books that explain how energy healers do what they do. Dr. Oschman's research has given everyone in the alternative and complementary field the latest scientific research and the validated proof of what many people have known for thousands of years. Dr. Oschman's books will have a profound effect on the medical establishment because he speaks their language.

Science and Human Transformation, by Williams Tiller, PhD., professor Emeritus at Stanford University in the department of Material Sciences and Engineering, gave me the scientific explanations of how subtle energy works and behaves. In his own words he says his book is a paradigm-breaking book for science in that it reveals in some detail a viable larger perspective and framework for a scientific description of nature and human evolvement in that framework.

The more you understand how universal energy and our energy field, the more you understand our connection to God...and that the connection can never be broken. Dr. Tiller's description of God is "consciousness pulsating through creation", a source echoing a rapidly pulsating energy of pure thought emitting vibratory sound or photons of light forming perfectly harmonic geometric shape of all living forms as well as the placement of the stars. Consciousness radiating in the form of information at an infinite speed could simultaneously be present in an infinite number of places in an infinite expanse of space. Thus "God" resides within the core of every atom.

Power vs. Force, by David Hawkins, M.D., Ph.D. According to Dr. Hawkins, "The universe is very cooperative–as much as it isn't different from consciousness itself, the universe is happy to create whatever we wish to find 'out there'. And, "To become more conscious is the greatest gift anyone can give to the world; moreover, in a ripple effect, the gift comes back to its source. These are challenging times in which every outer solution seems to spawn more problems. Many feel that this downward spiral is being reversed that earth's vibration is rising."

Dr. Richard Gerber, author of *Vibrational Medicine* and *Vibrational Medicine for the 21st Century: The Complete Guide to Energy Healing and Spiritual Transformations,* says, "Within the quantum model there can be no separateness, because it is all energy. When we come to understand that "Believing is Seeing", we can see how the concept of Faith works. When we choose to have faith in the existence of a Universal and Divine Presence, or God, we can understand that God is nothing more than the energy matrix that makes up our Universe. God then, is the very Life Force Energy (Chi, Prana, or Breath of life) that flows into and through us. This God, or Life Force Energy, is the very fuel that keeps us alive. The degree to which we allow this life force energy to flow (or put another way, the degree to which we are willing and able to see ourselves as part of, or co-creators with this Universal Energy), determines how healthy we are. With this idea in mind, we don't even need any outside tools or therapies to create or enhance our body, mind, and spirit. We can simply call it into existence through the use of meditation and prayer. Unfortunately, not too many of us have been willing to take the time or energy required manifesting our health through the discipline of prayer and meditation so it's good that there are also other tools available to assist us on our journey to health.

Light Years Ahead The Illustrated Guide to Full Spectrum and Colored Light in Mindbody Healing by Brian Breiling is a compellation of articles by the nation's leading experts in the use of light in optometry, mindbody healing, and phototherapy. This book like the other books mentioned has an excellent bibliography and resources that you should consult.

Principles of Energy

Everything in the universe is energy; everything radiates energy.

Your personal energy is connected to everyone and everything in the universe.

Energy conforms to the principle "That which is below reflects that which is above". Hermes Trismegistus, the architect of the Great Pyramid, believed that all things small and large abide by the law of correspondence.

You are electrical, magnetic, and crystalline just like the universe.

You have the ability and force to direct, transfer, and release subtle energy.

The energy of the heart is the connection to the soul. When you connect your heart to the Mind of God and the Love of God you will produce your most powerful energy.

Flowing energy creates health, happiness, and success. Blocked energy creates disease, sadness, and failure.

You become a powerful force when you learn how to align your energies with your higher self.

Synergizing people with high vibrations can influence and change the reality of the world.

Thoughts are energy. Energy is information.

You get what you give your energy to.

The level of your thinking, breathing, being determines your life energy.

Our power increases what we become through Intentionality. Intention sets the results.

1. What Is Energy?

Energy Principle: Everything in the universe is energy; everything radiates energy.

Energy is the universal substance, the glue that holds everything together.

Everything visible and invisible is Universal Energy.

Energy can differentiate itself into stars, trees, rocks, water, humans... everything in the Universe, but all energy is still One Universal Energy Field. All matter is surrounded by its own energy field. Each form of matter emanates a unique vibration. Both physical and subtle energy penetrate all coarse materials, metals and organic substances.

Dr. John White and Dr. Stanley Krippner list the properties of The Universal Energy Field as being: it permeates all space, animate and inanimate objects, and connects all objects to each other; it flows from one object to another; and its density varies inversely with the distance from its source. It also follow the laws of harmonic inductance and sympathetic resonance. This is what occurs when you strike a tuning fork and one near it will begin to vibrate at the same frequency, giving off the same sound.

"Everything in the entire universe is one thing... **Energy**."

There are two types of energy: physical and non-physical (subtle) energy. You will read about all the types of physical energy and what is meant by physical energy in Chapter 2 Chapter 3 deals more with non-physical subtle energy.

Physical energy and subtle energy are universally present in all the celestial bodies–the stars and planets–the earth, in non-living matter on earth, and in living human bodies.

Physical Energies

Solids, liquids, gases and plasma are the usual recognized states of matter. The following physical energies are the universal substance that take several different forms such as: natural gas, electricity, hydrogen, petroleum gas, heat, light, magnetism, electromagnetism, sound, gravity, vibration, kinetic energy of motion, and elastic energy.

Subtle Energy

Recently people were encouraged to simply think "outside the box". I encourage you to think outside your perceived world, that is, to explore the world beyond what you now call the physical world. Metaphysics is called "beyond the physical world," but since there is only one universal energy that contains everything, how can there be anything outside of it? Physicists tell us that everything in the universe was created at one time. That means that everything in the universe is already in place. For instance, the waves to send radio and TV signals were there long before radios and Television were created. Thank goodness we now have the technology to measure invisible, subtle energies so we can prove what we have known all along–that they exist.

Subtle energy is now being researched by some eminent scientists involved in cutting-edge human energy research. Dr. William A. Tiller, Professor Emeritus of Stanford University, Department of Material Sciences and Engineering, author of *Science and Human Transformation*, and Dr. Vladimir Poponin, formerly of the Institute of Biochemical Physics of the Russian Academy of Science and co-discoverer of the DNA phantom effect, are now working with the Institute of HeartMath.

Dr. Victor Inyushin at Kazakh University in Russia, who has been researching the Human Energy Field since the 1950's, says there is a fifth state of matter he calls bioplasmic energy (subtle energy). Chemical processes in the cells constantly renew bioplasmic particles that keep them in constant motion. He suggests the existence of a bioplasmic energy field composed of ions, free protons, and free electrons. When there are too many negative charges or too many positive charges, illness occurs.

Subtle energy exists in seven grades or orders of fineness, corresponding to the seven grades of physical matter, which are solid, liquid, gaseous, etheric, superetheric, sub-atomic and atomic. Dr. Tiller and his colleagues at Stanford developed a subtle energy detector–an ultra-sensitive Geiger counter–with which they demonstrated the existence of an energy field that is not in the electromagnetic spectrum. With this special detector, Dr. Tiller demonstrated that this subtle energy field responds to intentional human focus.

Every physical atom floats in a sea of subtle matter, which surrounds it and fills every interstice in physical matter. Subtle energy is that which moves between the spaces of physical atoms. About 99% of your subtle energy is compressed within the periphery of your physical body while only 1% fills the aura. Every physical object has its subtle energy counterpart. But because the subtle energy is in constant movement, it is not affiliated with any specific physical part of the body. [1] Inyushin

When a person is healthy, some of this bioplasma, the person's subtle energy we are always talking about, is radiated into space. These particles are subatomic and when they are charged they move together in clouds. In addition to bioplasma, we are sending out thought forms from our energy fields.

Physical energy is transformed into subtle energy by the chakras which will be discussed in Chapter 5 Energy Is Moveable And Transferable When you transform physical energy into subtle energy, or vice versa, the energy is not as strong as subtle energy from your energy field. There is a barrier, a kind of insulation that you have to cross over so that you won't be overwhelmed by the physical energy. In the same way there are protective barriers between the subtle energies. The subtle energies are blocked in the body by what we call insulations, gaps, or exclusions zone that keep the full impact of the subtle energy out of the physical. The insulations keep you from short circuiting. The right amount of energy has to be moderated. Chapter 8 on auras teaches you how to measure the seven levels. When you do this, you will feel the barrier between each of the levels. However, information is easily transferred through the barriers with no loss of that information.

When you set your intent as you do when you are doing healing or when you are setting your goals, the intent is focused information. You have to modulate the energy to get the information to pass through. To modulate physical energy you control how much it flows, polarization. To modulate subtle energy you use your thoughts. For instance, you modulate your thoughts to change the emotion of hate to love.

Physical energy gives you impressions that you are more familiar with. Physical energy is going to have a physical effect. For instance, heat (physical energy) will really get hot and melt inorganic objects. On the other hand, subtle energies trigger actions more so in living organisms than inorganic. This next statement is important for you to understand. **Subtle energies work at the levels that they exist. This is why it is important that you know that there are seven different levels of subtle energy vibrations,** which will be discussed in detail in Chapter 8 Subtle Energy Called The Aura.

Learning about the difference between physical energy and subtle energy will explain how people are able to do what are called paranormal and psychic acts. These people are simply utilizing different levels of subtle energy. My friend Johnny has visions prior to events that are going to occur. He says that he saw a vision of his nineteen-year-old sister dying at his father's funeral. She died two weeks later and the autopsy revealed no apparent reason for her death. Other people have visions, but they are not necessarily projecting in the future and could relate to any time. These visions are just as valid. What would happen if you stopped looking at time as linear and saw time as relative to what you were observing? We've all had experiences when time moved in slow motion or appeared to stop. What if you believed that all time was occurring at the same time? This would enable you to go back in time and see or experience events like many people are able to do.

You know more about subtle energy than you think. As a matter of fact, when you think, you are using subtle energy. Thoughts are energy. Neither thoughts nor emotions are physical. The heart that we describe as being broken, a heart of gold, or the one we wear on our sleeve are different descriptions of heart energy as subtle energy. Remember this the next time that you get depressed. Subtle energies can be transformed, directed and focused.

Many of us try to change things through will and desire. What we need to realize is that neither will nor desire operates the body. We cannot will that we are slender. Thought is the only power that deals with things. It is with thought-power that the body is created and how all the activities that are not reflex are performed.

Using subtle energy you can learn to do the following:

Precognition–advance knowing
Scan people's bodies to know where they are losing energy, blocking energy, or where the energy is balanced and flowing
Do energy healing
Feel if a person's intentions toward you are good or bad
Contact the spirits of people who have passed over
See or sense angels, guides, and disembodied spirits who hang around the earth Channel–receive information from Universal Mind
Do remote viewing–a person leaves the physical body and their mind energy is able to view other localities
Psychometry–the ability to read people by looking at their photographs or by holding a possession of theirs, such as jewelry, clothing, or an heirloom, without having the person present during the reading. The person doing psychometry is reading the energy transmitted by the other person and translating it into words.
Dowsing– the process of locating objects or resources usually buried underground or hidden from sight. The dowser holds a diving rod, a forked stick or pole, in order to connect with the energy of the buried object. There are several uses for dowsing, including finding people who are lost.

The Subtle Energy Of The Aura:

- The aura sustains us mentally, physically, and spiritually.
- All of our resources come from the aura.

What Is Energy?

- Our empowerment comes from the aura.
- It connects us to our cosmic origins.
- The totality of our individuality is encoded in our aura.
- It is an evolving chronicle of our past, present, and future.

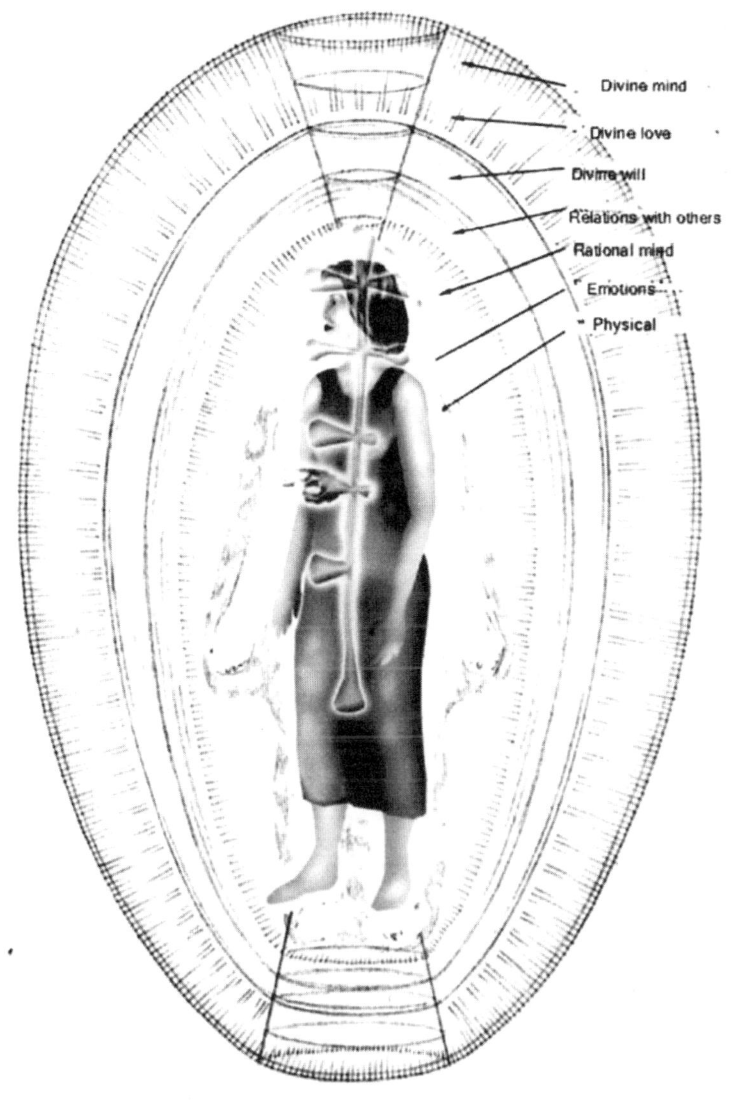

The Seven Bodies Of The Aura

- It is an interactive link between our innermost self and the external environment.
- Our aura is able to connect with the aura systems of others.
- The aura is an indicator of our personal development.

Physical Energy	**Non-Physical Energy/Subtle Energy**
Forms: gravity, nuclear (strong and weak), electrical, magnetic, and chemical, pressure, temperature	No gravitational qualities-moves out infinitely, is strong nuclear
Matter is a condensed form of energy	Subtle energy can be interpreted
Can penetrate physical matter	Can penetrate physical matter
Matter such as steel or quartz can have memory depending upon what stage it is in	Subtle energy can leave an imprint in matter (example: crystals) psychometry
Cannot access universal mind via physical energy	Can access universal mind (subtle energy) via subtle energy
Physical energy does not have the same aspects as subtle energy	Subtle energy has the following aspects: mental, physical, emotional, and spiritual (comes from higher level, source energy) These aspects interpenetrate each other and influence each other
Physical energy is not connected like the web of subtle energy	All subtle energy is connected; therefore, it is always non-local
Thoughts create changes in the nervous system	Thoughts, intentions, feelings and emotions can change the color, vibration, shape and size of subtle energy
Physical energy has no intelligence	Subtle energy is intelligent and has information
Does not contain information about the past, present, and future	Subtle energy can contain information about the past, present, and future
Has patterns, standing waves, or shapes	Has patterns, standing waves, or shapes
Different kinds of physical energy have different perceptual sensations	The perceptual sensations of subtle energy are warm, cold, tingling, shock, pressure and different levels of vibration
Positive and negative energy can not flow in the same space at the same time	Positive and negative energy can flow in the same space at the same time
Cannot exceed the speed of light	Can exceed the speed of light

What Is Energy?

Polarized	Polarized differently than physical energy
Can not move in both directions at the same time	Can move in both directions at the same time
Needs physical matter to create light	Does not need physical matter to create light
Chakras take in physical energy Different kinds of physical energy cannot exist in the same space	Chakras take in subtle energy
Most physical energy moves in waves	Subtle energy moves concentrically waves rather than linear
Some kinds of physical energy cannot be touched or smelled. Physical energy does produce a vibration; therefore a sound	Subtle energy can be touched, tasted, smelled, and heard
Can harm, destroy, or heal the body through: X-rays-too many can create cancer Ultra-violet rays-too many can sunburn the skin and cause cancer Chemicals and hormones-the body functions through the production of chemicals and hormones. Over production or under production create illness.	Can never destroy or harm the physical body because you can never have too much subtle energy-you are subtle energy
Physical energy permeates matter	Subtle energy permeates matter
Physical energy is carried by the nerves in the body	Subtle energy moves through the meridians of the body
The colors of physical energy are changed by refraction, i.e. prism	The colors of subtle energy can be cloudy or clear
Can be contained, i.e. electrical energy is sent through wires	Cannot be contained. Subtle energy in the meridian is a natural confinement. The energy moves rotationally.
Can be used to heal via electrical pulsating devices, magnets	All kinds of subtle energy can be used to heal
The magnetic poles of physical energy are the opposite and repel each other	The magnetic poles of subtle energy do not repel each other
A few psychics can manipulate physical energy	Remote viewing, psychometry, telepathy, distant healing, clairvoyance (seeing), clairaudience (hearing), clairsentience (feeling) and other so called "paranormal" events are

	achieved through subtle energy
Physical energy such as electricity and fiber optics can carry information	Through your thoughts you can send, direct, focus and receive subtle energy
Physical energy enters the body via food, water, air and via the chakras	Subtle energy becomes denser inside the body

Energy is the underlying, forcible glue that keeps the planets in orbit, that puts our chemicals and hormones into action, that fuels the fires that heats our houses, and fuels our bodies via water, food, and sound, even entering our bodies through unseen passageways. Energy can simultaneously have the aspects of being physical, mental, emotional and spiritual yet be considered only one thing–**Energy**. You need to know everything you can about how to get your microcosmic energy in sync with the macrocosmic energy of the universe.

Everything in the universe is One.

When we are in touch with being whole, we feel at one with everything. When we feel at one with everything, we feel whole ourselves. *Wherever You Go There You Are*, Jon Kabat-Zinn, Ph.D.

The holographic model of the universe gives a new foundation for comprehending the unseen energy interconnections between all things. The Einsteinian viewpoint of matter as particularized energy shows us that we are all constructed from the same subatomic building blocks. At a microcosmic level, we are each complex yet uniquely arranged aggregates of the same particularized universal energy.

Einstein's Theory of Relativity essentially states that light, energy, and matter are all of equal importance. Where matter once ruled, energy is now taking its place in the thinking of physicists. They related to energy in the universe but not how it affected human health. In the last 30 years, technological advances have created a new paradigm shift so that now the general public understands how energy works. Energy always precedes matter and indeed, matter accounts for only 2% of the Universe. Essentially the only difference between physical matter and etheric matter is the electromagnetic frequency at which it vibrates or resonates.

In 1905 Albert Einstein published his Special Theory of Relativity. Most people have heard of this but they don't know what it is. Basically Einstein said that space is not three-dimensional; rather it is a four-dimensional continuum. He states that there is no universal flow of time. This means that time is not linear nor is it absolute. Linear means that one thing appears to happen right after another thing. Time, according to Einstein, is relative. Two observers will order events differently in time if they move with different velocities relative to the observed events. In certain conditions two observers can see two events in reverse time.

Einstein's Theory of Relativity taught us that matter and energy are interchangeable. The fact is that everything, all matter, is slowed down or crystallized energy, what some call "frozen light" that is connected to all other "frozen light". Matter is a form of energy. How can we successfully live in a universe when we do not understand how it operates? Quantum physics has moved our understanding far beyond the Theory of Relativity.

The word light is a good example. Science might study white light going through a prism and separating into different rays of color–red, orange, yellow, green, blue, indigo, and purple. Technology talks about light in the use of fiber optics to transport massive amounts of data. The energy worker also knows ability of the electromagnetic field of matter to transport massive amounts of data. Physics teaches about light as indestructible energy while quantum physics says that light is both a particle and wave and that the smallest unit in the universe is strings of energy. The theory is called "string theory" and like gravity and air, you know strings of energy make up the universe because they are there and working, though you can't see them.

Everything in the universe is both organic and inorganic in that everything has an energy field that is part of a universal energy field. Understanding the form and structure of the energy fields is somewhat complicated, but it is necessary so that we may access that information possessing energy and change our lives. Through this study we learn full self-empowerment.

The point is that we are seeing science, physics, medicine, and spirituality moving closer and closer as we learn more about energy. A "New Thought Movement" is growing, and it proposes that we see ourselves as energy beings who know how to take responsibility for our actions and our outcomes. The secret to knowing how to do this is simply to understand energy.

Energy is life. It is the connecting force that penetrates the whole universe. Energy is the medium we use to connect with everything. You must understand this concept to get anything out of this book. You have to understand how energy operates to know what to do with it. You begin first by learning about universal energy and cosmic energy. Then you learn about the different kinds of energies in the atmosphere, the levels of energy in your HEF, the **Human Energy Field**, how energy enters the body, how it moves through your meridians, and finally how each cell in your body has its own energy field.

Your energy is a part of the Universal Energy Field. Because you are a part of the universal energy field, your energy is infinite and eternal. This is good news. You come into contact with all of the other bioplasmic fields; people, the energy fields of nature, plants, minerals, power lines, and thought fields from the beginning of time, extending into the future. You are protected and shielded from the energy of all of these fields or you would be overloaded. You are given the ability to access the energy fields that you choose.

Those who view the **UEF**, (**Universal Energy Field**) describe it as a highly organized series of geometric points and as isolated pulsating points of light, spiral, webs of lines, sparks and clouds. The more adept person can sense it by touch, taste, smell and sound.

Energy is pure and perfect–it has positive and negative aspects that do not denote goodness or badness. Its natural state is to be in constant movement and flux. Energy is always in its purest state, neither good nor bad, but forms of energy–water, air, fire, waves, particles–can enliven, energize, and activate or it can flood, burn, and destroy. Air is all around us, but in some places it is still and in other places it is blowing or creating hurricanes. So it is with energy.

A rock you hold in your hand, though it appears "non energetic," is energy because it is composed of atoms, neurons and protons which makes it vibrate, though at a low frequency. Different frequencies of energy reflect varying rates of vibration. All the previously mentioned objects are constantly receiving, sending, and communicating their energies. Each of the objects has a mutual influence from the energies of all other objects. Every plant, animal, gemstone and human has a distinctive vibrational frequency.

Gravity, nuclear, electrical, magnetic, and chemical energy are all different forms of energy. Energy is in water, the atmosphere, and in the cosmic particles that land on our planet. Energy is a comparatively fine substance of particles and waves that range from the slow wavelengths of telephone poles to the high vibration of angels. Energy is the light that shines from the stars; it is all forms of visible and invisible light. Energy is the force that ignites the cells of plants, animals, and people to be alive. When it becomes trapped in parts of the body, it creates illness causing excessive heat or cold. The flow of energy in your body can be damaged by emotional and physical traumas, infections, unhealthy foods and drinks, too little exercise or even too much exercise.

What Is Energy?

Energy is an equal opportunity creator. We all reside in the same sea of universal energy. Therefore we all have equal access to it. It is a magnificent thought that we all have equal access and connection to the Creator. Authors Stephan Caldwell and Cailen Richardsen write in *Insights,* "We are part of an inseparable energy that creates the stars, a child-life itself. We are one with an infinite power. Our purpose in life is to choose peace and love."

As energy beings all our energy fields have equal access. There is never a reason for a power struggle. No sense of lack should ever exist. Every energy field is a connected part of the universal energy field. The energy supply is infinite. For this reason you need never again to feel lonesome, weak, abandoned, or worthless. It is impossible for you to feel any of these things unless you choose to.

What is not understanding energy costing you? Everything!

As you will learn from reading this book, everything that you do in business, in your home, in your relationship with yourself and others, with your Creator, with your health, happiness and success is based on your knowledge and use of energy. The level of your vibration determines everything that happens to you. Everything about you will transform when you understand that ***all you are is energy.*** This is what you base your self-worth on.

How high energy gives you the health, happiness and success you desire:

Motivational speakers are always promising you health, happiness and success. Basically they give you the same formula about achieving your dreams and goals. First, they tell you to be who you are. Second, they tell you to have confidence in yourself. Third, they tell you to focus all your energy on achieving your goals and dreams.

The problem is that we, along with the motivational speakers, do not know the true scientific basis and the "how to" for doing the three steps in the formula. Let's start with the "be who you are" statement. If you ask 100 people "who they are" would even one of them say, "I am pure energy"? Most people believe that they are the events that have happened to them, or another way of saying it, that the events that have happened in their lives have caused them to be the way that they are. Other people have let their environment, their family, or what others think they should be determine "who they are". You will learn in this book that being "pure energy" gives you entitlement. It gives you undreamed of capabilities to create and manifest. When you start seeing yourself in this new "light" and when you start utilizing the light and energy around you and within you, you will be empowered to your full potential.

You are a powerful force field already. It is just that no one has told you so. Your force field is pure energy. When charged particles interact, a disturbance or condition is created. Pure energy has different aspects: emotional energy, mental energy, physical energy, and spiritual energy. While there may be different aspects, there is still only one energy. Because very little energy information has been written outside of metaphysical books, most people do not understand it. They know little about how to control these different aspects. If you think your energy is only inside your physical body, you are missing out on understanding the other 99% of your energy.

The second step in the formula is to have confidence in yourself. What we, especially, and the motivators don't realize is that when we begin we don't have a lot of history or success in what we are doing. It is in the fulfilling of our dreams, goals, and purpose that we gain confidence. Our confidence should be based on the belief that we have all been given the gifts, talents, and abilities that we need to accomplish our purposes. The main reason that we come to earth is to gain knowledge. Hopefully you will never fulfill all your dreams and goals because you will always be getting new ones. We get hung up on fulfilling purpose not realizing that our lives keep changing as we continue to grow mentally, emotionally, and spiritually.

Thirdly, we really haven't been taught the right way to focus all our energies on achieving our goals and dreams. Learning to focus and direct your energies requires the mental and physical dedication of an Olympian, emotional and spiritual balance and alignment. Have you ever heard the phrase "with ease and grace?" The perfect plan for happiness, health, and success is to really feel that life is not hard and that what you do is really not work. Our doubts in our worthiness are what block our happiness, success, and achievements. We are innately worthy when we come solely from the place of worthiness. We keep our energies flowing, and we learn to operate our powerful energy.

The present time has been described as the Information Age. We need to know more about universal energy because it contains information about everything past, present, and future. We can learn how to access that information by getting into what is called an altered or relaxed state. The main problem with the Information Age is information overload. It is important that we learn how to discern information and how to judge the truth of the information without prejudices.

We say that energy and information are synonymous and that energy (Universal Mind) is everywhere. We also know that mind and brain are not the same thing. Mind is both outside of the physical body and inside the physical body. Chapter Seven will discuss "What Is Mind?" "Where Is

Mind?" Energy carries information everywhere in the body Cells in the heart contain energy telling it to beat, white blood cells *know* to go where to attack invading viruses and bacteria, and endocrine glands know when to produce more hormones for your body's different needs.

We will soon be entering the Energy Age. We are becoming more multisensory, meaning that we won't receive information just through our five senses, but we will receive information through intuition. The ways to receive information are clairvoyance (seeing), clairaudience (hearing), and clairsentience (feeling), telepathy, direct knowing, and psychometry. These abilities will help us redefine our understanding of ourselves and our Universe.

In the Energy Age we will use our multi-sensory abilities to connect with everything in the Universe. For instance, we may connect with other people through the senses by feeling their vibration; we may connect with another person through thought–another form of vibration. We already know when someone is thinking about us. Or we know who is calling on the phone...without caller ID. In this Information Age our main problem is that most of us are getting our information outside of ourselves, and we are paying attention to unimportant information.

Secondly, I believe that it is paramount that we take responsibility for our health. Our spirit is the determiner of our health on all levels, and it reflects our connection with our Creator, others and self.

The third main idea is that the memory of everything that has ever happened to us is stored simultaneously in our energy field and in our physical bodies. When emotional energy from feelings, words, events, or traumas, attaches to a memory, it becomes extremely powerful, positively or negatively. When we place a judgment on the feelings, words, events, or traumas, we are placing a value or worth and this determines whether the stored memory will be positive or negative. All of this stored information determines our perceptions that then influence the information we will discern later. Everything that has ever happened to us is stored in our energy field. For instance, witnesses to crimes are often put into hypnotic states to help them remember more details of a criminal event. ***Secrets of Energy*** will teach you how to quickly and easily release all the negatively stored energy in your bodies that stagnates your energy and creates diseases.

What is evolving in our information about our personal energy is that as mind/body/spirit beings we are light beings giving and receiving energy. The fact is that if we do not have our energy (mentally, physically, spiritually, and emotionally) in alignment, balanced, centered, and flowing nothing works in our business, money, health, happiness, relationships, and spirituality in optimum abundance. How many people can you name that have it all together? More importantly, would you like to be one of the people who have **optimum abundance?** The amount of flow of that energy determines our physical, mental, and emotional health, business and financial success, and happiness.

It has taken a few centuries, but now almost everyone thinks that we are spirit-mind-body. Thinking that this is all we are is another limiting belief. **What you are is pure energy!** Astrophysicist Stephen Hawkin is the perfect example to explode this idea. If we hold on to the idea of the power of the "mind-body connection" we would wonder how Hawkins's twisted body affects his mind. Obviously it does not. The consciousness of Stephen Hawkin is his energy. The next step is to get people to understand that the connector, the medium, the force that holds us and everything else in the universe together is energy.

To get more energy, let more energy flow to you. Let the energy that you already are flow. The Creator has endowed each personal energy field to receive as much energy as it needs. We have all the systems in place to focus and direct, expand, release, and send energy within our own energy field.

Every culture has a word for energy. How is it that we know so little about something that is everything? How can the word "energy" have so many meanings, be used in so many different ways, and yet, most of the time we understand the kind of energy the speaker is referring to? Are we talking about the same energy when we say, "I am going to put all of my energy into that project," and "I like that guy's energy," or "My mother drains all of my energy?" We think we can't see, smell, or touch some forms of energy, and yet, you will read the stories of people in this book who say they can. Once you know how energy operates, you will believe them. Energy is not elusive, but our knowledge about how we can manage, increase, focus, direct, and control it is.

You have a unique individual signature vibration called your spirit– your energy that is constantly changing because of your thoughts, movements, environment, food, water, relationships, and cosmic influences.

Everything in the universe has a rhythmic pulse of vibrating energy. You send out an individually unique signature vibration. All of our attributes are energetic to make up our signature vibration. The attributes are our cells, bones, muscles, and hormones, which are chemical energy carrying messages and information sent through the neuro-transmitters, and finally our words and sounds. Information is sent through the body's tissues, through the cell membrane and its nucleus and finally down to the gene level where, did you know, specific changes can be made. Much speculation has been made about the human DNA, deoxyribonucleic acid, and what we will learn from it. Scientists know that DNA carries information about the color of our eyes, hair and skin; everything that comprises us physically. Cellular biologist Dr. Bruce Lipton notes that neither our DNA nor our genes determine our "genetic determinism". This is because we are much more than physical. Energy causes DNA to enliven; it does not explain all of our aspects.

The combination of all your vibrations is pulsed through your aura. The seven levels of your aura each have a different vibration with the lowest beginning at the first level and getting higher as your move up to the seventh level. Your vibration is a combination of your entire energy field.

Your energy field is creating your personal signature–the tone and vibration of your energy field. There is not other signature like yours because no one else has had your experiences, your feelings, your history. Because everything in the Universe is energy, everything is also vibrational. We are not only energy beings sending out our unique star core light, but we are also vibrational beings with messenger systems that possess a specific tone. We have an individualized signature tune that vibrates our sound and our message. Our vibration is constantly rising and falling, vibrating at high or low levels, binding and unbinding depending upon our thoughts and our emotions. Some people can see the colors displayed in our electro-magnetic field, while others can ***feel*** and ***hear*** our body music.

The universe has a rhythmic pulse, is info-energetically rhythmic. Scientists will agree that rhythmic energy carries information, and as humans we are constantly receiving millions of bits of information from everywhere. All of the animate and inanimate objects are in a constant state of vibrational resonance and harmonics, which generates energy-fields of an electrical and electromagnetic nature. All of the life force systems of nature, animals, trees, flowers, and rocks pulsate with energy. The molecules of all these life forms put out frequencies that enter our physical bodies. As you walk around in a forest or stroll down the beach, you can feel the energy moving in your body.

Energy Principle: Your personal energy, Human Energy Field, is connected to everyone and everything in the universe.

The molecular structure of everything in the universe, both animate and inanimate, is in constant motion because it is energy. The densest type of energy is matter, which is energy confined to physical form. Early philosophers called the human body a microcosm of the macrocosm because we represent the universe. That is to say that just as the cosmos is orderly and rhythmically vibrating, everything in our body, even at the cellular level, is orderly and vibrating. Neils Bohr as far back as 1913 theorized that the structure of the atom is like a tiny solar system with the nucleus representing the sun and the electrons representing the planets.

The components of the Human Energy Field can be measured as electrostatic, magnetic, electromagnetic, sonic, and thermal energy. You are a physical structure made of molecules. You are composed of millions of electromagnetic energy fields created from your physical matter, your thoughts, and your spirit that are constantly changing and flowing in and out of your energy field. Each of the fifty trillion cells in your body has an energy field! It has been said that we have 60,000 thoughts each day. Most of our "new" thoughts are created from the thoughts we have been holding onto. These thoughts create our beliefs and our perceptions. Thoughts are vibratory energy and therefore every thought has an energy field.

Dr. Stone, the developer of Polarity Therapy used the design in Figure 1, which is often seen in nature, to illustrate the essential form of energy fields. Note how the center resembles The Caduceus, Figure 2, the ancient symbol

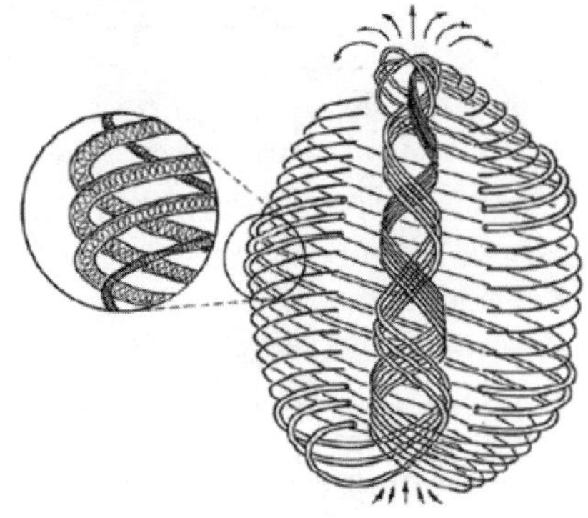

Figure 1

Figure 2

of energy in the body. The Caduceus is an Egyptian and Greek symbol also known as the Staff of Hermes or Staff of Life. The Romans called it the "magic wand" of Mercury. The wings of the Caduceus represent the two hemispheres of the brain. The knob in the center is the pineal body. The pineal gland is considered to be the most important gland in the body because it controls the light (energy) intake. The upright staff is the path of the finer energy of the brain and the spinal cord below it. The two serpents represent the Mind principle in its dual aspects.

Consciousness

"The conclusion is always the same: love is the most powerful and still the most unknown energy in the world." Pierre Teilhard de Chardin

Your state of consciousness transforms your energy level. Our spirits create subtle energy fields filled with high vibrating unconditional love or low vibrating fields of fear and lack of love. Energy has a vibration that ranges on a scale beginning with low frequency and moving to a high frequency. Shame, guilt, fear, anger, and revenge are low frequency thoughts. Love, sympathy, and truth are examples of higher frequency thoughts. The highest state of energy is transcendence. Scientists cannot locate our consciousness. The problem is that they are looking at the energy of the brain, movement of ions and chemicals to try to find consciousness. Our consciousness cannot be activated by anything in the physical body because when the physical body dies, our consciousness is not destroyed. Consciousness is outside the limitations of the physical body. Our goal is to connect with the consciousness that has already been created in a state of perfection at the highest level.

Consciousness creates the body, the brain and everything else around us that we interpret as physical. Keith Floyd, a psychologist at Virginia Intermont College, has pointed out that if the concreteness of reality were but a holographic illusion, it would no longer be true to say that the brain produces consciousness. The truth would be that consciousness produces the brain. The way we view biological structures has done a complete turn about that has caused researchers to point out that medicine and our understanding of the healing process could also be transformed by the holographic paradigm. If the apparent physical structure of the body is but a holographic projection of consciousness, it becomes clear that each of us is much more responsible for our health than current medical wisdom allows. What we now view as miraculous remissions of disease may actually be due to changes in consciousness, which in turn effect changes in the hologram of the body. Similarly, controversial new healing techniques such as visualization work well because in the holographic domain of thought, images are ultimately "reality".

This book will show you how to keep your mental, physical, emotional and spiritual energies in balance and aligned. To do this, you need to learn how to manipulate the energy in your aura. For instance, some people are very intellectual. They know how to control their emotions. They are transcending spiritually and yet they are ignoring their physical bodies. The physical is just as important as the spiritual. These people are not "grounded" and they are not able put their goals and purposes into action.

On the other hand, some people may be so in touch with the physical world that they have only ten percent body fat. They do their thinking from the cerebrum rather than from the heart. They are so emotionally controlled that they do not know how to express them; and their spiritual aspect is almost void. The way to balance and align your energy in your personal human energy field is to learn how to connect to and expand it by receiving more universal energy

The beginning of this chapter discussed **Universal Energy** and how it contains all the different kinds of energies, cosmic energy, and what most people do not realize,–**Universal Mind.** There is only One Mind and it is called Universal Mind. Mind is energy. The thoughts the mind produces are energy. We forget and we think that we are One Self. However, our One Self is just a speck in the infinitesimal One Energy Field.

We access Universal Mind when we receive information that is outside of what we have been taught or read. Accessing Universal Mind gives us our intuition, our genius, our insights to solve difficult problems, and our creativity gifts in the arts, in writing, in thinking.

How We Come From The Stars

When we scan the universe, from the largest known galaxy to the smallest particle of matter, we find a magnificent system that is comparable in many ways to the wondrous design of our own being, including the make-up of our aura system. Like the cosmos, we are a complex creation of many elements, all designed to function in harmony. Joe Slate, Ph.D. *Aura Energy*

All living and inorganic things are shaped from the same matter that exists throughout the physical universe.

We are all made from the same "star stuff", the basic building blocks of the universe. Whether that material comes from aggregates of cosmic dust, reformed primordial hydrogen, or even astral matter, its basic nature is that of particularized frozen energy. Astral matter is another name for subtle energy. It is so called because medieval alchemists described it as starry because of it luminous appearance. All matter is energy and light in it myriad forms and manifestations. We are multidimensional beings of energy and light whose physical body is but a single component of a larger dynamic system. Humans are mind/body/spirit complexes which exist in continuous dynamic equilibrium with higher energy dimensions of reality.

We could not have been created without the creative process of the stars. Astronomers say that the earth and humans could not have been without the metals of younger stars and I found this fascinating. Astrophysicists have now surmised that the matter from which the Earth and its inhabitants have evolved was born in the cosmic incubators of second and third generation stars similar to our own sun. Massive stars that formed early in the history of the Milky Way finished their principal stages of evolution several billion years ago.

The first stars were created out of hydrogen and helium particles. Inside the star, fusion converts some of the original hydrogen and helium particles like carbon-12 and oxygen-16. At the same time, the carbon, nitrogen, and oxygen nuclei that were originally present in the star's fuel are converted into heavier, neutron-rich nuclei, like neon-22 and magnesium-25.

When this burning has exhausted all of the nuclear fuel in the core of the star, the star explodes as a supernova. The shock wave generated by the explosion produces additional heavy nuclei and ejects most of these products of nucleosynthesis back into the interstellar gas. Repetition of these events in each generation of stars steadily enriches the interstellar gas in carbon, nitrogen, and oxygen, and in heavy nuclei with an excess of neutrons.

Near the end of the existence of these stars, heavier elements, fused from hydrogen by nuclear reactions, may have spewed back into the interstellar gas and dust. Younger stars contain higher proportions of metals, which we in turn needed, to be created. The vast array of physical elements on our own planet had their origin in the building up of matter from molecular evolution. Earth formed from gas and dust ejected by ancient, dying stars. These elements, including carbon, oxygen, nitrogen, and iron, form all the known substances in our world. The solar fusion of hydrogen to form helium the triple alpha process of helium recombining to form carbon, and so on up the elemental ladder have provided the primal ingredients for planetary evolution and the emergency of life on Earth.

Cosmic and Solar Energies Send Us Energy

Everything in the universe is constantly throwing off infinitesimal particles of itself. The stars are constantly sending out heat, light, and sound vibrations (energy), just as we humans are sending out heat, light, thoughts, smells, and sounds, These are all different forms of energy. The energy, or currents of force, passing through any form throws off infinitesimal particles charged with that force. The fact that every thought we create affects the energy of the universe should make us more mindful and responsible for our thoughts.

We connect to the oneness through our **unique vibrational rate**. They list the heart pulses in the order of their velocities in an article for the Mind-body Journal. [2] Russek. Linda and Schwartz, Gary The electromagnetic pulse, measured by the electrocardiogram and magnetocardiogram is the fastest signal. The next vibration is the sound pulse recorded by an audiogram, next is the pressure pulse recorded by the kymogram, and lastly, the heat pulse, measured by a thermogram. Even inanimate objects are drawing in and sending out energy just as the objects described as animate. The result is that everything is interdependent on everything else.

It is empowering to realize that we are infinitely connected with all matter in the universe through energy. As energy beings we possess the same qualities of energy–that is we can never be destroyed or changed, and we are forever linked to universal energy. We can manipulate all of the energy that is around us. For instance, light is energy and it comes in various colors depending upon its frequency. If we decide to increase green healing light energy into our bodies, we need only to think about it, and it is done. Once you read about all the properties of energy you will understand how this happens.

Electromagnetic fields

Electromagnetic fields were first discovered in the 19th century, when physicists noticed that electric arcs (sparks) could be reproduced at a distance, with no connecting wires between them. This led scientists to believe that it was possible to communicate across long distances without wires. The first radio transmitters made use of electric arcs. These "spark transmitters" and the associated receivers were as exciting to people in the early 20th century as the Internet is today. This was the beginning of what we now call wireless communication. People have always been doing wireless communication called telepathy. Many times you know when someone is thinking of you so it is not surprising when you get a phone call from him or her. Connected people literally know what is on each other's mind.

Electromagnetic fields are typically generated by alternating current (AC) in electrical conductors. The frequency of the AC can range from one cycle in thousands of years (at the low extreme) to trillions or quadrillions of cycles per second (at the high extreme). The standard unit of EM frequency is the hertz, abbreviated Hz. The wavelength of an EM field is related to the frequency.

Kinds Of Electromagnetic Energy

Short waves, radio waves, TV waves, high frequency rays, cosmic rays, radium rays, gamma rays, microwaves, infrared radiation, hard rays, grenz rays, x-rays, visible and invisible light, erythemal rays, florescent rays, and ultraviolet rays are all kinds of electromagnetic energy.

Ultraviolet light affects the body in the following way: helps regulate the blood pressure, improves the electrocardiogram and cardiac output, and blood cholesterol, aids with glycogen storage in the liver, and helps energy endurance and muscular strength. Ultraviolet light increases lymphocytes and the phagocytic index thereby increasing the body's resistance to infections and resistance to skin infections. It promotes the oxygen carrying capacity of the blood and also increases adrenalin in the tissues and tolerance to stress.

They all move at 186,000 miles per second, the speed of light, which is also a part of the electromagnetic spectrum. The only difference between them is their wavelength, which is directly related to the amount of energy the waves carry.

On one end of the spectrum are radio waves with wavelengths billions of time longer than those of visible light. On the other end of the spectrum are gamma rays. They have wavelengths millions of times smaller than those of visible light. Different frequencies of energy reflect varying rates of vibration. Science knows a great deal about these different energies, but it knows very little about how they came to be.

Did you know that microwaves are really radio waves? Microwaves are emitted from the Earth, from objects such as cars and planes, and from the atmosphere. Humans also send out microwaves. This will be discussed in the information about auras. Radio waves can also be used to create images. Radio waves with wavelengths of a few centimeters can be transmitted from a satellite or airplane antenna. The reflected waves can be used to form an image on the ground in complete darkness or through clouds.

Infrared waves include thermal radiations; i.e.: charcoal which burns but which doesn't send out light. Gamma rays have wavelengths more penetrating than X-rays because they are generated by radioactive atoms. They are used in nuclear explosions as well as in many medical applications.

Electromagnetic energy ranges from the slower, longer waves–electrical power, telephone, ultrasound, radio waves, TV waves, microwaves, fluorescent and incandescent lighting, ultraviolet, photography, CAT Scans, X-ray, deep tissue waves, progressing–to cosmic rays vibrating the shortest and fastest. Visible light and the seven colors of the rainbow are within the electromagnetic field and they have a specific frequency range. Beginning with the slowest, red, the frequency of the colors move higher from orange, yellow, green, blue, indigo and violet, the highest vibrating. Each color has a different frequency. The same colors are in the rainbow and the body's chakras. These same colors in subtle energy carry meanings: Violet-spiritual power, Indigo-intuition, Blue-inspiration, Green- healing energy, yellow-wisdom, orange-health, and personal power, red-life.

Energy Principle: Energy conforms to the principle "That which is below reflects that which is above". Hermes Trismegistus, the architect of the Great Pyramid, believed that all things small and large abide by the law of correspondence.

References

Inyushin *"Questions of Theoretical and Applied Biology, Possibilities of Studying Tissues in High Frequency Discharge, Biological Plasma of Human Organism with Animals, The Biological Essence of the Kirlian Effect" 1967-1970, p. 259.*

Nelson, Roger D., Bradish Johnston, , York H. Dobyns, Brenda J. Dunne, and Robert G. John. "Field Anomalies in Group Situations," *Journal of Scientific Exploration,* v. 10 pp. 111-141, 1996.

Russek, Linda, Schwartz, Gary, Mind-Body Journal, 1996, p. 59.

2. Subtle Energy

Energy Principle: You have the ability and force to direct, transfer, and release subtle energy.

All matter is condensed light.
Matter is in a constant state of inhalation and exhalation of light particles, photons, at infinitesimal speeds.

Energy Is Infinite

Your electromagnetic field is sent out into space through the movement of any part of your body. This helps us understand the statement that we are a part of the sea of energy in the universe. We are sending and receiving energy from the Universal Energy Field at the same time. Bio-magnetic and electromagnetic fields extend indefinitely into space though their strength diminishes. Energy can never be destroyed.

Energy Has Relativity.

The universe as a whole, including all of living nature, forms a seamless dynamic web of interrelated and interconnected parts and rhythmic processes. Just as touching a web in one place will cause vibration, the events, motions, relations and energies in the universe are an unbroken and interconnected network of energy points. None are more important than or more isolated from the other points of energy.

We can affect the energy levels and vibrations of those around us. Scientists compiled information from ten separate gatherings, ranging from business meetings to scientific conferences or religious events, and found that the effect was strongest during periods when the group's attention was focused, or when the group's cohesion was high, or when the group's members were sharing a common emotional experience [1]Nelson, Roger

Everything About Us Is Relative

We must stop trying to separate the activities of our souls, the feelings of our emotions, the thinking of our mental mind, and the physical body from our own energy field and the universal energy field. All of these activities take place in our energy field. Nothing in the universe exists by itself.

Both Physical And Subtle Energy Are Measurable

Energy Measurement In The Body

Different forms of physical energy can be measured in different ways. For instance, electricity is measured in kilowatts; energy from food is measured in calories.

We speak of the body putting out "vibes" meaning vibrations, or electricity.. The electrical output of the brain can vary from 0 to 100, 225 in the muscles, and 250 in the heart. **The interesting part is that the measurement of the skin above the body's seven chakras can range in frequency from 100 to 1,600 cycles per second.**

If you look at the Gas Discharge Visualization Camera images, the colored pages in the middle of the book, you will see that when a person has a lot of brain activity, the energy sticks to both the front and the back of their head. The GDV (Gas Discharge Visualization Camera) is also called corona discharge. The GDV shows the increased energetic shifts as a result of yoga, acupuncture, qi gong, meditation, relaxation, exercise, certain foods, water intake, deep breathing, energy psychology techniques such as Thought Field Therapy and the Emotional Freedom technique, and energy healing.

Energy healers are able to increase the energy flowing through their hands in the same way mediators are able to project more energy through their chakras which in turn causes the energy of their electromagnetic fields to increase. The palm of the right hand is positive and stimulates energy, which has a strengthening effect. The palm of the left hand is negative and has a sedating, soothing, and cleansing effect. By using both hands you get the combined effect of both hands. Conversely, the back of the right hand is negative and the back of the left hand is positive. The back of the head is positive while the front of the head is negative. To release the pain of a headache or to send energy to the head for other reasons, remember, the back of the head is positive and the front of the head is negative. So when you work with someone, place the palm of your right hand on the lower part of the back of the head and place the palm of the left hand on the front part of the head. Energy healers are also able to see magnetic fields the same way a biomagnetic device does.

Subtle Energy Measurement

How are the subtle energies measured and even their existence proven? **There are over one thousand technological devices available to measure or influence subtle energies.** This book will discuss the MRI, CAT, spectroscope, GDV camera, SQUID, and other technologies. **The electromyography records the electrical fields produced by all the muscles of the body except the heart. Magnetomygrams record the magnetic field of these same muscles.**

Hiroshi Motoyama, author of ***Measurements of Ki Energy, Diagnosis and Treatments***, has spent several years researching subtle energy in Japan. He attaches electrodes to the hands and feet to provide a complete assessment of energy flowing through each meridian and the corresponding internal organs. There are twelve meridians or "pathways" that energy flows through the body. They will be discussed in Chapter 9.

With a movie camera in a darkroom Hiroshi Motoyama has measured low light levels coming from people who have practiced yoga for many years. He also studied the strength of a sender's and a receiver's energy meridians before and after different kind of energy treatments. Most of the time, the sender's energy level dipped and then rose again. Motoyama has several exercises to increase the human energy field in his publication *"The Functional Relationship Between Yoga Asanas and Acupuncture Meridians"*.

CAT scans and MRI instruments are diagnostic instruments that can read bioenergy fields through the use of the electromagnetic spectrum. Doctors use these devices all the time without really knowing how they work.

The SQUID Magnetometer (Superconducting Quantum Interference Device) can detect minute biomagnetic fields around the human body as each organ in the body generates an electrical field that can be detected on the surface of the skin. In 1963, two coils, each with 2 million turns of wire, connected to a sensitive amplifier, were able to detect the biomagnetic field projected from the heart. Every cell, every organ and all the tissues in the body create electrical current and therefore have a corresponding magnetic field. [2] Baule, G.M. The SQUID also showed how electrons are not only particles but they are also waves, as contended by quantum physics. Brian Josephson, an English physicist, received a Nobel Prize for his work in this area in 1973. The SQUID can detect where diseases have caused the energy to incorrectly flow in sick patients. It also measures biomagnetic pulses of varying frequencies coming from the hands of energy healers and practioners. Medical laboratories are using SQUIDS to show the biomagnetic fields produced by physiological processes in the human body.

Secrets Of Energy

The spectroscope shows the angular rays of light characteristic for its color absorption and emission. It uses a prism that separates frequencies of an element for analysis.

A conventional Langmuir type device can be used to measure the electrostatic fields and provides the voltage distribution in time and space.

A dielectric polarization detector gives the magnitude and orientation of the electric field in space and time.

Humans Are The Best Detectors of Subtle Energy

> ***Some energies have not been detected with scientific instruments because these instruments have no parts above the (physical) level. Humans have all the parts and can therefore detect a greater spectrum of energies. Instruments are made of minerals, and lack the transducer components needed for detection...In other words, living beings are coupled to the cosmos better than scientific devices, which are, after all, quite limited tools.*** [3] Dr. Elmer Green of the Menninger Foundation, *Beyond Biofeedback*

Self-Directed Empowerment Technique: How To Sense Energy

1. Balance and center yourself by putting yourself in a relaxed, calm state and quieting your emotions. If you are interested in learning more about how to get into a theta state, you need to read about Autogenic Training.
2. As you send out your mind (your aura) to other people, you may notice a change in your pulse, perhaps a change in your body.

Subtle Energy Is Positive and Negative, Yin and Yang, Masculine and Feminine

Positive and negative refer to ions that are positively and negatively charged. Energy is neither good nor bad. See if this sounds logical to you. Since everything in the universe is energy, you are also pure energy. Your energy is neither good nor bad. However, you can use your energy in productive or non-productive behaviors. You may have positive or negative thoughts.

Energy has two poles, yin and yang, which are constantly fluctuating in dynamic balance and expressing the interdependence and relationship of opposites. Peace and harmony exist in nature and in your mind and body when the yin and yang principles are ebbing and flowing in the waves of creation. For anything to function optimally there has to be an energy balance. The body operates electrically–heartbeats, brain activity, hormones and chemicals. When there is an imbalance in the electrical system of the nervous system, we get strokes, an imbalance in the cardiovascular system causes heart attacks, an imbalance in the cellular system results in cancer.

Yin, feminine, subtle energy, corresponds to that which is: dark, moist, cool, receptive, yielding, Yin is intuition, and structure. The moon is considered to be yin energy. Yin energy is on the left side of the body.

Yang, masculine subtle energy, corresponds to that which is: light, dry, hot, active, and penetrating, Yang is rationality and analysis, and function. The sun is considered to be yang energy. Yang energy is on the right side of the body.

Subtle Energy Is Nonlocal

Energy does not exist in one place at one time but everywhere all the time. Picture a sponge submerged in a bucket of water. The sponge represents matter and the water represents energy. The same water is inside the sponge as is surrounding it. Now picture the sponge in the bucket and putting the bucket in the ocean. The water in the bucket is one with the water of the ocean the same way our energy is one with all energy, except unlike the ocean, energy is infinite.

My brother Scott has a sway back that gives him problems. I did energy work on him while visiting him in Chicago. About a year and a half later I saw him again and he said his back was beginning to hurt, so I did energy work again. Scott doesn't quite understand how energy healing works but he knows it does. Recently when I called from Atlanta and talked to him in Chicago, he said that his upper back was sore so I volunteered to work on him over 800 miles away. He knew immediately that I had removed the blocked energy and got the energy flowing in his muscles, but now he really doesn't know how I did it. Using the same illustration above and the illustration about how cellular phones work without wires, he understands that we are both transmitters and receivers of electrical and magnetic energy connected in the sea of energy. All energy is connected like a web.

Where Does Your Mind Exist?

Does your mind exist inside the body or perhaps at the outer layer of the Human Energy Field? I believe that mind extends infinitely...it is your energy field. **Mind is inside every cell, tissue, organ and system in your body and at the same time mind is operating throughout your entire energy field and connecting with Universal Mind and with all other minds.** That is an awesome thought. One thought from your mind (energy) joins the universal energy field and goes on infinitely! And in the reverse, mind energy from the universe joins your mind energy. The best solution to all your problems is to stop putting up barriers and blocking the wisdom of Universal Mind Energy.

Psychologists talk about a conscious mind and subconscious mind because they do not understand subtle energy. There is only mind. Mind is your energy field. It permeates your body. When you are taking in information through your five senses, and when you are consciously aware, your mind is active. It is the same mind that is receiving information, though more subtly, from higher levels and different dimensions. When mind thinks, it is operating at the mental level of subtle energy; when mind feels, it is operating at the emotional level of subtle energy. When mind is operating on the levels of divine will, divine mind, and divine love, it is spiritual. All of these subtle energy levels make up our beliefs. Further discussion in Chapter 7 What Is "Mind"? Where Is "Mind"?

Proof That Energy Is Nonlocal

To understand the impact of a nonlocal invisible form of info-energy that the brain finds very difficult to accept, consider the results of an experiment done in 1993 under the direction of the United States Army Intelligence and Security Command (INSCOM). White blood cells (leukocytes) scraped from the mouth of a volunteer were centrifuged and placed into a test tube.

A probe from a recording polygraph–a lie or emotion detector–was then inserted in the tube. The donor of the cheek cells was seated in a room separate from his donated cells and shown a television program with many violent scenes. When the volunteer watched scenes of fighting and killing, the probe from the polygraph detected extreme excitation in the mouth cells, even though they were in a room down the hall.

Subsequent repeats of this experiment with donor cells separated up to fifty miles, and two days after donation of the cells, showed the same results. The donated cells remained energetically and nonlocally connected with their donor and seemed to "remember" where they came from. [4]J. Motz

Subtle Energy and Information Are Interchangeable

Subtle Energy Is Intelligent

Energy follows thought follows energy. Subtle energy, according to Dr. Pecci in the forward of *Science and Human Transformation: Subtle Energies, Intentionality and Consciousness,* carries messages which unlock or modify the already existing energy potential within every cubic centimeter of space.

Subtle Energy

Everything that was needed in the universe was created at one time. Accessing the messages of subtle energy gives us the all the information that will ever exist. Is that not the most powerful statement!

Everything is energy, so thoughts are energy. What you are thinking, where you are focusing your attention and your will, and what you are imagining and visualizing, will manifest depending upon how much energy you are expending. **All of our ideas and feelings are flowing energy.** The things which we have the individual power to change, our success or failure, our health, our happiness, are the results of the expectations which we hold in our mind. Chapter 7 will discuss "What Is Mind"? And Where Is "Mind"?

Look at the GDV images in the middle of the book. People who mostly utilize their mental energies (illustrated by the yellow color) and are always trying to figure things out rationally have energy stuck to the front or back of their heads. The three-pound brain uses 25% of our energy, so when we are always just thinking, thinking, we feel so exhausted.

The GDV images of Dan (Figure A) show the power of our thoughts through guided visualization. Dan was attending a weeklong Neuro Linguistic Programming Seminar taught by Ann Daniel, a certified teacher. His first image Figure A shows Dan's exhaustion because he was awake most of the previous night. He has wide expanses of energy breaks that show no physical, mental, emotional or spiritual energy. The energy at the back left side of his head looks like a rooster's comb. This energy flow shows someone distracted in his thinking. The instructor did a fifteen-minute visualization with the class. You can see Dan's amazing changes. During the visualization he said he imagined his daughter. His thoughts were so strong that they created the expanse of purple mental energy around his head and lots of his physical, mental, emotional and spiritual energy was renewed.

Using Thoughts And Prayers To Promote Healing

Larry Dossey, in *Healing Words: The Power of Prayer and the Practice of Medicine,* discusses the healing effect of prayer. The important discovery was that the person doing the praying does not have to be near the person they were praying for. Other forms of mental activity can influence plant growth, fungi, bacteria, blood stability, and healing. A person can be taught how to influence the GSR (electrodermal activity) of a distant person who is unaware of the first person's efforts.

How Distant Healing Works

This is the same principle as how staying in touch with other people works. When you connect with a person simply by thinking about them via a picture, a piece of clothing, or a piece of their jewelry, you establish an energetic connection in the same way that a cellular phone or networked computer establishes an energetic (electrical) connection. The cellular phone has no wire connecting it to a transmitter. It connects and operates using a negative and positive charged battery. Remember: we are pure energy beings–both electrical and magnetic. Our battery is the billions of negatively and positively charged energy cells in our body and in the seven levels of our subtle energy bodies. This means that we can choose our connections if the other person is willing to be open.

Energy Has Memory

It is foolish to think that what we see in movies and on TV doesn't affect us. After seeing the movie *Psycho,* it took some women several years before they would take a shower instead of a bath. Until recently I could still recall the electrocution scene of a movie I saw as a child. It was a black and white movie at a drive-in theater. I could see the terror and feel the pain of the character as he faced electrocution. I used the Emotional Freedom Technique to remove emotional blockage that occurred.

When we become emotionally involved in a movie, the cells in our body are not able to discern whether the event is real or not. Our children see over 12,000 deaths on TV. It has been proven that everything that happens to us is stored in our energy field–the place where our beliefs are determined.

Subtle Energy Can Be Directed, Focused, And Increased Wherever You Want To Send It

Thoughts are the doorways to sensing and sending energy. Being able to focus your energy on one thing like a laser, rather an ordinary light that diffuses its light energy, makes you very powerful. Focusing is concentrating on one idea to the exclusion of all others. The more you are able to focus, the faster you will be able to do what you want to do in all areas. Dr. Tiller, in his book, *Science and Human Transformation: Subtle Energies, Intentionality and Consciousness,* says that through mental focus alone, people can increase the activity of the electrons.

Self-Directed Empowerment Technique: Take a few minutes each day to practice focusing your thoughts, seeking information, and sensing energy... whatever you need to do most. Write down the results so that you see your improvements.

Quantum physicists and scientists have discovered that the person administering any kind of test or experiment can consciously or unconsciously influence the test results simply by watching and, more so, by sending their own energy. The quantum physics principle of nonlocality says that, in the minuscule buzzing world of which our body's cells are a part, there are no barriers, time is relative, that mass, and information are one and the same, that objects once connected forever retain the info-energetic memory of that connection, and that the separateness of any kind in the world, human or otherwise, is mere illusion. [5] Pearsall, Paul

This is the reason that we have to be so careful about our associations and relationships. We pick up the energies of the people we are around even for a short period of time. The aura produces bioplasmic streamers that are sent out to other people. For instance, a positive person lifts another person's vibrations and brings clarity and lightness through what we call harmonic induction. We may unconsciously do it, but we are trying to make the other person's energy field pulsate like ours. A "kinesthetic," is a person who is very sensitive and who feels subtle energy more than sees it. Because they are more open to receive other people's energy, they attract strangers who come up and tell them all their problems.

In our auric interactions we are doing one of the following with our subtle energy allowing the energy to flow naturally, push, pull, or stop. You've played this game–if someone is trying to pull you in, you pull back or you disconnect with the person to stop the energy flow. If someone tries to push their energy into your field, you may push back or dig in your heels to stop them.

Many of us feel that we have to be in defensive mode most of the time to stop other people's negative energy. The problem with this is that we get reactive and begin sending negative energy back. Then the aura of both people gets distorted and both people begin to project and imagine things that are not truth. When we do battle this way, we get wounded. Then we suppress the wounds. Think about what happens to your energy when you repeatedly have bad interactions with a spouse, children, relatives, friends, or work associates.

The following procedure will tell you how to block other people's negative energies from entering your energy field.

Step number one: Remember subtle energy is everywhere, and it will do what you want it to do.

Step number two: Visualize a clear cylinder around your body that will refract negative energy. Fill the cylinder with subtle energy of different colors of light or white light, because it contains all the colors. Visualization is a powerful way of directing energy and stopping energy drain. Anyone involved in massage, chiropractic, or healing helps clients by releasing stored energy. You do not want that released energy to settle in you because it will drain your energy. It works!

How To Change Other People's Subtle Energy

Any time we are around other people there is an energy exchange. Would you like to soften the hearts of the people who are angry with you? You can do so if they have not closed their heart chakra and if their heart is open to receive. When one heart sends energy to another person, that energy becomes a part of the receiver's heart memory. The amazing thing is that you don't have to be in the presence of the angry person or a person sending you love to receive that energy..

Whenever we come into contact with a group of people, we either feel in harmony or discord with them. The principle like begets like applies here. If you are attracting people with negative traits, you need to look within to discover what is inside you that is drawing these people to you. A circle is formed and whatever is thrown off, more of the same returns again to the source. We can control ourselves, our surroundings, and our future. Our feelings radiate from us in circles or waves. When a thought connects with a similar thought, a vortex of energy is formed. You can watch as people in a group enter into a similar thought. The energy vibration of the entire group will rise or lower depending on the level of thinking.

Subtle Energy Can Be Scattered

Veronica's GDV image (Figure B) is best example I have of scattered energy. The day the images were done, Veronica was in charge of an exposition at work, getting ready to go through a divorce, and at odds with a co-worker. Her images look like someone took an eggbeater and literally scrambled her energies. Veronica's face showed the stress. She didn't argue with the results of her images because she felt the scrambled energy in her body. As a quick remedy I told her to walk backwards across the room several times to unscramble. However, if nothing changes in her life, her energies will scramble again. Over the next two weeks she saw a counselor, spent time in meditation, and made a decision about the divorce. When I took her second GDV images, she appeared more balanced.

We know that we send out vibrations. A spiritually evolved person emits five rates of vibrations from his subtle energy; while most people send out nine rates of vibration. When people are overly emotional and worried, they may send out 50-100 rates of vibration. Their subtle energy is broken up into many whirlpools and cross-currents of energy causing them to lose both their physical and subtle energy.

Subtle Energy

Electromagnetic Energy Is Visible And Invisible

You might want to read the information about the electromagnetic spectrum in Chapter 1 again. The following information is just about the visible and invisible light, which is in the middle of the electromagnetic spectrum. Visible and invisible light contain all the colors.

Visible, Physical Light

The shorter the wavelength of the radiation, the higher the energy is. The range of colors in the rainbow are red, orange, yellow, green, blue, indigo, and purple. All other colors come from these main colors. Red has the slowest frequency and orange has the next. As you go through the order of the colors previously listed, you end with purple being the fastest frequency. The same colors vibrate in areas in the human body. You will read more about this in the section of chakras.

The rainbow of colors that we see in visible light represents a very small portion of the electromagnetic spectrum. Physical invisible light becomes visible when it interacts with matter (like the human body.) Look at a red flower in the sunshine and you will see red light refracted off the petals of the flower. This is not the same light that is created by subtle energies because subtle energy is not refracted and it does not move in a straight line. The light coming from subtle energy moves rotationally and the subtle energy is the source of the light.

Humans are heliotropes. This means that one of the ways we receive energy is from the sun's rays. We receive ultraviolet light, the seven rays, the colors of the rainbow–red, orange, yellow, green, blue, indigo, and purple, through our skin, eyes, and through seven major metabolic centers and hundreds of smaller metabolic centers called chakras. I prefer to call them stars as the Egyptians did. We all feel more energetic on sunny days and less energetic on cloudy days. When we don't receive enough energy from the sun in our energy field and in our body, disharmony results on all of our levels. Too little sunshine creates depression, physical, mental and emotional illnesses.

References

Baule GM, McFee R 1963 *Detection of the magnetic field of the heart. American Heart Journal* 66 95-96

Green, E. and A. Green. 1989, *Beyond Biofeedback.* New York: Knoll Publishing Co. p. 304

Motz, J. "*Everyone an Energy Healer:* the Treat V Conference in Santa Fe." *Advances* Vol. 9,1993, pp. 95-98.

Pearsall, Paul, *The Heart's Code, Broadway Books, New York, 1998, p. 42..*

Nelson, Roger D. G. Johnston Bradish, York H. Dobyns, Brenda J. Dunne, and Robert G. John. "Field Anomalies in Group Situations," *Journal of Scientific Exploration,* v. 10 pp. 111-141, 1996.

3. Properties Of Subtle Energy

Categories Of Subtle Energies

Geopathic; the meridians of the earth, Biological fields (other than orgone)
Orgone: vital energy
Ethers: First three levels of the aura etheric

Systems Utilizing Subtle Energies

Meridians, geopathic lines, bioemissions, thought forms, crystals

Examples of Subtle Energy Phenomena

If you interested in learning more about subtle energy phenomena you should begin with an in depth study of several of these areas: Homeopathy, remote viewing, precognition, levitation, telepathy, dematerialization/ materialization, healing/Qigong, dowsing, clairvoyance, clairaudience, psychokinsis/telekinesis

Properties Of Subtle Energy

Subtle energy is visible to many people.
Subtle energy interpenetrates matter exuding in layers that infiltrate one another. The layers are created by the level of vibration beginning with the slowest vibration and moving up to the highest. Some properties and actions of subtle energy have not been listed because they were not particularly applicable to the purpose of this book. (Subtle energy is a negative space/time lattice. This is an aspect you might want to research.)

Subtle energy is not physical

Plato said that the physical is but a shadow of higher dimensions. He insisted that we have receptors within the mental and sensory systems of our physical body that are receptive to and can be trained to bring into conscious awareness the energies of the negative space/time lattice. What does this mean? Negative space/time means that since all subtle energies are connected, what affects the subtle energies in one place affects all subtle energies; therefore, there is no time differential.

Many of the colors of subtle energy are different from physical light and there are many more colors. The colors have an opalescent quality, which means that the light comes from within the colors

Subtle energy is mutable. It can change colors, form, and attributes.
Each level of subtle energy can exist with each other level. Lower levels cannot extend out to the higher levels.
Subtle light is not refracted or reflected.
It can move in straight lines that are scintillating, which means that the light spirals around the straight line as it moves up and out the straight line that goes infinitely.
Subtle energy has patterns, standing waves, and shapes.

All of creation exists as energetic patterns of waveforms what can be described in terms of frequency (vibrations) and form (geometry). Physicists say that there are eleven dimensions of reality. We live in what we call the third dimension. Most of us can only see 3-dimensional shapes and configurations, others can see patterns in other dimensions. For instance, the 4th dimension acts as a transformer of vibrational energy that creates patterns in the shape of Plastonic solids. The shapes that subtle energy takes are the shapes of sacred geometry: circle, triangle, square, rectangle, tetrahedrons, pentagram etc. You can research more information on this interesting topic.
Thoughts, intentions, feelings, and emotions can change the color, vibration, shape, and size of subtle energy. You determine the level of your thinking by getting into a state, which then determines what level you are on.
Keep the following subtle energy characteristics in mind as you read about the aura.
Subtle energy can be cloudy or clear. Darker shades of subtle energy colors indicate negative thoughts, emotions, and memories.
Subtle energy contains information about the past, present, and future.
Magnetic forms have subtle energy

Interactions:
Subtle energy influences the biological activity of the body
The subtle fields interact with one another. There is an intermixing across different fields. Subtle energy forms a connection that piggybacks, one on top of the other.
Subtle energy has interactions with physical properties
The perceptual sensations of subtle energy: pressure, warm, cold
Subtle energy may be conducted by materials and retained by materials

Actions: (specific descriptions) (physics)
Subtle energy can have opposing polarities without cancellation–positive and negative energy can flow at the same time.
Counterflow of currents is possible with subtle energy.
Fast propagation phenomenon (can exceed light speed).

Properties Of Subtle Energy

Subtle energy has intrinsic flow properties as a result of its different forms: gas, liquid, fluid, and lines.
Subtle energy behaves as if it had infinite frequency.
Positive aspect: expands, Negative aspect: balances, diminishes.
Subtle energy, unlike physical energy, can move in both directions at the same time. Physical energy would explode if it moved in both directions.
Both physical and subtle energy penetrate matter, but subtle energy does not need matter to be created as does physical light.

Subtle energy can be in fluid form. It can take the form as gas so it looks vaporous and cloudlike. As you study the seven layers of the aura you will find that levels of subtle energy are transferable locally and non-locally.

Your Aura Is Your Human Energy Field

Humans emit ultraviolet waves, microwaves, radar and radio frequencies. Science states that the movement of any electric charge involves the emission of electromagnetic waves. The movement of electrons in atoms leads to emission in the ultraviolet. The movement of molecules in cell membranes leads to emission in the microwave region. The movements of cells in muscles and body organs generate emission in the radar and radio frequency ranges. The larger the entity causing electric charge displacement, the lower the frequency of electromagnetic emission. (EM) Invisible light can carry intelligence through telepathy or other forms of communication by distance. Tests conducted by Dr.Valorie Hunt and others at UCLA showed the following frequencies for subtle light: Blue 250-275 Hz, Green 250-475 Hz, Yellow 500-700 Hz, Orange, 950-1050 Hz, Violet, 1000-2000, plus 300-400, 600-800 Hz and White 1100-2000 Hz.

Self-Directed Empowerment Technique: Put yourself into a theta state by doing meditation.. Ask and get permission from the higher self of someone you know before you tune into his/her energy. You can understand the other person or perhaps help them heal if you feel their energy. Subtle energy can feel warm, cold, prickly, slimy, soft, and loving. You already pick up a person's energy subconsciously. Trust to be aware of what you are feeling and to trust your feelings.

First, a discussion of light...
Light may be spontaneously emitted from an atom when an electron changes its state. Or, a light beam may be directed toward an atom from outside, and either scatter from the atom or be absorbed, causing some change in atomic state.

Physics teaches us that a light beam of a definite frequency is made up of a large number of particles of definite energy and momentum, called the photons. The photon energies are comparable to the energy of the outer electrons in the atom.

How Atoms Create Emissions Of Light

When an atom is in its ground state it cannot emit photons because it would lose energy. When there is a collision with another atom, one or more electrons are raised to an excited orbit and a *transition* occurs and photons (light energy) are emitted (spontaneous emission).

Atoms in solid matter affect one another, as well as the light they emit, in such a way that the light emerging from a solid body bears little resemblance to that which the atoms composing the light would emit in isolation. Now isn't that interesting!

The photons emitted in a transition have both spin and orbital angular momentum as well as energy associated with them. The atom's angular momentum must change in order to balance the energy carried away by the photon. In some cases **the emission of photons does not depend on anything outside the atom. There is an internal mechanism in the atom that makes it emit the photon.** There is a lot more to be learned about atoms that physicists do not understand. I believe the answers will be resolved through quantum physics.

Bottom line, the aura is created by electron orbit changes and the result of physical rotations and vibrations of molecules, flexture of cell membranes, and pulsations of organs and body movement.

The Absorption Of Photons By Atoms

Imagine a direct light beam sent to a group of atoms. What can occur is resonance absorption. Resonance energy, the energy between ground energy (when no energy emissions are given off) and excited states, is absorbed by the atom. The shortened version of what can happen is the energy of the photon ends up being converted into the heat energy of random motion of the atoms in the body. Again, this explains energy healing. The person sending the energy sends a direct beam of light through the chakras in their hands or through the heart chakra that is a higher vibration than the person receiving the energy. The receiver's energy becomes higher and resonant with the sender, and thereby healthier. The more intense the light beam, the better.

The Aura

Your personal energy field has an egg-shaped protective shield approximately six feet in circumference that keeps you from being bombarded with too much cosmic energy and with too much information from universal mind. What if your mind tried to take in information about everything that ever happened or will ever happen? What if your senses reacted to everything that was going on in every place? Talk about sensory overload!

The energy inside this protective shield, now referred to as **aura,** is also called "subtle energy" because it is not as high voltage as the power of the electrical energy that runs the electronics in your home. Subtle means that the energy hasn't been harnessed into a small wire, but this is still powerful energy, especially when several like-minded people send their group energy–synergize.

What Causes The Colors In The Aura

Different kinds of atoms emit different colors of light. The exact pattern of the light can be studied with a spectroscope, which uses a prism to separate the light into its many component colors, each of which corresponds to a wave of a definite wavelength. The particular pattern of colors emitted by a specific element (or compound) is unique, and rather independent of how the atoms are excited. **Different atoms will generally have different emission spectra because their energy levels are different.** When the temperature of matter is increased, the rate at which the collisions of atoms occur increases. This is the reason that people feel heat when energy healing takes place

When pure light intermingles and integrates with the atoms of matter, colors, hues, and intensities are created. Subtle energy contains several different forms and colors or no color. The colors are opalescent. Look at a beautiful opal gem and you will see what I mean. The colors come from within the opal; they are not a reflection of outside light. The colors are not cloudy when the person is healthy and clear thinking. Have you seen the new clear kind of neon lighting? The difference in the light within the aura is that there isn't just one filament of light creating the color. Millions of points and particles of light moving in waves are creating the light. For this reason the light is in constant, revolving motion. The light energy is constantly changing in response to our thinking, emotions, metabolizing food, air, water, energy and all the other activities going on in our body, our energy field, and the universal energy field.

The beginning of Quantum physics began when Dr. Albert Einstein won the Nobel Prize for his discovery of the photoelectric effect. Simply put, he discovered that light is both a wave motion in space, and it carries particles with it called photons–small particles that integrated with electrons and caused displacement. **There may be ten billion photons for each electron. Photons are constantly intermingling, interacting and radiating within the**

molecules of matter. They animate the inanimate making such molecules as calcium, magnesium, and sodium, vital to all life processes. Sitting out in the bright sunshine the other day I noticed thousands of gold points of energy, each smaller than a pinhead, constantly moving in the atmosphere near my body. When they moved they produced beautiful streams or strings of energy. Quantum physics says that everything in the universe is made of strings of energy.

Subtle energy can be white light, black light, or different colors of light, many that are not found in physical light. It can be formless or it can have the form of scintillating lines. The light in scintillating lines begins inside the body and it rapidly fires and moves along the line quite beautifully. Sometimes the light is gaseous. Sometimes it is reflective light, like the light around a light bulb.

When you were first created, seven levels within a protective shield were created. They are templates, which means that they are the energetic design, the form and structure of who you become mentally, physically, emotionally, and spiritually on the physical level when you incarnate each time. Each of these seven levels contains all of the information about you past, present, and future. They contain all of your physical, emotional, mental and spiritual experiences. They contain all of the organs in your body on an energetic level. They contain all of your emotional issues that you carry from lifetime to lifetime. They contain your patterns of thinking as well as your patterns of doing.

In order to think differently, behave differently, feel differently, connect differently we have to change the energy in each of these seven levels. It is important to note that your human body exists within these seven levels. The human body does not create your aura. The physical body in which you now reside is just the vehicle that you are presently traveling in. The energy inside the body is a continuation of the energy outside the body, only more compressed. You have seven levels of energetic bodies that are interacting; fields that envelop and penetrate your physical body and govern its functioning and extend out into other energy fields.

Energy travels in waves and particles, and it is able to freely travel through matter. If your energy in your protected shield is not free flowing, it will not be free flowing in your body. The energy inside the body is determined by the energy outside the body.

Science currently accepts the following general categories of energy –gravity, electromagnetic energy, strong and weak nuclear energy. You cannot see gravity or air, but you know that both are present and that they are energy because of the "work" or "effects" they produce. Most of the electromagnetic field is invisible except for the visible light and seven color rays. We know that there are microwaves, x-rays, radio waves, TV waves etc. because we use them. An **electromagnetic field**, sometimes referred to as an **EM** field, is generated when charged particles, such as electrons, are accelerated. All electrically charged particles are surrounded by electric fields. Charged particles in motion produce magnetic fields. When the velocity of a charged particle changes, an EM field is produced.

We talk about the "vibes" or vibration people send out. The level of your vibration depends upon your energy output. Negative thoughts such as anger, revenge, worry, and depression are low vibrating energies that stagnate the energy flow in your body and lower your vibration. People who are very sensitive about picking up other people's energy or the energy of objects such as clothing, furniture, and different localities should stay away from negative people, places and objects. People who are not knowledgeable about how energy operates scoff at people who might hug a tree to get energy or place their hands on a tree to release energy. You can put your hands on a wooden door to release energy if you don't have a living tree around.

Quantum physics teaches us that we constantly receive energy (light) from the stars in the form of waves and particles. We have chakras and meridians that act as energy portals that metabolize energy sent from the universe. Have you ever waved your hand over your head to signify that something went "right over your head?" You were illustrating a second principle of energy; it has information. If your mind was blocked with stuck, blocked energy, the information could not enter the sixth chakra, better known as the Third Eye, the place where your receive intuitive information and knowledge from the universe.

When I speak on the topic Energy Management, ™ I may have an audience of two hundred people whom I have never met. I take a quick three minutes to teach them how to see my aura. Then I tell them I am going to take another two minutes to change to color of my aura. Over 75% of the audience can see my aura and then see it change colors. How so? We have the power of our minds to focus and direct energy. Like sound, color, and everything in the electromagnetic field, thoughts have different vibrations. So when I have higher thoughts, such as unconditional love, I imagine a soft pink color with my Third Eye and I create lots of pink in my aura and raise my own vibration.

Pure Energy

ergy Principle: You are electrical, magnetic, and crystalline, just like the niverse.

Here is what is going on in your body that makes you pure energy:

You are always sending out various colors of light: Each of the organs creates a different color of light. For example, the liver creates yellow light, the heart creates green, gold, and pink light, the hypothalamus creates purple light.
Your heart is producing an electromagnetic pulse, a sound pulse, a pressure pulse, and a heat pulse.
You can send out infrared radiations from your hands that increase cell growth, cell respiration, plus DNA and protein synthesis.
You are sending out microwaves.
You are sending out sound waves created by the organs, bones, cells, and muscles.
Your bones are sending out an electromagnetic field.
You are vibrational, magnetic, electrical, and crystalline.
You are a force field that influences others and is influenced by others through touch, words, sounds, and vibrations.

You are light–which means you are electrical, vibrational, and magnetic

The physical body takes in and sends out light. We are energy and light, meaning that we are affected and nourished by light. **Light is energy**. The more open, aware, and sensitive to light vibrations we are, the more we can be influenced and healed by the basic nature of light. Each color in light has it own vibration. We need all the colors to be balanced. The more light in your physical body and around you, the more you are like the Source of your energy and the more sustainable and influential your power is.

When I speak to groups of nurses I always ask nurses who work in critical care if they have seen the energy leaving a dying person. They all give a similar response. The nurses say the second that the patient transcends this life, they see light leaving the patient's body and going up in the air. Many nurses say that patients, no matter how sick they are, perk up right before they transcend and talk about seeing departed relatives and angels around them. Family members mistakenly think they are going to revive, but it is preparation for transition.

Sound creates vibrations in the body...the body creates sounds and vibrations

them. The sound wave created is a million times slower than electromagnetic waves because its neutral mass movement. [1] Oster, G.

You Are A Totally Crystalline Being

I have a collection of crystals bought at rock and mineral shows. People who realize that you are going to use them for energy and healing begin to look at you a little weirdly only because they do not know the first thing about their bodies or about crystals. Read on and you find a new appreciation for crystals.

Mined crystals–The energy of crystals and gems have been used by all cultures throughout the centuries to heal, calm, influence, radiate, protect, and help you instill favorable qualities, just to name a few. They store, amplify, absorb, and transmit energy.

Crystals are mentioned over two hundred times in the Bible so it is hard to understand why people consider those who use crystals to be weird or unspiritual. The high priests in the Old Testament wore breastplates containing amethyst, amazonite, serpentine, lapis lazuli, quartz crystals, citrine, onyx, and jasper.

Melody says in her book, *Love Is In The Earth*, "crystals are universal energy and when one contacts them and receives their energy via exercise of the Higher Will, one can contact and synthesize the energies from which the entire universe is comprised." [2] Melody

Crystals from the ground and those in our bodies function as energy amplifiers, transformers, capacitors, modifiers and focusers of energy. For this reason when I do energy healing I send my energy through a crystal to do all the functions listed above. Our bodies are crystalline structures that assimilate the inflow and outflow of energy. **Solid and liquid crystals are contained in every organ, gland, cell tissue salts, protein structure in our bodies.**

Connective tissues such as bone cartilage, tendons, and ligaments, plus other tissue in our bodies such as teeth, artery tissue, keratin in skin, and elastin have piezoelectric properties. Glycine, proline, and hydroxyproline, amino acids crystals do also. **Piezoelectricity is the quality whereby electricity, and sometimes light, is produced via compression.** Collagen and proteoglycans, the extracellular matrix components of bone, possess piezoelectric qualities according to Andrew Basset in "Biological Significance of Piezoelectricity" written in 1968.[3] Medical research by Dr. Basset's professors at the College of Physicians and Surgeons, Columbia University has been going on for over 30 years. **His hypothesis is that alterations in a cell's electrical environment will create a change in the cell's physiological behavior.**

Even The Membranes Of Our Cells Are Polar

We need to know something about cells since we have trillions of them in our body. Cell membrane appears as a vanishingly thin and is tri-layered black-white-black "skin" enveloping the cell. In science we were taught that the membrane was simply a passageway. Recent research shows that membranes possess both a globular *polar* phosphate head and two stick-like *non-polar* legs. So what we find is that even the membranes of cells are polar. The membrane protects the cytoplasm (all the structures inside the cell) in the cell from its external environment. It also gives a way for the active exchange of metabolites and information between the cytoplasm and surrounding environment. It is energy/information that travels in and out of cells.

Each of the approximately 100,000 different proteins providing for the human body is comprised of a linear chain of linked amino acids. The "chains" are assembled from a population of twenty different amino acids. Each protein's unique structure and function is defined by the specific sequence of amino acids comprising its chain. Synthesized as a linear string, the amino acid chains subsequently fold into unique three dimensional globules. The final conformation (shape) of the protein reflects a balance of electrical charges among its constituent amino acids.

The three dimensional morphology of folded proteins endows their surfaces with specifically shaped clefts and pockets. Molecules and ions possessing complementary physical shapes and electrical charges will bind to a protein's surface clefts and pockets with the specificity of a lock-and-key. Binding of another molecule alters the protein's electrical charge distribution. In response, the protein's amino acid chain will spontaneously refold to rebalance the charge distribution. Refolding changes the protein's conformation. In shifting from one conformation to the next, the protein expresses movement. Protein conformational movements are harnessed by the cell to carry out physiologic functions. The work generated by protein movement is responsible for "life."

A number of the twenty amino acids comprising the protein's chain are non-polar (hydrophobic, oil-loving). The hydrophobic portions of proteins seek stability by inserting themselves into the membrane's lipid core. The polar (water-loving) portions of these proteins extend from either or both of the membrane's water-covered surfaces. Proteins incorporated within the membrane are called *integral membrane proteins* (IMPs).

Membrane IMPs can be functionally subdivided into two classes: *receptors* and *effectors*. Receptors are *input* devices that respond to environmental signals. Effectors are *output* devices that activate cellular processes. A family of *processor proteins*, located in the cytoplasm beneath the membrane, serve to link signal-receiving receptors with action-producing effectors.

Receptors are molecular "antennas" that recognize environmental signals. Some receptor antennas extend inward from the membrane's cytoplasmic face. These receptors "read" the internal milieu and provide awareness of cytoplasmic conditions. Other receptors extending from the cell's outer surface provide awareness of external environmental signals.

Conventional biomedical sciences hold that environmental "information" can *only* be carried by the substance of molecules. According to this notion, receptors only recognize "signals" that *physically* complement their surface features. This materialistic belief is maintained even though it has been amply demonstrated that protein receptors respond to vibrational frequencies. Through a process known as *electro- conformational coupling.* [4] Tsong Resonant vibrational energy fields can alter the balance of charges in a protein. In a harmonic energy field, receptors will change their conformation. Consequently, membrane receptors respond to both physical and energetic environmental information.

A receptor's "activated" conformation *informs* the cell of a signal's existence. Changes in receptor conformation provide for cellular "awareness." In its "activated" conformation, a signal-receiving receptor may bind to either a specific function-producing *effector protein* or to intermediary *processor protein*. Receptor proteins return to their original "inactive" conformation and detach from other proteins when the signal ceases.

How does this happen? According to cellular biologist, Dr. Bruce Lipton, the cell membrane is an organic information processor. It senses the environment and converts that awareness into "information" that can influence the activity of protein pathways and control the expression of the genes. Two things to remember–energy contains information...and it is possible to change our DNA.

The membrane of a cell is a *liquid crystal*. And the fact that information is transported across the membrane of a cell makes it a *semiconductor*. As a **liquid crystal semiconductor with gates and channels**, the membrane is an information processing *transistor*, an organic *computer chip*.

We Are Pure Energy

Each receptor-effector complex represents a biological BIT, a single unit of perception. Though this hypothesis was first formally presented in 1986, the concept has since been technologically verified. Cornell linked a membrane to a gold foil substrate. By controlling the electrolytes between the membrane and the foil, they were able to digitize the opening and closing of receptor-activated channels. The cell and a chip are homologous structures. [5]Lipton, Bruce, PhD.

The cell is a carbon-based "computer chip" that reads the environment. Its "keyboard" is comprised of receptors. Environmental information is entered via its protein "keys." The data is transduced into biological behavior by effector proteins. The IMP BITs serve as switches that regulate cell functions and gene expression. The nucleus represents a "hard disk" with DNA-coded software. Recent advances in molecular biology emphasize the read/write nature of this hard drive. Indirect support for this idea of the overall living system as a complex of synchronistic oscillating crystalline structures has slowly been accumulated by the scientific community. In ***An Atlas of Cellular Oscillators,*** by P.R. Rapp, research in over 450 papers is cited in cataloguing an atlas of biological and biochemical oscillators with a periodicity of one hour or less. [6]Rapp, P.R.

This includes oscillations in cell membranes, secretory cells, neuronal cells, skeletal cells, smooth cells, heart muscle cells, and cell movement. In a healthy state, the body structures are a multileveled series of interacting systems and subsystems that resonate harmoniously. Disease occurs when this synchronicity is thrown into disharmony. **Appropriate crystal balancing of the total system through the chakras or of subsystems with a particular organ or gland can be very beneficial for healing this dies-synchronicity.**

Energy And The Cellular Body

Energy Principle: Flowing energy creates health, happiness, and success. Blocked energy creates disease, sadness, and failure.

This is a must read section. Right now your child's textbooks are teaching outdated information about the cells.

We have forgotten our history. A split formed in the healing arts of medicine that is slowly reuniting. Until the 1930's medicines were derived from plants. We didn't have to worry about side effects that are worse than the cure. The apostles of the Christ went from town to town performing miracles of healing. But many of today's churches have forgotten their role in healing the sick. Science has just invented the technology to prove what people have known innately about energy for 5,000 years–that our level of energy determines our health. Spirituality, science, and medicine are slowly coming together.

Your Body Has Innate Intelligence In Every Cell.

The moment the father's sperm fertilizes the mother's egg it produces an ***electrical charge*** and physical life begins! So we begin life with an electrical charge; we even say "the spark of life". From this union on the etheric level, millions of cells begin to grow. But what is it that causes the cells to divide into all the different kinds–muscle cells, cartilage cells, gland cells, nerve cells and others that ultimately create tissue in our bodies? It is energy. Energy is the basic ingredient of our whole body. DNA predispositions all our ingredients, but energy puts it into action.

Your body has over fifty trillion cells. The organelles of each cell have physiologic functions associated with the activities of specific organs. Cells literally have components that can be called bones, tendons, and muscles, digestive system, an excretory system, a respiratory system, an immune system, a reproductive system and a cardiovascular system, among others. Cells also contain their own little musculosketal system called the cytoskelton.

In humans, all of these physiologic functions mentioned above are associated with the activity of specific organs. These same physiologic processes are carried out in cells by diminutive organ systems called *organelles*. Therefore it is true to say that cells have the equivalent of a "brain" and a "nervous system". This explains how white blood cells can move to an injury and also the fact that they have mind.

Dr. Bruce Lipton, Ph.D. says in an article for *Bridges* that each cell has its own nervous system that reacts to environmental stimuli. Previously it was thought that the cell's brain was located in the nucleus of the cell. It is the cell's membranes, however, that represent the cell's brain.

Also, cells are embodied in the connective tissue and information flows in and out of the cell membrane continuously. Not only do we have information flowing in and out cell membranes, but also the cells are able to communicate and break apart from their connections. The action of the cells forms a molecular network connecting every part of the body. This is the reason we say that the body is not only connected, but it works cooperatively and synergistically.

The millions of cells in the body are connected. This helps us understand why energy healers are able to help people heal. It also explains how energy sent to one part of the body can then travel to other parts of the body and heal. Also important to note is that the energy level of the healer must be higher than the person they are sending energy to because the higher energy of the healer raises the energy level of the other person. It has been proven that all substances in the body are semiconductors of energy. The necessary material for all transmission of energy is water. The more water tissue holds the better its conductivity. Today doctors prescribe electrical conducting technology called Pulsed electromagnetic field (PEMF) therapy. This is a device that produces a magnetic field that induces currents to flow in nearby tissues and bones to increase the speed of healing broken bones.

Vibrations And Sounds

Every time a cell moves or changes its shape, specific sets of lattice vibrations (photons) travel like waves throughout the nuclear and cytoplasmic matrix and then into the extracellular matrix. Likewise, muscle contractions produce specific sound vibrations that travel through tissues.

Cells Are Bipolar

The nucleus of the cell is slightly acid and the cytoplasm is slightly alkaline. Enzymes do a large part of the work of the cell, assimilating nutrients and generating electric charges through the mitochondria. These large molecules are light (energy) catalysts; they trigger reactions within the cell. They donate energy to reactions as in breaking down sugars and fats for electron energy. Enzymes are depositories of light/energy particles. The membranes of muscle and nerve cells conduct alternating positive and negative charges along their surfaces. These cells make up our neuromuscular network, a relay system of our thoughts, sensations, and motor responses. Scientists use a voltmeter to register the charge, which is slightly more negative, about-70mV, when they are at rest.

Cell membranes have intelligence because they decide what can enter the cell or what they must keep out, for example, toxins. Cells contain more positive potassium ions (K +) while the fluid outside contains positive sodium ions (Na+). To put it simply, the cell's membrane allows the potassium ions to enter. But when a nerve or muscle is stimulated or "charged" in about one thousandth of a second, the measurement moves to -30mV. Energy is created by our thoughts that in turn produce our emotional chemicals.

Ions are an electrically charged atom or molecule. They are created when atoms and molecules exchange tiny negatively charged articles called electrons. Calcium ions are essential for muscle contraction. Sodium ions are essential for conduction of nerve impulses. Electrolytes are substances that easily release ions when dissolved in water. The pineal gland is situated just above the thalamus in the area of the brain known as the epithalamus. It produces melatonin.

When a cell becomes "***excited,***" it produces neuro-transmitters, such as acetylcholine, which moves from cell to cell via synapses and dendrites. Neurotransmitters are chemical agents, enzymes and hormones that carry information. In order to send a rippling effect throughout the body several cells must be stimulated. When the cells create the electro and magnetic fields they circulate through the body's nervous system, the connective tissue sheaths, and the circulatory system which extends into every part of the brain and into every part of the body. Cells can learn to ***inhibit*** neurotransmitters through conscious mental processes or as a result of a traumatic experience. We learn how to *control* our nerve cells and muscles through training, experience, and attitude.

Thought is processed, interpreted, and evaluated in the central nervous system based on our physical habits, patterned ways of thinking, and our present mental attitudes. It then moves throughout the body at about two hundred fifty miles per hour. **The body responds to our thinking commands.** When the flow of energy through the body circulates inefficiently, our thoughts become cloudy, and parts of the body become numb, unable to feel sensations and work efficiently.

Our Bones Are A Solid Crystal Structure

Our skeletal bone structure has been proven to be a solid crystal structure. **It is able to convert sound or light, forms of vibrational energy, into electrical magnetic and electric energy that pulsates throughout the body.** Our crystalline bone structure as an antenna for all incoming and internal vibratory energy and information, including direct thought from energy. Do you ever think that your bones are picking up your thoughts? This is one of the causes people get misshapened as they grow older. When a bone is physically stressed or for some reason pushed out of its normal shape, a piezoelectric effect is created which causes an electromagnetic field pulse. Medical intuitives are able to see this field pulse. You can also use a pendulum to find field pulses.

What Is A Piezoelectric Field And What Are The Effects?

Piezoelectricity is the quality whereby electricity, and sometimes light, is produced via compression. They could negatively affect cell nutrition, local PH control, enzyme activation and suppression, orientation of cells, synthetic capacity and specialized function of cells, contractility and permeability of cell membranes and energy transfer. [7]Basset, Andrew. Piezoelectric fields are created in the anti-gravity muscles, the cardiovascular system and the voluntary muscles. The heart and muscles act as a result of electrical impulses. We receive impulses from outside of the body–the reason you don't want to live close to power lines.

Our bones create an electrical-magnetic field response called streaming potentials. This electric field is created by the flow of ions, charged solutes, and cells such as red blood cells through the tissue, carried by extracellular fluids such as blood through the extracellular matrix. When bone is even subtly bent from pressure by something like walking or even the pulse of our arteries, the extracellular fluids are pumped through the bones. An electrical potential is created as a result of the electrostatic interaction of the electrically charged fluids past the fixed charge in the crystalline bone structure. These electrical fluids can also interact with the piezoelectric fields (pressure created fields) of the bone. [8]Basset, Andrew

Depending on the generating sources, electro-magnetic field intensity, pulse characteristics, and the combination of the electrical interactions with the bone structure and fluids, a particular electromagnetic field will be generated in the bone.

It is also important to understand that the energy being discussed is not simply mechanistic, heat, and electron transfer. As pointed out by McClare in Resonance in Bioenergetics, there is a level of organization in bioenergetic systems to operate rapidly and yet efficiently. [9] McClare, C.W. F. He points out that energy release via resonance is exchanged so quickly that it is not thermally available, but remains a form of stored energy. This implies that 100 percent of the resonant energy is transferred and that no entropy (loss of energy) occurs.

Muscles And Energy

Muscle and nerve tissue exist as liquid crystal systems held in shape by bone and skin systems. The muscles, by nature of their structure, are held in shape by bone and skin systems. The muscles have also been shown to have some piezoelectric (pressure created) properties. Muscles and nerve tissue also exist as liquid crystal systems held into form by bone and skin systems. On the cellular level, all cells and cell membranes are considered liquid crystals. These include the plasma membranes, mitchondrial membrane, smooth and rough endoplasic reticulum, nuclear membranes and chloroplast membranes. [10] Johnson, J.F. and Porter, R.S.

Here's how muscles work. Muscles have fibers that draw together in the center. Muscles attached to bones spread out along the bone. The muscle may attach to another bone or muscle. When the body is in a steady state of contraction, it is holding its posture or firmness (muscle tone). Movement is unbalancing of tone. Movement is a relaxation of one muscle while the other muscle contracts. When muscles are working perfectly all of the body's energies are flowing freely.

Muscle weakness is caused from turned off muscles due to toxins, tightness, lack of use, and lack of nutrition. Reflexes and reflex points relate to different systems in the body. You can learn in Chapter 9 how to gently pressure them into allowing the energies to flow to the muscles and other parts of the body. When our muscles are tight or in spasm, they cause pain because they are pulling the spine out of alignment. A weak muscle on the one side of the body causes the spasm and tightness in the muscle connected to it. You may rub, relax, and stretch a tight muscle and temporarily release it, only to find the problem return because you have not addressed the cause–the weak muscle. For each motion a muscle makes, there is a corresponding muscle that opposes that motion. For instance, if you have a tight muscle in your leg, look for a weak muscle that extends or straightens it.

Since everything in the body is connected, let me give you an example of how one tight muscle in the hip can affect your whole body and the positions of your internal organs. As we noted in the preceding paragraph, tightness in one muscle means there is weakness on the other side that causes us to favor the other side. This puts a strain on the foot because it is in a different position causing strain on other sets of muscles. Another result is that the posture will change and affect the position of the internal organs that then restricts the nutrition to the organs and changes the excretions and hormonal functions. This results in a change in the body's cells caused by a chemical/psychological imbalance. Again, another result will be that the person will think and feel differently because of our mind/body connection.

Body Fluids Also Have Crystal Qualities.

The water molecule contains in itself the potential forms of all crystals in its primary form of a tetrahedron. Water can bring all different forms of ions into a crystalline state and hold them in solution. In addition, the more structured water is, the higher concentration of ions it can hold.

One of the most important of these ion solutions is the dissolved cell salts. In Norm Miksell's paper on structured water, the author points out that when the body cells and tissues become disease or cancerous, the crystalline protein structures no longer have the proper configuration to maintain the water in an optimal structured state. [11] Miksell

If the water in the cell, extracellular fluid or blood plasma becomes structured, it will then be able to attract and hold more ions by virtue of its hydration shell patterns. When structured water is organized around a particular ion, as it is with cell salts, it is able to move the ions more easily into the more structured cytoplaic water inside the cell. Once of the ionically structure water is within a cell; it helps attract the same cell salt or ion into the cell. This is probably how the ferrum phosphorum cell salt works to help people who are anemic draw more ions into their intracellular and extracellular fluids.

The Mind And The Body–Within It Is A Crystal Transmitter

Self-Directed Empowerment Technique: You are like a radio or TV receiver that can receive many different levels of energy of your choosing. What you receive is what you pay attention to. Make a specific list of the negative things that you do not want to receive into your energy field and consciously decide not to pay attention to them.

When we become a clear channel for the Divine God Force of unconditional love, it comes through us in a way analogous to a gem or crystal being activated by our thought forms. In this enhanced state, a strong resonant field is created which is capable of reprogramming the subtle energy of a person's crystalline structure. We create a new and healthy field that then reorganizes the person on a spiritual, mental, emotional, and physical vibratory level This higher love force helps release negative thought forms which are stored as dissonant vibrations within a person's system at any of these four levels.

What You Need To Know About The Electromagnetic Fields

The following scientific information about electromagnetic fields doesn't appear to be very exciting until you apply it to how electromagnetic fields work in your body and then it gets very, very interesting.

What causes you to be vibrational, magnetic, and electrical? Thousands of mini crystalline transformers in your body transmit vibrational, magnetic, and electrical energy. But what decides at what level of vibration all these different kinds of energies are moving in and out of your body? You do.

Study the following information carefully because you have to understand the differences in electrical energy and magnetic energy to know how they work together in your body. Electric and magnetic energy can be in fluid form. When they do not have charges, they are at rest. Electric fluid and magnetic fluid act differently. Electric charges act either as sources or sinks of the electric fluid. Magnetic liquid, on the other hand, has no sources or sinks: nothing can pour out or suck up magnetic fluid.

An electron is constantly absorbing electric fluid around it at some rate, call it ε. In the reverse, **protons constantly pour electric "liquid" towards the surrounding space** at rate ε, so liquid moves away from the proton with speed. (Keep these facts in mind as you think about the millions of fields operating in your body.) See that energy moving in circles. (You will learn later that subtle energy is also in fluid form.)

Both electric fluid and magnetic fluid are incompressible, which means that their density does not change: it is not possible to compress a lot of electric or magnetic fluid into a smaller space, or to squash it out of a given volume. If magnetic fluid is standing still, it can be stirred up, making it move in closed circles and closed loops called vortical motion. For the magnetic fluid to keep moving in the same loop, though, some force has to keep stirring it up: otherwise the energy of its circular motion will dissipate and the magnetic fluid will stop moving and will return to rest.

Two things that cause magnetic fluid to be stirred up are thoughts and emotions. **Thoughts and emotions are very powerful energetic forces that pull in the electromagnetic fields of other people–their thoughts, emotions, mental and physical energy and their spiritual energies.** This is the reason that we need to be careful of the close connections and relationships with other people. You need to carefully choose the people that are being magnetized to you and that are magnetizing you to them.

You Are Magnetic–Proven By Magnetocardiograms

There is a new science called neuromagnetics. It says that crystals of magnetite exist throughout the body and permeate our brain cells. The pineal gland, called the "king gland" because it regulates the endocrine system, has a unique magnetostatic sensitivity. The pineal gland, located in the middle of your head, is the fastest vibrating part of your body. The brain produces biomagnetic fields that pass undistorted through the cerebrospinal fluid, across the connective tissue of the brain, and through the skull bones and scalp. This is the basis of how our brain functions.

Contractions of muscles produce electrical fields that are recorded by electromyography. Every muscle in the body produces magnetic pulses when it contracts. The larger muscles produce larger fields and the smaller muscles produce smaller fields...of course.

Biomagnetic fields indicate the events taking place in the body. MEG (magnetocardiograms) are the most sensitive devices to measure brain activity because magnetic fields can travel through tissues without a distortion. This is the reason doctors order MRI's.

Note: If electric fluid starts to accelerate in a certain direction, it will cause a vortex. It causes magnetic fluid to move in circles around the direction in which the electric fluid is accelerating As soon as the electric fluid stops accelerating, the vortex of magnetic fluid vanishes. Note: electric fluid will not accelerate spontaneously. Something has to force it to accelerate. This same thing then thing then causes (indirectly) the magnetic vortex to be stirred up. A magnetic vortex will not arise spontaneously. Finally, if magnetic fluid accelerates in a certain direction, it causes electric fluid to move in a vortex which circles around the direction of acceleration in the direction opposite to the right hand rule. An acceleration of the electric fluid causes a positive vortex of magnetic "liquid" to move around it, but an acceleration of the magnetic liquid causes a negative vortex of electric liquid to flow around it. Magnetic Fields, unlike electric fields that positive and negative energy coming from monopoles, do not have magnetic monopoles.

> Self-Directed Empowerment Technique: **Now this is important: In order to magnetize whatever you want to bring into your life you must focus on a higher level of reality.** That is to say, you must use your mind energy focused on the 5th, 6th, and 7th levels of your subtle energies (aura) to draw to you whatever you want.

You Are Electrical

We are electrical beings because every metabolic process, every enzyme reaction, muscular movement, food digestion, fat burning, and thought processing is an electrical process. Illness and disease occur when our bodies have an electrical slow down; there's reduced metabolism and fat burning, reduced energy and immunity.

The gases, liquid, and solids in our bodies are made of atoms–just different forms of energy. Although they appear inert, they are transformed when integrated into life forms. Light particles are constantly intermingling, interacting integrating and radiating within the particles of matter. Elements are the smallest particles of matter and they are individual atoms that we also call oxygen, carbon, hydrogen, nitrogen, etc. When elements bond together they form molecules. Molecules are two or more atoms electrically bonded together forming compounds, such as, water, carbohydrates, proteins, fats, etc. When the electrons orbit at infinitesimal speeds and share, they create chemical bonding. Bonding of elements creates the molecules of matter in water, fats, sugars, toxins, plastics, minerals, vitamins etc.

All matter emits radiations of energy. We are transformers of energy and we operate by radiant and electrical energy. Our electromagnetic waveforms indicate whether we are vibrating at a higher or lower vibration because they reflect our physical, mental, emotional, and spiritual levels.

When we are healthy and balanced, negative and positive vibrations are in equal strength. Illness occurs when the energy in any organ is disturbed. Health returns when a healer uses any number of various vibrational healing approaches, like homeopathy, acupuncture, and aromatherapy to balance the person.

Ever wonder why you feel so good on bright sun shining days? The sun, our closest star, charges the atmosphere with prana (energy). To see this energy, take off your glasses, if you wear them, and defocus your eyes softly gazing at the sky. You will see a entire field of dots pulsing together and moving in curved trajectories. On sunny days the dots are bright and fast moving. On cloudy days they are darker and slower moving. After several days of cloudy weather you will notice that you are moving even slower and are not as happy. This is the reason why so many people vacation in very sunny mountainous regions to recharge their energies. I have friends who suffer from light deprivation in the winter and they go to highly charged areas in the mountains or to the ocean to get revitalized. Your auric field can actually double in size as you walk along the beach because the salt air clears out low vibratory frequencies. If you can't swim in the ocean's salt water, you will benefit from a saltwater bath to clear out blocked energies.

Actually the ocean's vibration is too high for me and I prefer a calm lake. The sight of a still lake helps me release scrambled, incoherent energies. Many people like watching, listening and being close to a fast moving stream because it gives them high energy. Probably the highest energy comes from standing at the bottom of a waterfall. You leave exhilarated!

How Do Electrical and Magnetic Energy Work Together?

Go back and read where we left off on the discussion of how electrical and magnetic energy moves. An acceleration of electric fluid causes a positive magnetic vortex. This means that the magnetic fluid has been accelerated to produce this circular flow. But this causes a negative vortex of electric fluid around the magnetic vortex. This reactive vortical acceleration of electric fluid is in the direction opposite of the original acceleration of electric fluid: hence a negative feedback loop: The positive feedback would cause the original acceleration of electric fluid to amplify itself continually, while at the same time the vortices around it would amplify as well: an explosive maelstrom of movement of electromagnetic fluid. According to the laws of electro-magnetism an initial disturbance (acceleration) of the electric fluid will cause feedback loop which, being negative, will tend to extinguish itself at its source but which will propagate outwards in what is called an electromagnetic wave.

Self-Directed Empowerment Technique: Make a list of everything you want to magnetize to your life. Find some pictures or symbols of those things and place them on a poster board. Visualize what it is that you want coming to you. Use your physical senses to start feeling how it will feel, see how it will look, taste it, touch it. Use the power of your subtle energies to magnetically attract the physical matter and the people with high vibrations and higher thoughts...everything that you want in your life.

Self-Directed Empowerment Technique: Here's an exercise to help you receive more universal and earth energy. Picture any one of the stars above your own head. See the star holographically, that is, from all sides and angles. It is not flat, but filled with bright, radiant energy of any color that you choose. If you really want to be powerful, choose gold. As you know, the moon was once a part of the earth and it represents your connection with earth. Visualize the moon beneath your feet. Move the energy of the moon up to the star above your head. Move the energy of the star down to the moon. Do this several times.

Energy Principle: You get what you give your energy to.

References

Basset, Andre C. "Biophysical Principles Affecting Bone Structure," The Biochemistry of Physiology of Bone. New York, NY: Academic Press, p. 1-76. 1971.

Basset, Andrew. "Biological Significance of Piezoelectricity." Calc. Tiss. Res. 1.252-272, 1968.

Johnson, J.F. and Porter, R.S., *Liquid Crystals and Ordered Fluids* Ed. New York: Plenum Press, 1970. p. 80.

Lipton, B, Nature 1997, 387:580-584.

Lipton. B 1986, *Planetary Assoc. for Clean Energy Newsletter 5:4.*

McClare, C.W. F. "Resonance in Bioenergetics" Annals of the N.Y. Academy of Science. 227:74-91, 1974.

Melody, *Love Is In The Earth*, and Earth-Love publishing House 2003 P. 32.

Miksell, "Structured Water: The Healing Effects on the Diseased State," San Jose, CA: PRI, 1985, pp. 1-10.

Oster, G. 1983 "Muscle Sounds" Contracting muscle generates distinct sounds that are not heard only because the human ear is insensitive to low frequencies. Such sounds are now studied for their possible usefulness in science and medicine. *Scientific American*, vol. 250, pp. 108-114.

Oster G. & Jaffe, J.S. 1980, 'Low frequency sounds from sustained contraction of human skeletal muscle', *Biophysical Journal*, vol. 30 pp. 119-127.

Pieta, K.J. & Coffey, D. S. 1991. "Cellular harmonic information transfer through tissue tensegrity-matrix system." *Medical Hypotheses,* vol. 34, pp.88-95.

Rapp. P.R. "An atlas of Cellular Oscillators, Journal Esp. Biol., 81 291-306, 1979.

Russek LG, Schwartz G. E., 1996, Energy cardiology: a dynamical energy systems approach for integrating conventional and alternative medicine. Advances: The Journal of Mind-Body Health 12:4-24.

Science 1999, 284:79-109

Secrets Of Energy

Tsong, *Trends in Biochem. Sci.* 1989, 14:89-92.

5. Energy Is Moveable And Transferable

"If we are beings of energy, then it follows that we can be affected by energy."

All living creatures are metabolic. Metabolism of food water, air and light produces heat and energy. All living creatures are composed of atoms that have a back and forth motion. Atoms form molecules, which form cells and cells are throughout the body. Our body is in our energy field which is also metabolizing universal energy, cosmic energy, the earth's atmospheric energy, and energy from all the other energy fields.

All of the different types of energy (magnetic, electrical, light, vibration, sound, etc.) are in constant flux, so they are movable, transferable. So how does energy move in and out of our bodies? First, you have to understand that **you are a light being.**

You are a system of light, as are all beings. When you shift the level of your consciousness, you shift the frequency of your lights. Gary Zukav, *Seat of the Soul*

I hope by this time you totally understand the statement: **The human body is an electrical biosystem, collecting and receiving energy from the atmosphere and the universal energy field.** The universe sends us cosmic energy from the stars, sun, and even from other planets. We receive energy from the electromagnetic fields produced by the radiations of power lines, all electrical equipment, and the energy from non-alive and alive matter, such as humans and plants.

The seventh level of the aura keeps us from taking in too much cosmic energy and will be discussed later. Seven chakras are inside each of the seven levels of the aura. There are seven chakras just outside of the body that determine the intake and outflow of energy. Activity in certain chakras triggers increased activity in others. I have noticed a correlation between the 3rd chakra, also called the solar plexus chakra and our body's center of power and the 5th chakra, the throat chakra. When we close the throat chakra we also close the solar plexus chakra because we do not speak our truth with the throat and we stop our power.

While the chakra colors are frequently described as kundalini red, hypogastric orange, spleen yellow, heart green, throat blue, third eye violet, and crown white, there actually may be several different colors entering the different chakras. As Chapter 3 discussed, light is one of the major vibratory forms of communication in the body and the amount of light in the body determines the high or low frequency we emit.

How Energy In The Form Of Light Is Transferred Inside The Body

Our bodies are transducers that are able to detect and metabolize subtle energies. The endocrine glands, the nervous system, and the person's own energy field are "coupled" converting a signal from one form of energy to another. There is a transduction system in the body based on the chakra system that interpenetrates the seven subtle bodies of the aura. The chakras and the auric bodies must both be in alignment so that the energy flow meets little resistance.

Self-Directed Empowerment Techniques: 1. Do meditation to increase right and left-brain synchronization. 2. Learn to control mental and emotional agitation for chakra alignment. 3. Begin at the root chakra and move your hand in a clockwise motion. Visualize the red light energy from the root chakra moving to the second chakra. Visualize the orange light energy from the second chakra moving to the third chakra. Go through the same procedure with all your chakras.

How Do You Align Your Chakras And Auric Bodies?

The best way to align your chakras is to repeat the Lord's Prayer. If you look at the words closely, you will see that different lines directly affect different chakras.
Our Father which art in Heaven, hallowed be Thy name (relates to the 7th chakra also called the crown chakra)
Thy kingdom come (relates to the 6th chakra, where we know the love of God)
Thy will be done (relates to the 5th chakra, where the will of God is expressed)
On earth and it is in heaven (relates to the 4th chakra, the heart and relationship chakra and connector to the soul)
Give us our daily bread (relates to the 3rd chakra, the solar plexus, which contains the stomach, spleen, pancreas, and liver–all organs which have to do with digestion of our food)
And forgive us our errors as we forgive those who trespass against us. ((2nd chakra, the relational power source center)
Lead us not into temptation, but deliver us from evil. 1st chakra, root chakra)
For thine is the kingdom, power, and glory forever.

Meditation balances the right and left hemispheres of the brain. Recent research by Brother Charles of MSH Associates in Virginia supports the idea that increased right and left brain synchronizations increase the flow of spiritual energy into your energy field. You can use the Brain Button Exercise in the Chapter 12 Human Performance and Energy. Moments of mental agitation or anxiety can misalign your chakras and aura. During times like this you must become **aware** of your thoughts and feelings and take steps to realign yourself.

Remember how each of the seven colors of light produces a different wavelength, red being the lowest frequency and purple being the highest. This is the reason that the slower vibrating colors begin lower in the body and go up higher as they ascend in the body.

Black light, like white light, contains all of the primary colors, but it moves more slowly. You literally can bring black light into your body from the earth's energy in the ground. It enters through the soles of your feet and you can take a few seconds and slowly move it up through your body.

In the same way you used your thoughts and visualization to bring in black light, you will want use your thoughts and visualization to bring white light from the universe down through the top of your head and into the middle of your body to meet with the black light. Or you can bring a specific color into your body by beginning at the top of your head, the crown, and moving it throughout your body. It is better to bring in only the higher vibrating colors through your head so you don't slow down your vibrations in the top three chakras. This will be discussed more fully in the next section.

I have taught this technique to several people who work in energy release occupations like chiropractors, massage therapists, and healers. They complain that after working they feel very exhausted. Putting up a shield works because you are setting your intention. Visualizing and verbalizing your intentions is doing all of the previously stated things about energy.

To be balanced, we must receive all the light of the seven colors in the body. For instance, minerals and enzymes in the body's cells are not activated if they do not receive the proper wavelengths. The result is that they do not fire and catalyze normal, cellular metabolic reactions. This translates into less energy exchange, glandular insufficiencies, and reduced ability to burn fats and toxins. Did you ever associate deep breathing with weight loss?

Every cell in the body is built upon the cosmic rays that operate its enzymes and metabolic exchanges. The health of the cells is dependent upon a state of equilibrium and an abundance of the sun's life giving photons. Its spectral balance translates into acids and alkalis that operate electrical exchanges. As cell colonies and tissue systems, they vibrate in unison with a predominate color ray hue. The infrared rays–red, orange, yellow, green, blue, indigo, violet and ultraviolet–are constantly adjusting themselves according to internal combustion, enzyme reactions of sugars and fats converging with oxygen (blue), generating acids (red) liberating free electrons, and external radiations brought in through the skin and eyes.

[1] Dr. Charles Mc Williams

Self-Empowerment Technique: 1. Get 15 minutes of sunlight everyday. 2. Drink water that has been in the sunlight. 3. Put pieces of colored film, like those used in front of spotlights, or colored cellophane in your window and then sit so that your body can absorb that light. Use the pendulum to determine which color(s) you need.

How Sunlight Affects Our Bodies

When pure light intermingles and integrates with the atoms of matter, colors, hues, and intensities are created. Direct light energy into your body creates a new spark of life. It heightens your perceptions and contact with your soul and your Creator.

You are a light being, which means you are very dependent on huge amounts of light and color as a nutrient. Light deficiency and metabolic inefficiency create several diseases such as cancer, obesity, and immune deficiency.

Sunlight carries intelligence factors or vibrations. These rays carry communicable knowledge. When the ancients practiced sun worshipping, the sun priests would absorb intelligence. **The direct intake of solar energy is the inhalation of intelligence. The intake of solar energy through the eyes and nervous system has a revitalizing effect upon the organism.**

The eyes, for example, are sensory receptors of photons (light energy). Photons of light/energy enter the body through the skin and the eyes. The eyes pathway of energy is the retinal tissue that goes directly from the pineal gland, which is located in the center of the brain and head for protection. The energy of the photons is then transmitted all over the body by the nerve ganglia, which act as our electrical wiring. They distribute energy to all of the organs and cells.

The skin is also a receptor of the energy from other energy fields; it is also light sensitive. The endocrine glands are affected via the pituitary master gland and thereby the whole physical organism.

Strenuous exercise and training create lactic acid in the body causing soreness and stiffness. Sunlight produces a metabolic effect that reduces the lactic acid. Sunbathing also helps the lungs absorb more oxygen and increases the blood's capacity to carry and deliver oxygen. Illnesses such as chronic fatigue and cancer are linked to oxygen deficiency.

Sunlight affects the body's endocrine glands. It stimulates the thyroid gland to increase its hormone levels, translating into increased metabolism and weight loss. The following is a warning for people who work in offices every day. When color rays are missing in artificial lighting, or sunlight is filtered through window glass, contact lenses, windshields, and smog, color hunger creeps in. Amazingly the tiny pineal gland, located in the center of your brain, vibrates faster than any other part of your body, allowing your brain to process impressions and create pictures in your mind.

> **Self-Directed Empowerment Technique**: 1. Suggest that your business purchase full spectrum light bulbs for the health of their employees. 2. Get out in the sunshine and walk during lunch.

How Energy Is Transferred Inside Your Body

The skin receives sunlight, sound vibrations, and energy from other fields. The importance of the energy entering the eyes was discussed in the previous section. The sound vibrations received by the ears affect your entire body.

Breathing: Shallow breathing denotes fear. Deeper breathing from the solar plexus enervates the body, keeps the mind clear, and keeps you healthier. Remember the information in the beginning chapters about how the atmosphere is **filled with visible and invisible light–the electromagnetic field and infrared light? You are breathing in and exhaling visible and invisible light when you breathe.** Doesn't it stand to reason that the deeper you breathe, the more light will enter your body?

> **Self-Directed Empowerment Technique**: Breathe deeply from the stomach and diaphragm several times a day to get grounded and centered, to re-energize, and to release blocked energy. Deep breathing is the great stress reliever.

Food–I would suggest reading *Spiritual Nutrition and the Rainbow Diet* by Dr. Gabriel Cousens, holistic physician, psychiatrist, homeopath, family therapist, Essene minister, Reiki master, meditation teacher, and international peace activist. He and his wife direct the Tree of Life Rejuvenation Center in Patagonia, Arizona.

Water and Energy

Lack of water is the #1 trigger of daytime fatigue. 75% of Americans are chronically dehydrated.

Water and Weight
In 37% of Americans, the thirst mechanism is so weak that it is often mistaken for hunger. Even mild dehydration will slow down one's metabolism as much as 3%.
One glass of water will shut down midnight hunger pangs for almost 100% of the dieters studied in a University of Washington study.
Water and Health
Preliminary research indicates that 8-10 glasses of water a day could significantly ease back and joint pain for up to 80% of sufferers.
A mere 2% drop in body water can trigger fuzzy short-term memory, trouble with basic math, and difficulty focusing on the computer screen or on a printed page.
Drinking 5 glasses of water daily decreases the risk of colon cancer by 45%, plus it can slash the risk of breast cancer by 79%, and one is 50% less likely to develop bladder cancer.

Water has everything to do with the health and energy of your body. We are not talking about carbonated water, or water with caffeine that the liver will have to filter, or water in sweet fruit drinks that will temporarily spike your energy level. We are talking about pure water, preferably highly structured water that can hold a higher concentration of ions.

The Benefits Of Structured Water

Everyone knows that the body is 75-80 percent water, and that body fluids have crystalline qualities. Positive and negative ions activate (energize) the cells. Water can bring all different forms of ions into a crystalline state and hold them in solution, such as body fluids. If the water in the cell, extracellular fluid, or blood plasma becomes structured, it will then be able to attract and hold more ions by virtue of its hydration shell patterns. When structured water is organized around a particular ion, as it is with cell salts, it is able to move the ions more easily into the more structured cytoplaic water inside the cell. Once the ionically structured water is within a cell, it helps attract the same cell salt or ion into the cell. This is probably how the ferrum phosphorumcell salt works to help people who are anemic draw more ions into their intracellular and extracellular fluids.

Norm Miksell's paper on structured water points out that when the body cells and tissues become diseased or cancerous, the crystalline protein structures no longer have the proper configuration to maintain the water in an optimal structured state. [2] Miksell

How do you tell whether you are dehydrated so that your energy level is low or your body diseased? Dehydration can affect how your brain and nervous system function. Semi-dehydration affects your coordination and concentration. By the way, thirst does not determine dehydration so you need to use muscle testing. It would be worthwhile sometime to have your hair tested because it reveals so much about your health status. You can lightly hold your own hair if you are testing yourself, or hold the hair of another person to test them. If your muscle switches off when your hair is pulled, you need to drink more water. After drinking water, you will find that the muscle response is switched on now.

How Energy Enters The Body Through The Chakras

There are several books that discuss chakras in much further detail than will be done in this book. Since they are so important because they absorb the life force energy, also called light or prana, break it up and distribute it through the nadis to the nervous system, the endocrine glands and the blood, I think it would be worth your time to find out more information. *Chakra Therapy For Personal Growth and Healing* by Keith Sherwood is an excellent book devoted to chakras.

Barbara Brennen in her book *Hands of Light* says, "The word chakra is taken from the Sanskrit word meaning wheel. These wheels can be seen as rotating energy centers, gates, or transformers within the body. They sense the subtle energy in your personal energy field. Tibetans call them *khor-lo*, which also means wheel. In the Sufi tradition, some call them *latifas*, or subtle ones. In the Bible, John refers to these centers as the "seven seals on the back of the Book of Life." In early Christianity they were often referred to as the "seven churches." The Kabbalists refer to these centers as "the seven centers in the soul of man."

Here is an overview of the chakras. There are seven major chakras and twenty-one minor chakras. According to David Tansley, in his book *Radionics and the Subtle Bodies of Man*, the seven major chakras are formed at points where the standing lines of light (lines of energy) cross each other twenty-one times. The twenty-one minor chakras are located at points where the energy strands cross fourteen times. Additionally, there are smaller chakras situated over the body where the energy lines cross seven times. These points are used in acupuncture.

The twenty-one minor chakras are located: one in front of each ear, one behind each eye, one on each clavicle, one near the thymus gland, one above the breast, one in the palm of each hand, one near the liver, one connected with the stomach, two connected with the spleen, one related to each gonad (male) or ovary (female), one behind each knee and one on the sole of each foot.

The seven major chakras are situated in line with the spine. They are: the crown center which is just above the top of the head, the brow chakra, the throat chakra, the heart chakra, the solar plexus chakra, the sacral chakra and the base chakra. Each of these major chakras works with one of the endocrine glands in the physical body.

These chakras can become blocked or partially closed in a person due to trauma. When this happens, the endocrine glands are unable to function to their full potential and the physical body suffers.

What Causes The Chakras To Close

The chakras are the repositories of colored, invisible light that allow the inflow of energy from the Universal Energy Field. They are photon centers that feed the Five Senses, and nerve plexi. These force centers distribute high-frequency energies to the appropriate organs of the body by the fine network of nadis. The *nadis* conduct *Prana* (life force subtle energy) through the seven chakras, subtle bodies, and through the *hara*, the fulcrum from which everything is balanced which is located three fingers below the naval. The higher vibrational input provides a subtle nutritional and organizational influence to the cells of the physical body, helping to maintain balance and order at the molecular level of expression. Their energy is replenished by exposure to sunlight, proper breathing, pleasant sounds, water rich and flavored foods, and caressing touch. Chakras also send energy out.

We close our chakras with our thoughts and feelings. When you are around people projecting negative thoughts and feelings it is wise to close your chakras to their energy. This is a good short-term answer, but you don't want to stay closed because when the chakras are closed, they do not receive enough life force energy. This causes depletion of all our aspects of energy. Energy not only flows in and out of the chakras, but it flows from one level of the chakra to the next. When the energy from one or more chakras energy is depleted, it takes from the energy in other chakras. When the energy from one or more chakras is blocked, it causes the other chakras to be blocked.

The total balance and health of the human organism is a product of a balanced and coordinated functioning of both physical and higher dimensional homeostatic regulatory systems. If there is a system failure at any level of the physioenergetic hierarchy, physical breakdown and illness may occur.

Energy Principle: The energy of the heart is the connection to the soul. When you connect your heart to the Mind of God and the Love of God, you will produce your most powerful energy.

The Heart Chakra–Our most powerful subtle Electromagnetic Energy

The heart chakra, the center of love, contains the heart and thymus gland and it is where our most powerful electromagnetic energy is produced. It registers the quality and power of love in your life. It is through this chakra that you achieve spiritual transformation.

The heart connects to the soul. **The heart and the soul are the center of subtle energy and the point from which everything originates.** The emotions of the heart control the production hormones and cells produced in the thymus, which directly influences the immune system. This is scientific proof of the healing power of spiritual love. People who experience a broken heart, or some event which causes deep depression, will manifest a physical illness or disease. If they decide to close down their hearts in response to whatever the experience was, they close down their ability to receive life force energy. We pay a big price in lack of health and energy when we close down our hearts for whatever reason.

I am a professional speaker to many associations and groups. To demonstrate the power of the heart when I speak, I ask the people in the audience to raise their hands if they are holding a grudge against someone. A lot of hands go up, but from that group I always choose the biggest man so that it really illustrates my point.

After he has agreed to be a volunteer, I ask him to think about the person he is holding a grudge against. I do muscle testing when he is thinking negative thoughts about the person by pulling down his arm to show his weakness when he thinks negative thoughts about the person he is holding a grudge against. Remember, the body does not lie, so muscle testing is a very accurate diagnosis. Then I ask him to send loving thoughts from his heart to the person he is holding the grudge against. At first participants seem reluctant and amazed I would ask such a thing. I promise him that he doesn't have to have dinner with the person; I just want him to send unconditional loving thoughts. He takes a few minutes to send loving thoughts; you can see anger go out of his body and softness in his face. When I do the second muscle testing, I am not able to move the arm because it is more powerful. Actually his whole body becomes more powerful. The audience is amazed. The energy of the man's heart has affected every cell in the body.

Want to increase your heart energy? Every time you send loving thoughts or healing energy, your own heart energy increases. Because most of us have an "open" heart, we are directly affected by the electromagnetic energy around us, especially the energy of other people. For this reason we need to be careful who we hang around or we need to learn how to protect our hearts. Doctors are aware that a pulse of electricity through the heart muscle creates each heartbeat. They have not figured out that what is going on with us mentally, emotionally, and spiritually is as important as what is going on physically.

The flowing of these particles, ions of potassium, chloride, calcium, magnesium, and sodium, across the muscle membranes makes them excite and cause contraction in the heart. These currents of electricity move into surrounding tissues and into the circulatory system. This causes electricity to flow through the blood that then goes through every tissue. The heart is constantly in touch with every cell in the body; and this is what permits us to actually hear, feel and sense with our heart. It is from the heart that we resonate our energy, and it is with the heart that we know the vibration of other hearts. The heart has long been believed to be the place where the soul resides. You can read in detail about this concept in Gary Zukav's book *Seat of the Soul.*

The Great Power Of The Heart

A friend told me that she wanted to make some significant changes in her life so she was sending messages to her brain about how she wanted her new life to be. But it wasn't working! I told her that the heart, not the brain, is in charge of the body. The brain acts like a computer, but the heart is the software that tells it what to do. The heart is constantly sending information from within every cell of the billions of cells within our body. Energy contains information, and it is the heart that sends the information, organizes and integrates it, and connects the brain and body. The heart chakra is the middle chakra connecting us to our souls and balancing the energy of the body.

A new field in medicine, cardio-energetics, believes our thoughts, feelings, fears, and dreams come from the heart rather than the brain. We've always talked about our "heart-felt dreams," "heart-felt feelings," and "hearts of gold." The heart and brain communicate via neurotransmitters–chemical and electrical messengers that travel through the nervous system.

This is why the heart chakra, located in the front of the chest and at the back, is considered so important. People who see colors around the heart say that they are green, pink and gold. So when electricity flows through the heart, it is not only producing electrical current, it is producing energy in the form of vibration, "heart strings," and colors. Physics teaches us that energy fields are unbounded. This means that the biomagnetic field of the heart extends indefinitely into space. Each heartbeat moves out 360 degrees into the sea of universal energy.

Every time our heart beats, it is sending out our vibration that contains information about which level we are on. You can feel an angry heart, a joyous heart, or a change of heart–it speaks of our soul. Heart transplant patients tell stories of feeling the presence of the heart giver. Because the heart cells hold memories, the heart receiver begins to like foods eaten by the giver, though they have never liked those particular foods before, or the heart receiver begins listening to new kinds music. Many heart receivers have said that they have new thoughts. What kind of heart would you pass on?

Remembering that everything is energy, we find the heart affected by hormones and neurotransmitters, both of which are kinds of chemical energy. The heart also takes in physical energy from the sun and cosmos plus subtle energy within the body and from the aura through the heart chakra. In this section you are going to be amazed to find out that the heart controls the body, not the brain. The heart actually has its own brain cells. **The heart's electromagnetic field is the strongest of any tissue in the body.** The energy of the heart can be measured 15 feet away. Each heartbeat begins with a pulse of electricity through the heart muscle. The electricity is created because charged particles flow across the muscle to excite contraction. The currents created by this action spread out into all the tissues in the body.

Our broken hearts affect our health. The images of Amy, Figure 3, were done several months after her stepbrother's death. She is an attractive young woman who is overweight. The gaps in her GDV image show where she is losing energy. Her physical energy, represented by the blue color, is not flowing freely from her body.

Amy's stepbrother died as a result of a drug deal gone wrong. Notice on the right side of her body, the yang, worldly side, how the energy in the heart area has been pushed very far out by emotional energy. Amy's worldly side is very angry and emotionally upset by the death. The left side of the body is the spiritual side; it sees the big picture about the brother's death and has resolved the issues.

You can tell that something emotional happened to a family member because the displaced emotional energy in the first/root chakra. This chakra always shows our family relationships. You can tell that this was a recent event, not a childhood event by viewing the energy displacement in the upper part of her legs rather than the lower part.

I always tell people when they are grieving over the loss of a loved one that the person is probably around them in spirit form. Amy said that she felt her stepbrother around her, but she still felt emptiness in her heart.

How Our Thoughts, Emotions, And Attitudes Affect The Heart

The brain acts as an information relay station to let the heart know about the body's energy status. ***Now this is so important!*** The heart produces Atrial Naturetic Factor (ANF), a neurohormone that connects with the brain and the immune system. We have known that people could die of a broken heart, but we just didn't know how it worked. The hypothalamus is the pea-sized gland located the middle of the brain that affects so many of our body activities, affects our emotional states as well. The hypothalamus controls 75% of our life processes, regulates the messenger molecules between the brain and the immune system in addition to coordinating the endocrine system, and the autonomic nervous system, which regulates cardiac, smooth muscle cells and glands. The pituitary gland, called the master gland, is actually attached to the hypothalamus.

Take a few minutes to find the important endocrine glands: pituitary, hypothalamus, and pineal.

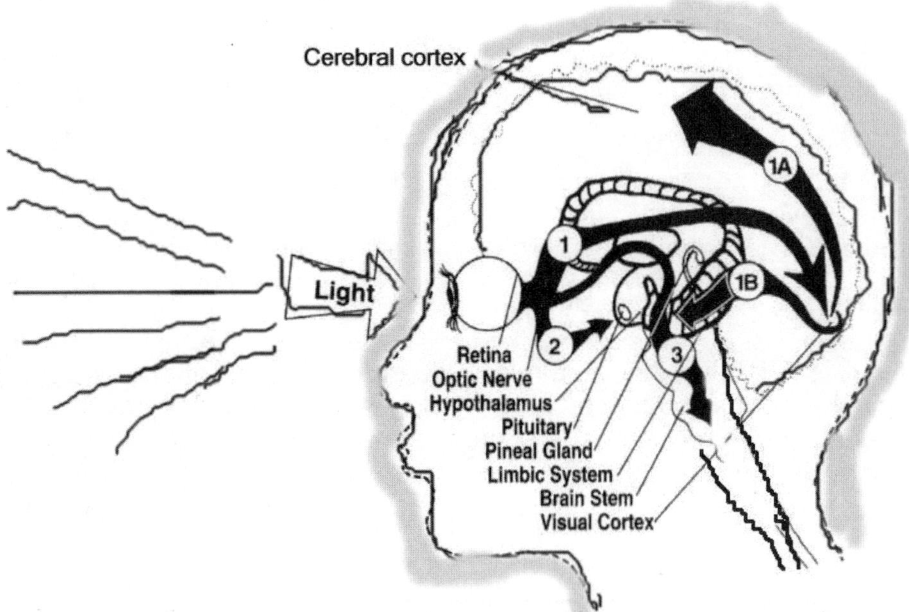

The heart's electromagnetic field is five thousand times more powerful than the electromagnetic field created by the brain. In addition to its immense power, the heart has subtle, nonlocal effects that travel within these forms of energy. Superconducting quantum interference devices, magneto-cardiograms, and magnetoencephlograms that measure magnetic field outside the body show that the heart generates over fifty thousand femtoteslas (a measure of EMF) compared to less that ten femtoteslas recorded from the brain. [3] Kargagulla, S. These devices can pick up the field of the heart 15 feet away from the body.

Energy Release And Transfer

Energy healing practitioners, massage therapists, and chiropractors help their patients release energy. The practitioner has to be careful that the released energy does not transfer and attach to them. **Every person is sending and receiving energy, which means that every person has the ability to be an energy healer and to receive energy to be healed.** Many of you already do healing in some degree when you send loving thoughts and prayers, or when you pat or kiss a child's hurt place. I believe that this is an innate ability that does not require certification. You may take some workshops, read some books about healing, or learn from other healing practitioners, but I do not believe that doctors or the government has the right to regulate something that everyone is doing innately.

My friend Julie went to a Native American sweat lodge ceremony and came back feeling rather sick and out of energy. This is not to say that you shouldn't attend sweat lodges, but you must install a protective shield around yourself before you go. Learn to check out how you feel after you have been. Using my pendulum I found that negative thoughts released from other people during the ceremony had attached to Julie. Thought forms can have cords that attach to your physical body and can enter your auric field. Thought forms will be discussed in detail in Chapter 8 Subtle Energy Of The Aura.

When we die and leave our physical body in death, our souls, our energy, can decide to go on to the Light while other souls with lower energy hang around the earth. Most of us believe that ghosts can hang around in different locations. If you have never heard of attachments, this sounds unusual. I have met several people who knew that a loved one had attached to them shortly after death. The person with the attachment said from that moment on they felt less energy and they knew exactly where the cord was located.

By moving the pendulum around Julie's body I found six attachments. I asked the pendulum to give me a "yes" where I should cut the attaching cords and then sent them to the light. The cords from Julie's body were sent back to her body. When Julie arrived she was energetically drained, but I noticed a definite energy renewal after the cords were cut.

Because energy is transferable we should never argue or be emotionally out of balance around others, especially our children. Their chakras are wide open and they easily pick up energy. Look at Figure 4 in the middle of the book and you will see the effects of a heated argument. Sandra's GDV was done after a morning argument with her husband. Sandra is young, short, feisty, and outspoken and she has repeated heated arguments with her six-foot husband. They are the parents of a nineteen-month old son who takes in the negative energy of their terrible arguments.

Look at all of the pink emotional energy throwing Sandra's auric field off balance. Notice how the physical energy, represented by the blue color, has been pushed out by the pink emotional energy. Beginning at the top of her head you can see all of the emotional energy "coloring" her yellow spiritual energy. The emotional energy right above her head pushes out the "blue" physical energy and causes her to be off balanced. At the front of her face, down into the throat area, the back of her head and neck and on down her spine is out of balanced emotional energy shown as pink. You can see sharp spikes of emotional energy sent from the back of the head, stomach area and the legs.

Remembering how the spine sends information throughout the body, look at all of the emotional energy and dark purple mental energy at Sandra's back. Look at all of the dark purple in the solar plexus (stomach area). Sandra's cells are filled with memories of lots of fights with her first and second husband and her parents. She is even more off balanced beginning around the feet and moving up the legs to the knees. When we are stuck in our past behaviors and unable to move out of them, stale energy collects in the feet. The legs tell our history. We store childhood traumas, beginning with our feet, and as we grow older, traumas are stored higher up in the legs. Sandra's images tell me that she grew up in an emotionally charged, fighting family and now she is passing this behavior along to her son.

Look at Sandra's left side. It is interesting that the left, spiritual side of Sandra has so much mental energy in the solar plexus area. So when we are in conflict in our personal relationships, we are blocking our spiritual relationships. The solar plexus area is the stomach area (3rd chakra), the location of the center of our power. Every time Sandra gets into an argument, her stomach recalls her past arguments because the memories are stored in this area. The energy is very dense so it is very dark purple (designated as mental energy by the GDV camera). Sandra doesn't know how to negotiate in a conflict, or come from the heart. She is thinking, how can I win this argument and be right. She is not thinking of how much it will cost her.

There are several other areas of dark mental energy around her body, especially at her back, around her head and in the leg area. When you are in a heated argument you are definitely not coming from the loving energy of the heart. You are thinking, "What can I say and do to beat out my opponent"? Look around Sandra's throat area and you will see the strong emotional and mental energy she is holding on to and causing her to be extremely off balance. The stored emotional energy held at her back will cause the shoulders and neck to tighten so she will feel the stress of the argument for several days. You can see why repeated arguments are unhealthy.

Look at Sandra's right side. This is the worldly, masculine, yang side of the body. The energy at the top of the head is not as rounded and full as the left side. The energy at the back of Sandra's head is stuck because she has been thinking so hard with her brain. You can tell that she has been arguing with a family member because of all the emotional energy held in the first (root) chakra.

Sandra's mother babysits her baby and she reported that the day of the argument the usually outgoing and independent baby boy was sad and clung to his grandmother all day. Everything you say, do, and feel has and is being absorbed into the energy field of your children. The chakras of children are wide open to collect negative energy and positive energy. Even if they are in the next room you are sending out your vibration. Remember, energy can travel through walls. It also collects in space like if we don't clear the area.

If you saw the colors in the aura of a person in such a highly agitated state, they appear like a dull discoloration. Besides arguments, insecurity, fear, and anxiety create an agitated aura. For instance, women who retain guilt feelings because of an abortion, have an agitated aura. Using the Emotional Freedom Technique with the statement, "Even though I had an abortion, I still totally love and respect myself," helps release the energy stuck in the meridians and the aura. It works for any kind of guilt feeling.

Cindy wanted to have her GDV images done because she felt that there was something blocking her success in life. She was in her late twenties, a massage therapist and expecting a baby in a few months. The first images didn't show as much energy around her as I expected. As we talked she told me that her father had been murdered when she was eleven years old, but her family never really talked about his death. She had always felt sadness and disappointment because she missed having a father. Of course she always wondered why his death was never discussed.

I did EFT, Emotional Freedom Technique, with her and then received a big shock when I saw the GDV side images, Figure 5. All of the feelings and emotions surrounding her father's death were caught by the GDV images. Cindy released years of suppressed disappointment of not getting to be with her father and all the sadness she felt because a co-worker decided to shoot someone. Note that all this energy was released from her back and spine, the location where we store so many of our emotions and the reason so many people have back problems. By doing the EFT technique, Cindy released the energy blocking her meridians.

Energy Is Moveable, Transferable, And Is Connected To All Other Energies

Subtle energy can travel faster than physical light energy, radiating out 360 degrees from you. Because energy is non-local, it means that we can send thoughts, prayers, love, and unfortunately, our negative thoughts, hatred, and ill will to others. All thoughts and actions are contained in the universal energy field and stored there. This is how telepathy, remote healing, and intercessory prayer are possible.

Baule and Mc Fee published an article in 1963 that discussed how scientists were able to prove that pairs of electrons are able to move through an insulator, material previously thought be impentrateable because electrons are both waves and particles. This is the basis of Quantum Physics. This is the reason that you need to protect yourself, especially if you are around a bunch of computers or your own home computer. You can put a coil of copper tubing or a crystal to collect the energy put out by the computer. The crystal will turn dark and cloudy. then you should cover it sea salt to cleanse it or put it out in the sunlight for several hours.

As a part of the universal energy field, our energies are intermingling with other people's energy fields. There are people who are too sensitive to live in big cities or be in crowded rooms. Our lack of comfort on an elevator is because too many other energy fields are encroaching upon our energy field. The energy field of a person averages around six feet in circumference, so this is why you feel so crowded even though no one is touching you.

People innately know how to move energy out of their body. The nervous person moves his foot back and forth to release nervous energy or he walks back and forth. Children lie on the floor while watching TV crossing their legs back and forth to release energy. You can watch a nervous person try to calm their energy by overeating, drinking too much alcohol, or smoking to release energy. A healthier way to release energy would be to shake your hands and concentrate on your naval. Chi Nei Tsand, internal organs chi massage, teaches us that all of the internal organs are connected at the naval, and by concentrating on the naval, we can discover where illness and energy blockages are in the body. The next step is to massage the naval area to promote healing.

Two Meditations To Powerfully Move Energy

The solar plexus area of the body contains the stomach, pancreas, and liver, and is the center of our body and the location where martial artists concentrate and draw upon physical energy. It is the source of our physical power. When I work with people who feel powerless, I teach them the following star visualization and meditation.

Visualize either a four or five pointed star in your solar plexus and see holographically so you can imagine it from all different angles and sides. Next, imagine streams of bright gold celestial light entering through the top of your head and in through the solar plexus, filling the star with the brightest light they have ever imagined. There is so much light that it pours out the points of the star in all directions. Powerful bright gold celestial light shines from the star and all the points leaving their body and going out of the room, out of the city and state, and then connecting with the light of the universe. Audiences can always feel this light energy surging past them. You can see the person grow more powerful and energized. GDV images before and after the meditation show the huge changes.

Pressing Your Solar Plexus Point

It is also a good idea to press on the solar plexus point on the bottom of your foot. Place your hands . When you gently squeeze the top hand, you will see a hollow space appear at the center of the sole of your foot. Release the squeeze and then press your thumb into the point for a few seconds. Breath in holding the breath a few seconds while you press the point. Exhale and slowly release the pressure. Rotate your thumb a few times on the solar plexus point. When we are relaxed we are able to do more physically and mentally. This is a wonderful exercise to create relaxation.

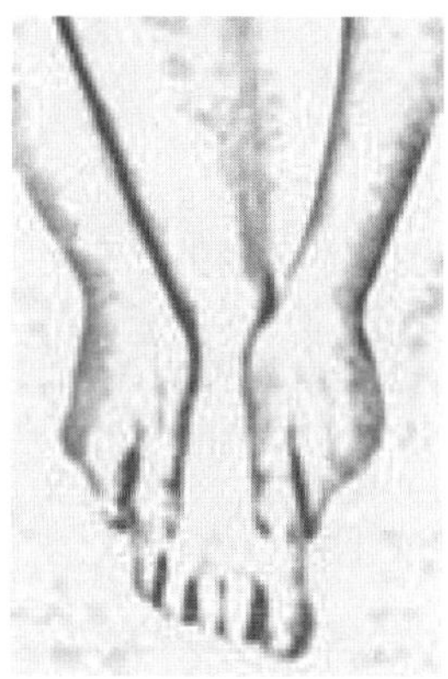

Energy In The Form Of Thoughts and Ideas Are Everywhere Around Us

How do people connect with great thoughts, ideas, and inventions? It may be when you are sleeping, driving, walking, out in nature, or doing anything that causes you to be in relaxed state. Dr. William A. Tiller and colleagues at Stanford University developed an ultra-sensitive gas-discharge detector that registers electron activity. The GDV mentioned earlier is also a gas-discharge detector. Dr. Tiller demonstrated that through mental focus alone, people can increase the activity of the electrons detected by his device. [4]Tiller, William

Energy Is Depletable From One Source To The Next, But Non-Destructive

Billy was eleven when I used my GDV Camera (Gas Discharge Visualization) to check out his physical, mental, emotional, and spiritual energies. His parents owned a school academy and were quite aware of energy. The first images I of took of Billy surprised me because the boy appeared to have no energy. I thought I must not have explained how to put his fingers on the glass plate correctly, so I took the images a second time. Same results. The third time I did the all too familiar procedures with slow motion accuracy. Same results.

"I hate to tell you this," I told the mother, "but something is sucking all of Billy's energy out of his energy field."

Billy's mother said, "Oh, we knew that, we were just wondering if it would show up with your camera. Before Billy was born my mother-in-law, my husband and I all saw and felt his grandfather's presence after he died. My husband's father was an alcoholic who died of lung cancer because of smoking. We believe that his grandfather entered Billy's auric field when he was born."

Children's auric fields and chakras are wide open when they are born and this is the reason that children are so impressionable. The grandfather was a low energy person while he was alive, so he chose not to leave the earth plane when he passed over. He hung around until he could attach himself to someone else. There is something that can be done to remove attaching spirits. Several different cultures use obsidian, the oldest rock on earth, in a ceremony to remove the invading spirit who is then sent to The Light.

Several people have described to me how it feels to have a disembodied spirit attached to them. Sometimes the spirit attaches just to one part of the body. One lady said that her father attached to her right shoulder seconds after he passed over. "Ever since I have felt a weakness at that location. I can feel my father and I wish he would go away," she said.

Observation of her body showed that her right shoulder and down her right side was losing energy and lower than the left side. I asked the angels to show me where her father's spirit attached cords and they showed me. Then I asked them where I should cut the cords. I used my index and middle fingers as scissors and set my intention that the cords would be cut. I sent the cords back to the father and sent him to the Light. I sent the daughter's cords back into her shoulder and body. She could feel the weight of her father's spirit lifted. When you hold a pendulum to an area that has an attachment, you can feel the energy being pulled out of the person. The GDV image shows an empty energy space.

Energy Is Moveable and Transferable

Energy Is Vibrational And Can Be Felt

If you want to be sure you can feel energy, take a minute and try this experiment. With your elbows bent, hold your arms out in front of you, with your hands facing each other as in prayer but not touching. Hold this position for a few seconds then drop your hand down to your waist. Put it back. Repeat the preceding procedure. Most people feel warmth and tingling when the hands face each other. Some people can feel the energy when their thumb and index finger are close to each other.

Halle Berry said in a TV interview that her movie *Gothic* was filmed in a unused jail in Canada. She noted that the jail's energy was low and negative. Also, she noted that she could feel the ghosts of the people who had been there. Many people say that when they have had to go to court they feel the negative energy in the room. I have talked to several people who work in courtrooms, and they complain of having more sickness and feeling a sticky energy where they work. If you work in any kind of negative environment, you should install a shield as mentioned before. Think about how you feel in a doctor's office or hospital. The reason most of us dislike going to these two places is because of the way we feel. People who are afraid of getting sick or dying are creating love vibrating, negative thought forms that linger in the office or building if they are not cleared.

Other places that hold slow frequency energy are battlefields, places that have had great disasters and loss of life. In these places the impact of the event has created a frequency or sound that is in disharmony with life forms in general. I could feel the chilling fear of death and all the pain that was suffered when I visited the Battlefield at Gettysburg. We will forever be able to feel the energy at the World Trade Centers location after September 11th.

The emotions of fear, anger, negativity and other slow frequency vibrations affect the first and second chakras of the body. You can travel to different parts of a city and feel areas of slow frequency energy where there are gangs and a lot of crimes. On the other hand, more buildings now are topped with a triangular structure to attract higher energy. The geometrical shape of the triangle has a higher frequency than the shape of a square.

Resonance

Sound transmits, increases and spreads energy. Resonance works on the principle that *like attracts like*. When the F string of a harp or piano is struck and it becomes a driving force, so all the other octave strings of F of other instruments or tuning forks begin to vibrate. They are in resonance with one another. The different parts of our physical, emotional, mental and spiritual being resonate to various frequencies of vibration. Low vibration signals disease and signals that energy is stuck, weak or depleted. Vibrational healing works because the person working with the sick person is able to send in the perfect vibration of sound (via tuning forks, voice toning, crystal bowls), color (depending upon which vibration is needed), or by using mind energy (in conjunction with the patient, preferably) to visualize energy flowing perfectly.

How To Scan Energy

After you have put your hands on someone else's body you can either use visualization, thought, or sensation to begin feeling their energy. To do this your hands must become receptive (yin) as you move them gently with the sway of the person's body. As you relax your hands, fingers, wrists, arms and shoulders more and more, you will be more sensitive to their energy. Don't place judgment on the experience, just feel it. With your thoughts, visualize your energy separating from theirs before you remove your hands. Remember how you feel around a depressed person. If you are not protected, their energy brings you down.

Energy Can Have Critical Mass

We are both space and form, or more accurately, space filled with form. Critical mass is the combined molecular waveform, comprised of many singular points, which moves consciousness, energy, or form. When many singular points of consciousness join together and create in the same wave or thought field, the corresponding answer or return from the universe is to join these points together and respond. As you put out a message, the universe listens. As a response, it is generally a creation index, or an answer that is held as a thought form. When many begin to put together their ideas for oneness, union, order or truth, there is a critical mass or molecular level of impact reached, which then goes out into the universe. The returning response, as well as the initial wave, is what is meant by the term critical mass–a level of impact that sustains a promise.

You can change the consciousness and the form of the earth and its people by joining other people with the same thoughts and energy levels. You can take control of your life by learning to use the natural energy in your body. We can use out natural energy to positively influence the health and attitudes of others. Every time we become part of the solution to challenges instead of part of the problem, we change mass consciousness.

How Can You Move Blocked Energy Out Of The Body?

Glen Rein, M.D. is a researcher at the Soma Psyche Institute International in New York City. His research shows that electromagnetic subtle psychic healing energies and crystal energies can heal the body by releasing blocked energy.

You can transfer blocked energy from your body to a tree, the ground, a rock, or a wall and that will allow the energy to move again. You can wash energy off your hands by washing them with cold running water. Most of our energy moves out the fingers because these are the beginning or ending points for many of the body's meridians. Check the index for more information on the meridians.

One of the best examples of transferring energy is the person who "lights" up the room when they enter. We've all seen the person at the party who everyone gathers around–the light of the party. There is an energy (plasma) exchange and everyone feels better just being around that person.

One of the most powerful examples of energy exchange is when people "lock eyes". Watch two people in a competition. The eyes take in lots of energy; they also send out powerful energy. When we talk about our eyes connecting, it's the resonant energy that's connecting.

The GDV images of Karl show a person with stuck energy. The only reason Karl (Figure 6) had his GDV images done was because he came to visit with a friend of mine. He wasn't really interested even in seeing the outcome. After you study his images, you can see why. Ever made the statement, "It went right over his head"? When energy is stuck, like in the balloon of energy at the top of Karl's head, no new thoughts or ideas can enter. Now look at figure two, which is the left side of Karl's head. See the big blank opening that illustrates what is going on in Karl's mind–a big blank nothing. The area in the very middle of our forehead is called our Third Eye. This is where we use our imagination, where we are able to visualize, and receive intuitive information. Unfortunately Karl obviously doesn't do meditation, does not imagine, or connect with his/her Creator.

References

Kargagulla, S., *Breakthrough to Creativity* Marina Del Rey, California: De Vorss, 1967, p. 39.

Mc Williams, Dr. Charles, Photobiotics , ProMotion Publishing 1995 p. 17.

Miksell, "Structured Water: Its Healing Effects on the Diseased State," San Jose, CA: PRI 1985, pp. 1-10.

Tiller, William A., *Science and Human Transformation: Subtle Energies, Intentionality and Consciousness,* Walnut Creek, CA. Pavior, 1997 p. 59.

6. History of Subtle Energies and The Human Energy Field Research

---

About a thousand years ago Zhang Dai, A Song scientist and Chi Kung philosopher wrote...

The cosmos is a body of chi. Chi has the properties of yin and yang. When chi is spread out, It permeates all things, when it coalesces it becomes nebulous. When this settles into form, it becomes matter. When it disintegrates it returns to its original state.

Hippocrates recognized the body's natural capacity for healing. He instructed physicians to find the blocking influences both within a patient and between them and the cosmos, in order to restore the healing life force. He felt nature, not the doctor, is the source of healing. The following quote comes from Hippocrates, The Father of Medicine (460-357 BC)

"It is believed by experienced doctors, that the heat which oozes out of the hand, on being applied to the sick, is highly salutary...It has often appeared while I have been thus soothing my patients, as if there were a singular property in my hands to pull and draw away from the affected parts, aches and diverse impurities, by laying my hand upon the place, and by extending my fingers toward it.

Thus it is known to some of the learned that health may be implanted in the sick by certain gestures, and by contact, as some diseases may be communicated from one to another."

It is puzzling to me that belief in the human energy is traceable back thousands of years ago and that every culture has a word for it and we still have people who are doubtful about the Human Energy Field. Early Ayurvedic references to a life force, or prana, go back to the eighth century B.C. In the West, as early as the sixth century B.C., Pythagoras conceived of a life energy or Pneuma visible as a luminous body. Until about twenty years ago scientists in the United States did not believe in the Human Energy Field but now they believe with absolute certainty that Human Energy Fields exist.

My interaction with people has led me to believe that the following groups in power and those responsible for educating have either been taught incorrectly or they believe that lack of knowledge about the Human Energy Field is a way to control people. Go look at your child's text books and you will find that education does not teach anything about Human Energy Fields. Some ministers teach their congregations that the aura or Human Energy Field is evil. I have been warned not to speak of the aura in certain churches, even if the churches contained pictures of Jesus and Mary with halos (auras) glowing around their heads. The good news is that medicine has changed its mind about the HEF and is now extremely interested in the biomagnetic fields around the body and hopefully soon this information will be widespread to all people.

Every culture has a name for the body's innate energy. John White in his book *Future Science* says that references to the phenomenon of the human energy field (HEF) or the aura of the body are in 97 different cultures. Similarly, we see a halo on statues and paintings of Buddha, and also we see energy coming from the fingers of many Indian gods.

It is interesting that the last few centuries of medicine are less fascinated and have less interest in the Human Energy Field than did medicine thousands of years ago. For instance, as far back as in 500 B.C., the Pythagoreans believed that there is a universal energy pervading all of nature. They taught that its light could effect cures in sick patients. In the 1100's, a scientist named Liebault said that humans have an energy that can react on someone else's energy, either at a distance or close by. According to Liebault, being near a person can have either an unhealthy or a healthy effect on someone else. The HEF of one person may be harmonious or discordant, nurturing or draining.

In India 5000 years ago Indians called universal energy prone, Shakti, or Prana. Prana is a Sanskrit word literally meaning life energy, vital force, that which keeps the body alive and healthy. This universal energy is the source of all life. The breath of life moves through all forms to give them life. Indians believe that prana is invisible particles constantly being inhaled and exhaled through matter. Yogis work with this energy in breathing techniques, meditation, and physical exercise to produce altered states of consciousness and longevity.

Both the Old Testament and New Testament often refer to the power of touch to heal. The words ***whole*** and ***holy*** come from the same Greek root word. Speaking of energy medicine is therefore also speaking of holistic medicine. The cure of the body and soul is a fundamental expression of our religious beliefs though I feel that many churches have lost their belief in healing miracles. God has great concern for human brokenness and how we can be restored to health. From the earliest times, the therapeutic power of touch has been recognized and has been raised to a sacrament in some religions.

Different names for subtle energy
Ankh–Ancient Egypt
Arunqsuiltha–Australian Aborigine
Num–The aboriginal Kung in the Khalahari desert raise num through ecstatic all-night dances, in which they perform healings and receive visions.

History Of Subtle Energies And The Human Energy Field Research

Nefesh– In the Jewish mystical tradition, it is also known as *Breath of Life. prone* or *shakti*. The Kabbalah, the Jewish mystical teachings written about 538 B.C., called these energies the astral light.
Biomagnetism–United States
Christians call the energy of God the Holy Spirit which is part of the Trinity that pervades everything. Christian paintings and sculptures show a halo around the head of Christ and other spiritual leaders.
Manitou– Algonquin
M'gbe– Hiru pygmy
Pneuma– Ancient Greek
Mana– Polynesian
Mulungu– Paracelsus
Ntoro–Ashantiu
Ntu–Bantu
Oki–Huron
Orenda– Iroquois
Prana– India
Ki – Japanese
Qi–Chinese (spelled Chi in English) 3,000 years ago the ancient Qigong masters in China were practicing their meditative discipline to balance and invigorate the human energy field. They called this vital energy and said it pervades all forms, both animate and inanimate, Qi is the vital energy of the body; while gong means the skill of moving this Qi and working with it.
Subtle Energy– United States, United Kingdom
Sila– Inuit
Tane– Hawaii
Ton– Dakota
Wakan– Lakota
Other names for energy are etheric energy, fohat, orgone, odic force, homeopathic resonance, life force, form giving force, vital substance, healing energy, archaeus, wakan, puha, kundalini, bioplasma, enteleckley, life force, guarding principle, and love.

Pranic healing began in the ancient civilizations of China, Egypt and India and is still practiced there. Cure is effected by simply removing diseased energies from the patient's subtle body and transferring vital energy to the affected areas with the hands. Pranic healing is used in more than 30 countries in five continents.

Early Greek and Roman texts wrote about the phenomenon of bioelectro-magnetism. Aristotle and Plato, plus other prominent scientists of the same period noted the shocking impact that the electric Torpedo fish had on helping humans heal. During the first century the first report describing the medical use of electric fish appeared. Before the Renaissance, physicians routinely used electric fish as a form of electrotherapy to treat sleeping disorders, migraines, melancholy and epilepsy.

Practitioners use mind, psychic powers, and spiritual development. The ancient Qigong masters developed Tai Chi, Kung Fu, and the martial arts. In addition, they made the first model for acupuncture. Acupuncturists insert needles, or use moxa, or put magnets at specific acupuncture points to balance the yin and yang of the human energy field. When the Qi is balanced, the entity has good health. When the Qi is unbalanced, the entity has poor or impaired health.

Paracelsus called energy, Mumia, saying that it was both the magnetic fundamental force and the nature cure force. He was a Swiss alchemist and physician in the sixteenth century who said "there is a healing energy that radiates within and around man like a luminous sphere."

The word mesmerism is named after Franz Anton Mesmer, the father of modern hypnotism, who in the 1800's suggested that a field similar to an electromagnetic field might exist around the human body. Mesmer thought that the power of this electromagnetic field, which he believed behaved as a fluid, might also be able to exert influence on the field of another.
German scholar, Burdach, called energy neurogomy–or "union of nerves."
Reichenback called energy the Od force. Klein called it vital electricity. Professor G. Kieser called energy, "tellurism" a "natural force of the earth."

Biophysicist Beverly Rubik, who is with The Institute of Frontier Science, says ."medicine has an emerging paradigm that celebrates the creative, subtle empowering, wise, and enduring features of life that were never acknowledged during the age of machines and mechanistic thought. Living systems are self-organizing systems that expend energy in order to maintain their coherence and integrity...Healing is ultimately self-healing, a natural response to internal dynamic shifts of external challenges."

7. What Is "Mind"? Where Is "Mind"?

If you were asked to define "mind", what would you say? Amazingly, some still think the brain in the physical body is mind. The brain is better compared to a mechanistic computer that is directed by the software of the heart. The brain is a limited information storage place of information in this lifetime.

Recently, we came to define "mind" as being in every part of the body. We learned that all of the 180 different kinds of cells in the body have "mind" in them. This concept will be discussed in the next chapter. But "mind" does so much more than just operate the human body.

We need to move beyond simply discussing the mind/body connection. This is such a limiting perception of "mind". Then what is "mind"? Mind is an energy field. Since all matter has an energy field, all matter has mind. The interactive level of that mind depends upon the level of vibration. **This book will focus on the human "mind" and propose that the aura or Human Energy Field is "mind".**

The physical, mental, emotional, and spiritual energies of which we speak are simply different aspects mind...but we each have only one mind, and as has been said over and over, our minds are a part of the universal energy field. Think of all the things mind does and then look at what the seven levels of the subtle bodies of the aura do. From this point in the book "mind" and aura are the same.

Look at how we describe our mind and then look at what happens in the aura... We say we are losing our mind, and we see the aura misshapened and out of alignment. We feel scrambled and mixed up and the energies in our aura are scrambled. When there is little light shining in our aura, we feel disconnected from our bodies, our spirit and our Creator because we have closed down the connections.

The aura/mind has memory just like universal mind. It is through the aura/mind that we can access the memory of universal mind.

The aura/mind is able to magnetize what it wants to come to it.

The aura/mind is non-local so its thoughts, prayers, and subtle energies are connected like an interrelated web with the subtle energy of the universe.

Secrets Of Energy

The aura/mind is infinite, eternal, and powerful. The most powerful energy of the aura/mind is love.

Why The Brain Is Not Mind

Thoughts come from mind. A brain wave is not an electromagnetic wave that radiates out from the brain, but rather the wave that is made on a paper chart when a person is hooked up to an electroencephalograph machine. We have no physical sensation connected with brain waves because thoughts are subtle energy originating in the aura. We can hear and feel out heart and our breathing, but no known physical connection with brain waves. What are detected are subjective states associated with different brainwave patterns.

Energy Principle: You become a powerful force when you learn how to align your energies with your higher self.

"All the body's systems relate to each other in a constant state of flux, with the hypothalamus at the center. The hypothalamus interfaces between mind and body, coordinating the readiness of both, affecting our consciousness, and thereby controlling our constant state of preparedness. This critical maintenance of body harmony is effecting by synchronizing the body's vital functions with the environmental conditions, or as some people say, 'becoming one with the universe." S.J. Ouseley

Energy Principle: Thoughts Are Energy. Energy Is Information.

The Power Of Thought

"Imagination is the beginning of creation. You imagine what you desire, you will what you imagine, and at last you create what you will."- George Bernard Shaw

The lower mental level (third level of the aura) is filled with thought forms. Each thought that we and the rest of humanity has creates a thought form. Whatever we think in the third level of subtle energy, the mental body, we set in motion. When you learn about how we are magnetic in addition to being electrical, you will realize how important it is to think positively because we will magnetize other positive thoughts, people and happenings to us.

The astral body is our emotional body. If you are a highly emotional person, this auric body is constantly fluctuating and out of balance. When you are overcome with strong emotions, you are temporarily out of balance and that emotional outburst will take a lot of energy from you. Look at the GDV images of Mya, Figure 7 in the middle of the book,. and you will see how being overly emotional will throw you off balance.

Where Is "Mind"? What Is "Mind"?

Energy Is Responsive To Our Consciousness.

Consciousness is the highest form of energy and is integrally involved with the life process. We should strive to be on an acceleration curve of expansion of human consciousness. If we consider consciousness as a fundamental quality and expression of life energy, we come closer to understanding how spirit interacts with and manifests through the many forms of physical matter. It is fact, the journey of spirit through the worlds of matter that provides the strongest driving force for the evolutionary process.

The rising tide of increased spiritual awareness will begin to affect larger numbers of people through a kind of cosmic resonance effect. When enough minds have changed to reach the critical threshold necessary to move the entire global consciousness to a new level of healing and awareness, we will have arrived at the New Age. Richard Gerber M.D. *Vibrational Medicine*

These subtle energies are hierarchical in nature. This means that the 7th level has the finest vibrating energy and it the highest level of our spiritual natures. The levels of the aura work from higher levels downward until they become manifest at the level of the physical body. The higher vibrational energies represent the organizing structures of consciousness that utilize the physical body as a vehicle of expression within our physical space/time/universe.

Each physical body and personality is an extension of a higher spiritual consciousness that seeks to evolve through learning experiences encountered in the school of Earth life. The drive of spirit to evolve toward a higher quality of consciousness is the motivating force behind the reincarnational system. This increased quality of consciousness can only be achieved through individual experiences and many lives in the physical body. When energetic disturbances occur at the etheric and higher frequency levels of structure, pathologic changes eventually manifest at the physical/cellular level.

In *Power vs. Force: The Hidden Determinants of Human Behavior,* Dr. David Hawkins correlates a 'map of consciousness' chart with levels of personal power, and levels of truth, and gives a technique for not only verifying the information yourself, but applying it to almost any question or situation. He calibrates levels that correlate with specific processes of consciousness-emotions, perceptions, or attitudes, worldviews, and spiritual belief. States such as, wise, merciful, grief, courage, and joy are assigned calibrations from as low as 20 to 1,000. Enlightenment he says is between 700-1,000. You can use his muscle kinesiology technique, or use a pendulum to determine where you are vibrating. By using the Emotional Freedom Technique that you will be reading about later, you will learn how to release stored emotions in your meridians and in your cellular memory that are lowering your vibration.

Hawkins, a psychiatrist, at one time treated about 1,000 patients a year from all over the United States. Later on he had 50 therapists and 2,000 outpatients. He said his practice became frustrating because he could on encounter one patient at a time. After giving up his lucrative practice and living as reclusive in a small town for seven years doing meditation and study, his book was written to teach people how to heal themselves. Additionally, he tells his story and experiences of very high states of consciousness, which has taken him years to be able to express in words. In *The Eye of the I,* Hawkins takes the reader deep into a non-religious spirituality that builds on the material presented in *Power vs. Force.* As you can tell, I would highly recommend reading both books.

Relationships

Sometimes we get into relationships where there is an unequal exchange of energy. If you feel that you are being taken advantage of, you need to change the energy of the relationship or get out of it. The kinds of relationships we have indicate our feeling of worth about ourselves.

Your sexual partner has a great deal to do with your energy level. During the intimacy of sex you are sending out and receiving the energy of your partner. Because sex is such an emotional act, memories are forever stored in your cells unless you choose to release them. It is extremely wise to decide if your want a person's energy.

Mind Energy

The mind is actually part of a continuum, a labyrinth that is connected not only to every other mind that exists or has existed, but to every atom, organism, and region in the in the vastness of space and time itself, the fact that it is able to occasionally make forays into the labyrinth and have transpersonal experiences no longer seems so strange. Grof

Mind energy is created from several different points of origin and processes –empirical, rational, critical thinking and inductive reasoning:
Mind energy is created from the independent thinking of the brain. This kind of thinking does not rely on conscious awareness and has no power to affect what is going on around us. This thinking process relies on our past experiences rather than new insights. The creation of new thoughts comes from conscious thinking.

Where Is "Mind"? What Is "Mind"?

Other Kinds Of Thinking

You can actually send an organ or area of your body energy by simply thinking about it. One of the Tai Chi exercises suggests that we smile and send loving thoughts to our various organs. How does this work? Remember it has been proven that mind is in the energy field and the physical body. Mind and the body listen to what we saying and thinking.

One of the methods to increase both physical and subtle energy is to learn how to do Autogenic Training, also called self-generated training. We may talk about different states–mental, physical, emotional, and spiritual–but we know that these states are really four aspects of our one state. When you look at the GDV images and you see a person totally out of energy in a part of their body, you will note that there is no energy from the other three states. Every change in the physiological state must be accompanied by an appropriate change in the mental-emotional-spiritual state, and every change in the mental-emotional-spiritual state must be accompanied by an appropriate change in the physiological state. This principle of balance made possible psychosomatic (psycho-mind, somatic-body) self-regulation.

For example, remember a time when you were over-charged emotionally; you had a heated argument with someone. This event not only caused you to be emotionally drained, but it caused you to be drained physically, mentally, and spiritually. You lose your ability to think clearly or not at all when you are over-charged emotionally. Look again at the GDV images of Sandra beginning with the individual finger images and you will see a faint background of yellow spiritual energy extremely overclouded with emotional energy. The bottom left image represents her heart and it is so negatively emotionally charged none of her spiritual energy shows.

The human brain is electrical and it emits brainwaves as it goes about processing data, responding to signals, and otherwise governing the internal and external life of the individual. The four principal brainwave patterns are alpha, beta, delta and theta. Alpha is associated with the normal and alert state of the mind. Alpha is the rhythm associated with a state of relaxation in which a person is thinking of nothing in particular. The beta rhythm is the fastest rhythm of the brain and usually relates to our active, thinking consideration of the outside world. Beta is normally seen over the frontal portions of the brain during intense mental activity. We are in beta when solving problems or when our attention is alerted. Delta occurs during deep sleep. Theta rhythm involves more deeply focused attention in which the body and mind are very quiet, near the almost unconscious state you experience just before sleep. Theta occurs during various stages of sleep in normal adults. The brain wave patterns are classified according to the number of cycles they make each second; these cycles are called Hertz. Delta waves vary between 1-3-4 cycles per second, the theta between 4-7 cycles per second, the alpha between 8-14, and the beta between 14-50.

Beta and alpha waves are associated with conscious processes, while the theta and delta waves are associated with the unconscious processes. Our attention shifts between conscious and unconscious nervous processes. The peripheral nervous system is divided into the autonomic (involuntary) and the craniospinal systems (voluntary). Control of the voluntary nervous system requires the use of active volition. Control of the involuntary nervous system requires the use of passive volition.

Alpha waves are produced in a relaxed state and create serenity, alertness, and a feeling of competence and well-being. When you become tense you go into the beta rhythm. Most people produce alpha rhythm with their eyes closed. Discovering this information has helped me so much as a healer because I understand why I do the things that come naturally to me. For instance, I always close my eyes when I send energy and it does strengthen my energy sending.

Theta frequency is correlated with reverie and hypnogogic imagery-words or pictures which are not consciously generated or manipulated, but which spring into the mind "full blown." Such imagery is the creative force of new invention, new art forms, and new enterprises. To reach a theta state quickly, make your eyes look up and then focus your eyes on that point on the wall. Become aware of the images in your peripheral.

What You Must Know About Synapses To Understand Flowing Energy And Blocked Energy

The electrical field of the brain is much weaker than the heart, and it is measured by an electroencephalogram (EEG). Brain waves are measured in the alpha state with the eyes closed. Closing the eyes causes more blood to go to the eyes and it help clear the mind a make a person more centered.

Brain cells have neurons. Synapses are the connections between neurons that store information and through which information flows. The interesting part is that **synapses are gaps**–it appears that nothing is there. Joseph LeDoux, a neuroscientist, says that synapses are spaces between brain cells. **I propose that what is there is energy**. Remember, energy ***is*** information and it is electrical. When a neuron becomes active, that is, it wants to send some new or stored information, an electrical impulse travels down a nerve fiber and this causes the release of a chemical neurotransmitter. In addition to being electrical and magnetic beings, we are also chemical beings.

Going on in your brain at all times is trillions of synaptic connections occurring in the billions of neurons. Wow! Sounds like things could get confusing. But they don't because there are circuits formed by synapses that link together neurons. Then there are circuits that form complex systems that perform different functions like hearing or seeing or the flight or fight response.

Joseph LeDoux in his book, *Synaptic Self*, says You are your synapses. Our knowledge about who we are, of the way we think about ourselves, of what others think of us, and how we typically act in certain situations is in large part learned through experience and this information is accessible to us through memory. The brain not only records the activities of our movements but also our attitudes about ourselves. [1] LeDoux

I agree with LeDoux, but I would like to add a further perspective. The synapses do hold information about the experiences and events that have happened to us. Conversely, we do not want what happened to us to determine who we are. We are more than just the events and the experiences that have happened to us. Unfortunately, we often let these times negative experiences or traumas warp our perceptions. New information that comes into our brains travels down the synaptic network that is most closely associated with the new information.

We have what some call a "higher self," or what others call the "soul," that is the real "who you are." To attain enlightenment and to live authentically, we need to release the emotions and memories stuck in the synapses of the brain and in the cells of the body. Self-esteem is something you have created based on your perceptions; it is not the truth about who you are.

Every form, whether it is physical or thought forms, has a nucleus that radiates a level of vibration depending upon the density of the substance that is attracted to it. The higher self is what changes any form, not the human mind. The higher self is the power to enact change. To me, this explains how the meridians, the channels of energy that run through our bodies, become blocked and how information is stored in our bodies as memories. Acupressure and acupuncture points are located in these meridians.

Acupuncture induced states of relaxation (meditation and hypnosis) are associated with brilliant and expansive electromagnetic emanations from the fingertips and feet called coronas. States of stress and tension are associated with the contraction and diminishment of the corona and darker colors at the extremities. Tension and upset magnetize more problems to you.

Mind energy is intelligent and carries information. We have approximately 60,000 thoughts per day. Our thoughts create neural pathways that become strong and more numerous with repetition. We only receive thoughts that we already carry within us or we have to create new "files" by changing our belief system. Thoughts similar to what we already believe resonate with us and are sent to complementary files. Most of the time new thoughts require repetition before creating neural pathway and the creation of new files. We can receive intuitive information. Still and receptiveness are required to receive intuition. Intuitive information many times defies logical thinking and helps us see beyond our perceptions. The word intuition is derived from the Latin *inturri,* which means to consider or look within.

Will power directs mind energy through the body. Emotions must be utilized with will power. Will power applied to paradigms not in a person's belief system causes stress.

Imagery facilitates new sensorimotor skills of extraordinary states of consciousness. Imagery is done through the practice of different sub roles or sub-personalities. It helps our concentration and focused intention. Imagery also helps us recall unnoticed or dissociated processes. Imagination is free flowing, unrestrained, and stress reducing.

How To Focus Your Mind Energy

In the same way an athlete trains mentally and physically for the Olympics, you can train your mind to focus and direct your mental energy. The following exercise will show the present level of your mind's ability to focus your thoughts. The more you do exercises such as this, the more you will improve your ability to focus and direct your mind energy (thoughts).

Exercise making the right hand hot. First, focus your mind energy on your right hand. Visualize your right hand near a fire or in a bucket of hot water. You might want to recall a past incident where your hand became very hot. Use all your senses if possible to feel the heat of the fire or the water, smell the burning wood, hear the crackling flames, and see your hand very, very close to the fire. If you have your hand in hot water, feel the wetness, even visualize the bucket as red. Visualize the color red in your mind's eye, the middle of your forehead where you see mentally. Then send the red color from the mind's eye down your neck, down your shoulder, and then down your arm to your hand. Imagine the red color as being warm liquid. Your right hand will actually heat up and your blood vessels will expand. This is actually a biofeedback technique to help people get rid of headaches and migraines.

Exercise making the left hand cold. First, focus your mind energy on your left hand. Visualize your left hand in a blue bucket of very cold ice water. Visualize the ice being so cold that a frosty cloud hangs above the bucket. Recall images of the characters in Titanic floating on blocks of ice. See your hand turning blue, frozen, and your fingers unable to move. They almost break. Visualize the color blue in your mind's eye, the middle of your forehead where you see mentally. Then send the blue color from the mind's eye down your neck, down your shoulder, and then down your arm to your hand. Imagine the blue color as being extremely cold, slow moving liquid. Your left hand will actually feel so cold that your blood vessels will contract and feel cold. Practice this technique several times so that you can see how easy it is to program your mind to immediately obey your directions to focus and direct your mind energy. You will get to the point that you only need to say the word "hot" to your right hand and "cold" to your left hand.

Use The Same Techniques For Relaxation

Mind Clearing We automatically place our hands on our faces to relieve tension and clear our minds. In the silent movies the heroine would often place the back of her hand on the forehead when she was in a dire situation. We rub our chins in contemplation, cup our hands over our eyes to help us think, and pull at our ears to release energy.

The best situation for the following techniques would be if the person receiving the energy work were lying on a massage table. Lying on a bed without a headboard is second best, lying on the floor or sitting in a chair is okay. Take between 1 to 3 minutes for each exercise using the fingers or the palm of the hand.

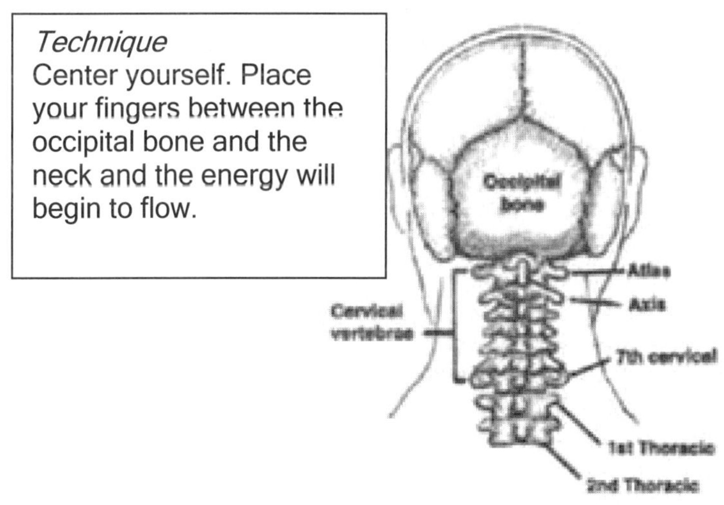

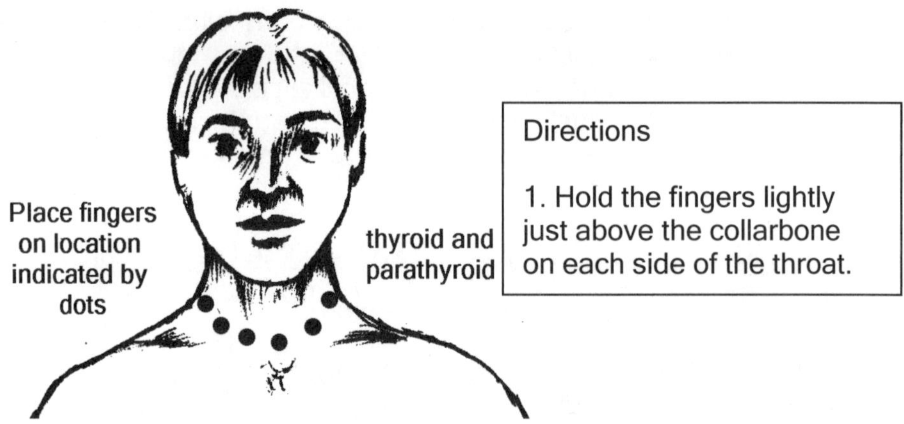

Directions

1. Hold the fingers lightly just above the collarbone on each side of the throat.

1. Put one hand on the center of the back of the head where the skull meets the neck. Place your middle finger in the notch in the occipital ridge.
2. Lightly place the fingers of the right hand as in the drawing.

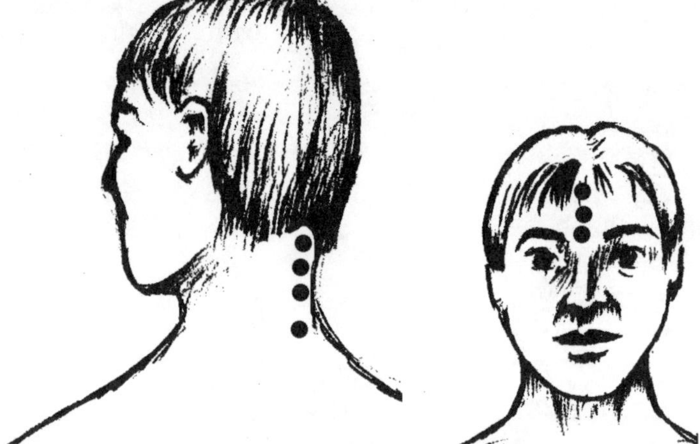

3. Find the notch in the occipital ridge. Place the middle finger in the notch. Two fingers of the opposite hand are held between the eyebrows.
4. The occipital ridge is where the back of the skull meets the neck. Place both hands under the head and wrap the fingers around the occipital. Put a slight tension on the muscles by pulling the neck toward you.

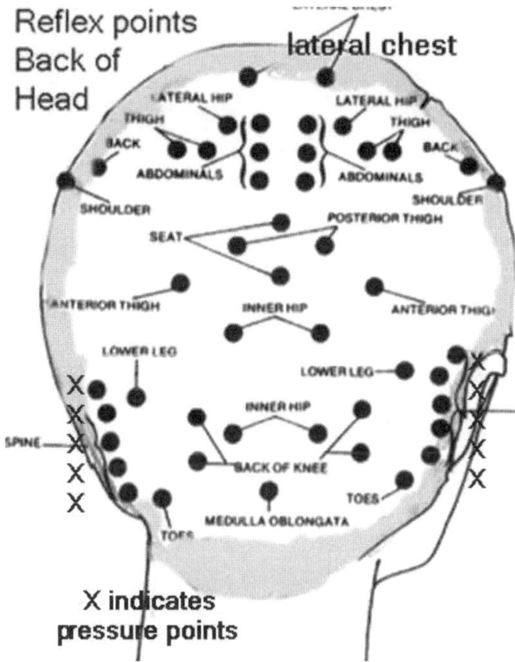

5. Place your fingers with the thumbs on the crown of the head (fontanel area.) This technique can reduce hypertension.
6. It is important that every part of your body be balanced and in alignment. You can balance the right and left hemispheres of the brain by placing three fingers of each hand where illustrated. You will know you are at the right place because you can feel a pulse. The location is at the hairline behind the ear. Hold the position until the pulse feels balanced.

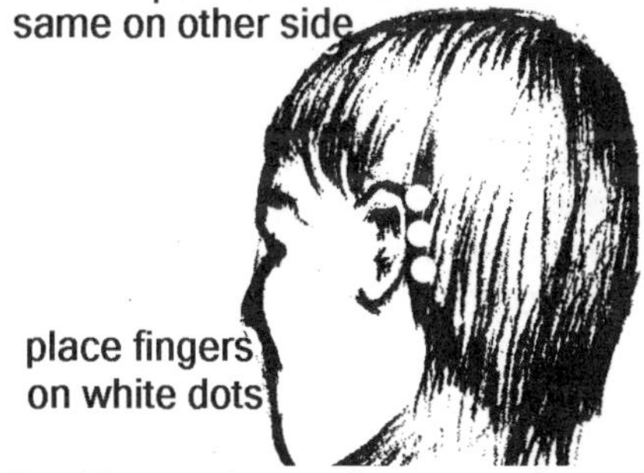

7. Place three fingers of each hand like the dots shown in the illustration (from the eyebrows to the hairline). Your elbows will extend out away from your body.

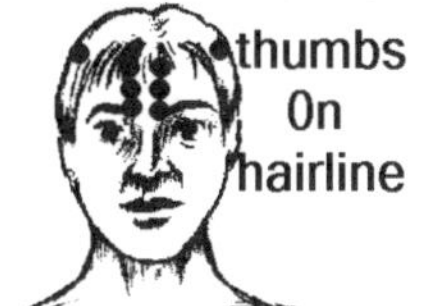

8. Placing your hands as illustrated opens the sixth Chakra, also called the Third Eye and intuitive center. This is where you visualize, imagine, dream, and see colors. Place index finger on the hairline

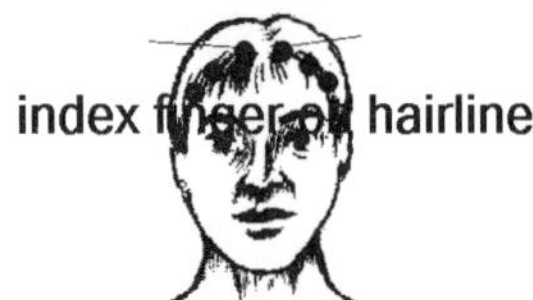

9. Have the person receiving the energy yawn to find the mandibular joint (located on the sides of the face where the jawbone and skull meet. Massage this joint as illustrated by rotating your fingers in a circular motion.

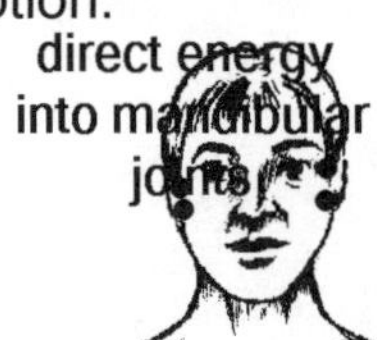

10. Stroke the face three times as illustrated beginning in the middle of the brow. An anatomy book will show you all the nerves in the jaws and you will see why softly brushing the cheeks with the palms and lightly cupping the hands around the jaws will improve your energy flow. Someone needs to do this for you because the fingers should point to the throat.

Exercises To Increase Your Mind Energy

You probably already do postures naturally that help your concentration. Some examples are: resting your forehead on the thumb and forefinger in deep thought, placing the hands behind the skull when lying on the back, and crossing the ankles while sitting.

Brain energy balance:

This exercise has three parts and each time you begin by holding the fingertips around the naval. For right/left balance, stimulate and hold the points on each side of the breastbone. For top/bottom balance, stimulate and hold with the thumb below the upper lip. For back/front balance, stimulate and hold directly behind the navel on the back.

Exercises For Stress Relief

Press and massage the hollow spot in the middle the medulla oblongata (the connector between the right and left brain), located where the base of your

Where Is "Mind"? What Is "Mind"?

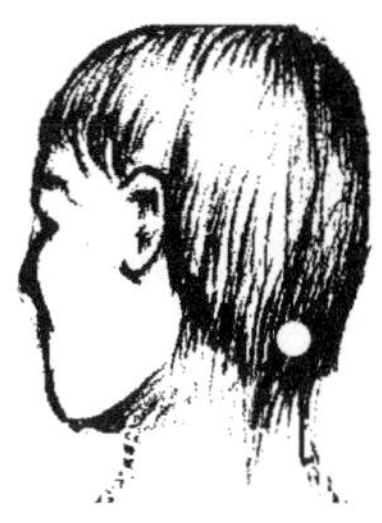

skull and your neck meet. White spot indicates medulla oblongata.

Exercise for emotional stress from past memories and the present: Positive Points-Gently place the thumbs of both of your hands at your temples and then put your index and middle fingers just above the eyebrows, halfway between the hairline and eyebrows. Hold this position until you feel emotional and stress release.

Emotional Energy

When we let the negative emotions of fear, worry, anger, anxiety, guilt, and depression create illness in our body; our life force energies are diminished. When our lives get out of balance and alignment because of overwork, bad relationships with family, at work, and friends, or lack of emotional release and control, or surgery, we create illness on all energetic levels. **Our belief in our self worth is at the bottom of every one of our issues, our addictions, and our problems. Our sense of our own self worth should be based on the fact that we are all made of the same "stuff" that everything else is made of...pure energy that comes from the Creator and Source of all that there is.**

I was teaching an aura class in Florida when I met Jack, a young man who preferred to sit on the back row and be disassociated with the others attending class. When he introduced himself to the class he said, "I work out about four times a week, play different forms of athletics, and I even enjoy sports such as skydiving." All of this surprised me since sports enthusiasts are usually very friendly and outgoing, plus, Jack had such a slight build and no muscles.

When Jack took his turn at going to the front of the room to let everyone see his aura, only faint white light appeared around his body–no colors were visible. How could this be I immediately thought? He says he does all this exercise. Then I noticed the arch in his legs–a sign many times that someone has been sexually abused as a child. When Jack and I were alone, I mentioned to him, "You need to let go of some things that happened in the past." He replied, "It would be hard, too hard." Jack was paying a high price for not forgiving his abuser. He had shut down his emotional and spiritual energies especially, and he was totally disconnected from himself and others.

Dissolving the Muscular armor

To protect ourselves as children from different kinds of threats (emotional abuse, verbal abuse, physical abuse etc.) we "armored" ourselves to stop feeling all the things that were hurting us. If you have one of these situations: backaches, are not sensitive to feeling energy, your chakras are closed, you lack energy, you lack happiness and success, and you have trouble with relationships, then you have armored yourself. Don't feel guilty; you had to do this to protect yourself, but as an adult you can learn how to protect yourself.

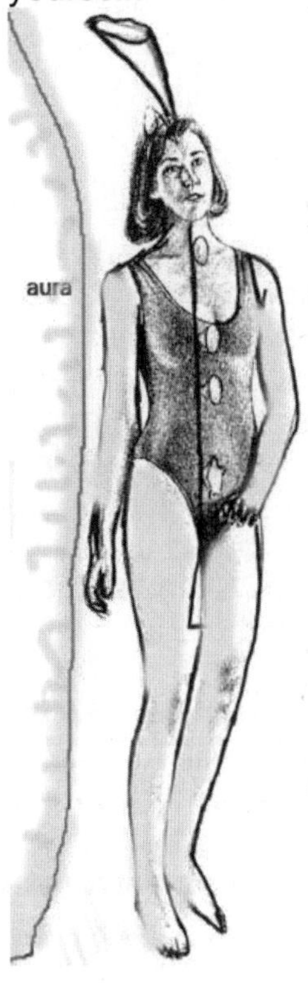

The second thing we do to protect ourselves as children is that our soul, also called our Spirit, steps outside or away from us. From the time that we are born until early childhood our chakras are wide open, receiving all the different forms in energy from those people around us. The child protects himself from negative energy and harm to his soul the only way he knows how at this time; he separates his soul from his physical body. By looking at the auric field, you can see his soul displaced to the right or the left or displaced to his back. The front of the body is more vulnerable to attack than the back. The child will protect his heart, which is the connection to his soul.

Spending Our Emotional And Mental Energy

I heard the author of a book about boxing talking on National Public Radio about how promoters pair a boxer with less ability to fight the hometown hero so that he will win. However, the author told an interesting story of a hometown boxer, who was really getting a little too old to box, being in a match with a younger, out of town boxer. The younger, out of town boxer looked physically better, but didn't have the experience of the older boxer.

Early in the match the younger boxer landed a punch above the eye of the older boxer, and blood started streaming down his face. "The younger boxer got overly confident that he was going to win," the author said, "and he got excited and began ***spending his psychological energy thinking that he was going to win."*** The older, wiser boxer knew this and waited until the younger boxer got mentally and emotionally tired out, and then he was easily defeated. In my book, ***Energy Management, How To Increase Your Positive Energy Levels,*** I discuss the *Principle of Flow* and how living and acting in the present moment is the great energizier. When we place judgment on a person or event, in this case the outcome of a boxing match, we are spending our present energy on future outcomes rather than present needs. Every moment you spend your thoughts or recapture your memories in the past or the future, you are wasting your current energy.

The Woman With The Ax In Her Head

Jennifer is a very delightful and intelligent woman who came for an all day healing session with me. She brought her 80-year old mother, Eve, who has suffered severe pain in her left leg for several years. Jennifer had a very difficult childhood so it was helpful to meet her mother even though her perspective of Jennifer's childhood was completely different.

Eve was a very frail and sickly child whose family pampered her and never required her to take any responsibilities. She married a man who broke off his engagement to another woman because he said that God directed him to marry Eve. He continued to treat Eve as a queen, but as time passed, he became very angry because he had to take all the responsibility for cooking, shopping, and cleaning. Jennifer was the first born of three daughters and she took the brunt of her father's anger. As she grew older she became the "mother" and had to take responsibility for her two sisters. They were treated differently by the father and did not harbor all the resentment that Jennifer felt. They did remember, however, that Jennifer had done all the things for them that a mother would have done. All three daughters suffered from the controlling father who would not permit them to be sick, express their emotions, or cry. Jennifer said that her sister never told her parents about a severe ear infection for fear of punishment. The school nurse finally sent her home because of the pus oozing out of both her ears.

Jennifer said that she too learned to have a high pain threshold which in doing so cut her off from her emotions. Now fifty-five, only in the last few years has she given herself permission to cry. When children experience traumas in their lives they learn to survive by moving out of their electromagnetic field. Until they correct it, by releasing the traumas stored in their meridians and organs, they forever feel out of balance and describe themselves as being out of touch or not really being or feeling who they are.

Jennifer's father was a teacher who was criticized by parents for being too harsh and controlling. He quit teaching to serve in the military where he again taught. The upper part of his body became "puffed up" as is the case with several military men in authority. Jennifer also described her father as a man who loved words and could use those words as swords. He knew how to use the energy coming from his eyes to force people into submission. In order to protect herself from that negative energy, Jennifer armored herself with several layers of shields that are as real as metal shields. The result was that her cerebral, logical thinking became divided.

You have heard about people using arrows to pierce out hearts and we all know how this feels. In this case, Jennifer had an "ax" lodged in the front of her skull that split her thinking. I worked for some time removing the layers of shields and the blocked energy that collected behind them. I placed my hands near the front of her skull, moved them counter clockwise several times and then I directed the energy to collect in the palm of my hands by seeing it and telling it to gather there. It is more powerful if the client can also direct and release the energy. By closing my eyes I can see the energy being released. In this case it was extremely difficult to pull my hands up because of all the barriers Jennifer had placed there to hold the negative energy. I removed the layers one after the other until the energy was finally able to flow again. Jennifer said that the pain had just about subsided but that some of it had moved to the side of her head. Energy healers call that "following the pain" because the healer may have to release the energy in several places before it is all gone.

After the death of her father Jennifer said that she could still feel him sucking energy out of her electromagnetic field. Her GDV images showed very little energy in her spinal area, and she noted that she felt her father sucking energy from her back. I removed five cords connecting her and her father.

Jennifer worked as a dental hygienist for thirty years and was absolutely passionate about her work saying that by cleaning people's teeth she was doing her part to restore their energy. A hygienist usually can only do their job for a few years because they must stay in the same awkward position while working on a patient, which is difficult for their posture, wrists and hands. Jennifer had corrected the problems with her posture and injuries, caused by rounding her shoulders to permit the strenuous tarter scraping, by having several Rolfing sessions. Rolfing is bodywork done on the body's connective tissues that are out of alignment.

Eve is a delightful lady who survived a lobotomy. Jennifer noted that her mother must have been very intelligent to be able to function so well after the lobotomy. She never took any responsibility for allowing the father to be so cruel to her children. She acted as if everything had been normal, however, she complained of severe stomach and leg pain. Her GDV showed that she had a lot of emotional energy stored in her stomach. I taught her the Emotional Freedom Technique and she used the statement, "Even though I feel powerless, I still totally love and respect myself." After tapping on her meridians as described in EFT, Eve released the emotional blockage. .

Visualization is a very powerful and successful technique to heal yourself, energize you, and create the future that you want. Go back to Figure 1 and look at the powerful energy created by Dan in his visualization. Remember, thoughts are energy, and when you create the thoughts you want to have to form your reality, you are creating the physical matter you want (house, car, etc), or the healing that you want (destruction of the tumor, creation of more white cells, blood cells, etc.) or the kind of relationships you want with your Creator and your loved ones.

How does this work? The eye looks at a symbol and electrical charges are stimulated so that the symbol is then amplified. We know an image on the retina, of a symbol or of any object in the visual field, results in a pattern of electrical activity that travels through the optic nerve to the optic lobes of the brain. The mechanisms involved have been carefully researched and much is known. The pattern of light on the retina is translated into a pattern of impulses on the occipital cortex. The retina is projected point to point onto the cortex.[2] Polyak.

In science class you learned that photons of light spark a nerve impulse that travels via the optic nerve to the brain. A few photons cause thousands of calcium ions to enter into the retinal cell membrane, leading into polarization of the membrane and nerve impulse. It is interesting that every aspect of the body is polarized from the head being positive and the feet being negative.

All cells, including the eye, have positive and negative charges. Science now agrees that anytime a neuron conducts an impulse, a magnetic field must be created in the surrounding space. So when a person sees anything, like a symbol, has a thought, or does anything else that would create charges, a

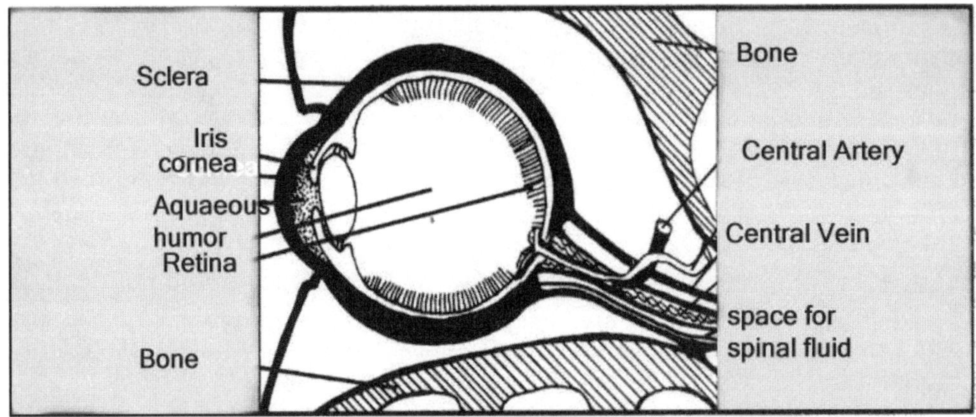

Note that spinal fluid goes to the eye; therefore the spine is affected by how much light enter the eyes.

magnetic field is created that emits light and vibration, and magnetic energy. Symbols are actually more powerful than words because they are not connected with your belief systems. Symbols affect direct healing of situations. We often have symbolic visions of people and situations. We may envision a person's words as barbs being thrown at us, or we may use ourselves as protective wall to stop the arrows being shot. [3] Marshall

To empower Jennifer I taught her the very powerful gold star guided visualization. You can read about the meaning associated with each of the different kinds of star symbols to decide which star you want to visualize.
Begin by visualizing a nine pointed star in your the stomach area, also called the solar plexus. The solar plexus area is the center of your body, where your strength and power originate Visualize it as a three dimensional star and see it growing brighter and brighter, bigger and bigger as it is filled with very bright celestial gold light. Visualize the star emitting light from its points, out the arms of the star, and then from the body of the star in 360 degrees. Send the light out from the solar plexus to the four corners of the room. It is so bright and filled with so much energy that it is sent out further to the city, to the state. Then connect your light with the light sent from the stars to really energize yourself. You begin to feel at one and connected with the entire universe, and you are open to receive the energy of the universe.

Feeling empowered, Eve released all of the stored emotions around the issue of feeling powerless as a child. As the energy began flowing through her body, the energy flowed freely through her leg and this immediately released the pain. Most of the time our emotions are so deeply stored that we are not aware that we have buried them. Like everything else in the universe, emotions are energy, and when they are stuck in the body, it becomes diseased.

Where Is "Mind"? What Is "Mind"?

Because human beings function through a physical body, the discovery by particles physicists that matter is a form of frozen energy has significant implication for science's ability to understand the subtle energetic intricacies of human physiology. Studies in the fields of laser physics and holography give us new ways of understanding how the brain may store information.

Thought Field Therapy And The Emotional Freedom Technique

It takes a lot of time and energy to release all of the lifetime traumas stored in our physical and subtle bodies, but it works. I have always felt that conventional talk therapy simple re-enforces bad feelings, emotions, and memories because it simply brings them up and has no way to release the stored emotions in the cells and tissues.

Energy psychology has several techniques all involving tapping on the body's meridians. Thought Field Therapy was discovered and developed by Roger Callahan PhD. Gary Craig modified it and created the Emotional Freedom Technique. You can research it on the Internet for more information. EFT works very well to relieve anxiety and phobias in minutes because it works directly with the stored energy causing them. Amazingly the relief rate is reputed at 85-90% even if the person has no confidence in the technique.

Thought Field Therapies open blocks in the meridians by balancing various body acupuncture points and actuating both hemisphere of the brain. This is done by having the client look to the left and right, rotate the head alternately in two different directions, hum a tune and count out loud in a systematic pattern coupled with tapping acupuncture points, while holding the phobic feeling in mind. The therapist must first correct any psychological energy reversal situation.

The client still needs to find and eliminate the initial causes of the problem because they will constantly reinforce negative programs in the mind. The bad things that happen to us are called Negative Forcing Functions that we hold in our mind. Every time the client's energy becomes unbalanced, they can learn how to rebalance it so that the energy becomes more stable and they get permanent healing.

Spiritual Energy

Any kind of disease should be considered as an alarm signal for disharmonies in spirit and soul...We have to turn away from our suffering and sickness, because they are the hindrances on our path towards the inner. We have to bid farewell to those frustrations and fears which prevent us from progressing and from coming into contact with our higher selves. Peter Mandel

"We are energy and even spirit manifested through this physical form. Once you embrace this you have a better understanding of how one can have an impact on health and illness from not just the physical level but the higher levels as well. The higher levels although you can define them on a mathematical level in terms of quantum physics and the existence of other levels, it is really more about understanding how the different energy components are part of information systems of the body and helps to provide the structure of our bodies. For instance, it is the etheric body and not just the memory within our genetic code which is the template that helps guide the development of each of us in the womb." Richard Gerber M.D.

References

LeDoux, Joseph, *Synaptic Self*, Penguin Publishing, 2003 P. 9.

Polyak, S.A. 1934, 'Projection of the retina upon the cerebral cortex, based upon experiments with monkeys', Research Publication of the Association for Research in Nervous & Mental Disease, vol. 13, pp. 535-537.

Talbot, S.A. & Marshall, W.H., 1941, 'Physiological studies on neural mechanisms of visual and discrimination'. American Journal of Ophthalmology, vol. 24, pp. 1255-1264.

8. Subtle Energy Called The Aura

Principle of Energy: Our power increases what we become through Intentionality.

One of the basic premises of this book is that each person has a HEF, Human Energy Field, that extends infinitely and that each HEF is a part of the Universal Energy Field. Every substance in the universe has a radiation, force field or aura. The auras of minerals, plants and animals as well as human bodies have special characteristics that will be discussed later.

Humans have two bodies–a physical and a non-physical body. We call the non-physical body an aura, Human Energy Field, or an electromagnetic field. All physical matter vibrates at a low frequency and is dense in appearance. The human body is physical matter. The subtle matter that makes up our etheric or seven auric bodies vibrates at a higher frequency and complements our physical form with a web of complex energy systems that are within and surround the human body.

The aura is compromised of the auric bodies. The order of the bodies moves from the etheric, astral, mental, higher mental, causal, and spiritual levels. They interpenetrate each other and the physical body. The aura is produced by the crystal transformers in the body that produce the electrical, chemical and magnetic energy that were discussed in Chapter 4 We Are Pure Energy. It explained that **we are vibrational, magnetic, electrical, and crystalline.**

Everything influences your aura from cosmic rays, the rays of electrical devices, your thoughts, your movements, medications you are taking, food you have eaten and any kind of liquid you have drunk. We can call subtle energy refined energy that comes from both cosmic energy and the virtual states just listed. Cosmic energy would be too much for the body to incorporate so the subtle bodies densify it. The seven layers of the aura break down cosmic energy into seven rays like a prism. The white light is broken down and each of the seven rays is the predominant energizing ray for one of the seven chakras.

There are 72,000 nadis in the body that carry energy from the chakras into the brain, the nervous endocrine, and organ system, the skeletal structure, and finally to the cell structure. The nadis intersect with the meridian lines and create the acupuncture points.

Within the HEF golden lines of energy are moving at a very high rate of frequency about six feet around the human body in an egg shape or ovoid.

The widest part of the aura is at the head because more electromagnetic activity is going on. The width depends upon a person's spiritual growth. This is the seventh level of your aura and its size, like the size of all your auric levels, depends upon how much energy you put into it. It is there to protect you because you cannot take in all of the information, past, present, and future, that is held in the universe. It also protects you from all of the cosmic rays, cosmic disturbances, and all of the energy transmission going on constantly.

The aura is filled with colors that are constantly changing according to our moods and well-being. The vibrations and colors closest to the physical body are the densest, gradually becoming higher vibration as they move towards the outer edges of the aura. The luminosity of the colors depends upon how advanced the soul is.

Bob Dubin, a chiropractor who has been using "Flashing Light Therapy" since 1985 was quoted by Dr. Jacob Lieberman in *Light Years Ahead* as having said, "Whenever there is a change within a system, the electron jumps states; it jumps to a different orbital ring." And when it does, photons are given off; light is given off. The photons are the informational substances. So, when you look deeply into the body, the way that the body communicates within itself is that every time there's a change in state, each cell gives off light. Light is the way the cells communicate. There are informational photons.

The energy in the aura is composed of highly structured patterns and designs. The GDV camera images show the energy symmetry in the following areas: the energy comparisons on the right and left side of the body, side views of the body show, especially above the head, whether the aura is in a balanced or agitated state. The images of Shana show an unbalanced aura. You can also look at the different images in the middle of the book and see streams of energy leaving a person's body. If the person is highly emotional, you will see the stream clouded with pink color. Clusters of energy develop where the energy is not flowing. If it is mental energy, the purple color will be very dark; if it is physical energy, a dark blue color will appear. The images of the woman with multiple personalities, Lynn and Emily, Figure 11, and of Susan, Figure 8, show arcs containing physical, mental, emotional, and spiritual energies. Interestingly, the large arcs located near Lynn's legs do not appear in her other personality's aura because Emily had forgiven her sexual abuser.

When most people see a person's aura they see the white light outlining their body and perhaps one or two other colors. However, some people can see people who have a rainbow aura enveloping the full body or just the head and shoulders. The rainbow consists of a variety of colors in soft tones. Joe Slate, Ph.D., in his book, *Aura Energy,* says that the rainbow aura is typically bright and expansive and it suggests a diverse combination of many positive traits–intelligence, humanitarian concerns, social interests, intuitive knowledge, integrity, generosity, optimism, and self-actualization. As a group, people with rainbow auras are usually intensely committed and successful in their careers and personal lives. Many great leaders and social reformers of today have rainbow auras. The flip side, Slate says, is that their aura is exceptionally sensitive to imbalance and discoloration. *Aura Energy* is the best aura book I have read. It gives great information about the colors in the aura. The author's contact information is in the bibliography.

The fourth level of the aura is a bridge between levels one, two, and three–the levels that metabolize energies from the physical world–and levels five, six, and seven–the levels that metabolize energies from the spiritual world. Energy from the first three levels must pass through the fourth level to go to the spiritual world levels. The spiritual energies must pass through the fourth level to the three physical levels.

Why does it work this way? You learned in Chapter 5, "Energy Is Moveable And Transferable", about how the 4th chakra is the heart chakra and that it is through the heart that we connect with our soul. When the spiritual energy of the last three auric levels passes to the physical levels or the physical energy of the first three auric levels passes to the spiritual levels, the energy must go through the 4th level and be transformed by the fire of the heart. You must be connected in all your different relationships: self, others, Creator, to connect with the person you are sending or receiving energy from.

The first level is a template for the physical subtle body, the second level is the template for the emotional body, the third level is the template for the mental body, the fourth level is the template that acts as a bridge between the fifth level, template for the will of God, sixth, template for the mind of God, and seventh, template for the love of God. You should memorize what each level does.

Living An Integrious Life

William Collinge, in his book *Subtle Energy*, says that through his work with energy, Einstein became a deeply religious man. He concluded that the continuously unfolding and dynamic nature of the universe could be understood only as the work of a higher guiding intelligence of another dimension. Indeed, the perennial wisdom of humankind holds that our physical world is embedded within a greater, transcendent dimension–that of Spirit or the Absolute. [1] Collinge, William

The Seventh Level Of The Aura

The seventh level of the aura, the ketheric template or causal body, can also be called the spiritual or the bodyless body. **It is the very essence of our**

being. It is the divine spark, that which is part of that ultimate reality or universal consciousness. It has no beginning and no ending. Interestingly the spiritual energy of the seventh level is generalized and does not have a pattern like the other levels; it is a non-specific energy. This highest source energy does not have form, no color etc Spiritual energy picks up the sensations of the other six levels as it comes down through the lower levels.

People who are able to see auras can see this level up to three feet from the body. The seventh level is composed of gold/silver light appearing as if it were woven in strong threads. The threads are pulsating so quickly with this shimmering light that it acts as a strong protective sheath. Unfortunately the protection can be broken when people are in drug or alcohol induced states and then tears or energy leaks can occur.

When you look at the chakras and the body form on this level, they appear as golden light. The main energy running through the body runs through the spine and then the energy flows to the roots of each chakra. As the chakras take in physical energy from the universe, if they are in alignment and functioning correctly, the energy from this level unites.

Sixth Level of the Aura

When you move your pendulum to the sixth level of the aura, you will again feel the change because the vibration will not be as high. The sixth level is called the celestial body and it deals with emotions, but on a spiritual level. This level extends around two and a half feet from the body. At this level you feel connected with all the universe. When we raise our consciousness to this level, the light and love of everything that exists appears. We experience that sense of being where we are at one with God. When you are around a person in a state of joy, bliss and harmony, they are experiencing divine love and those charged feelings radiate into other energy fields.

In order to express unconditional love, the heart chakra must be open and in union with the unconditional love of God. The result is that the person loves all humans with a higher spiritual love.

The colors in this level are soft pastel colors that appear as shimmering light. Beams of light exude through a mist of soft glowing light. If the sixth level is weak, the lines become thin and undercharged. The colors are dark and do not look opalescent. What occurs in the body has first occurred in the auric field or subtle bodies.

Fifth Level of the Aura

The fifth level is called the etheric level. The physical body appears in this level in a reversed blueprint form. That means that the forms that would usually appear blue, like the skeleton, appear white, and the spaces that usually would appear white appear blue. When this level is in perfect form, the physical body is in perfect form. When the physical body is diseased, healing work must be done on the fifth level.

Many healers, who work with tuning forks, chants, mantras, and toning, work in this level because it is where sound creates matter. To observe this level in someone's field you must focus on the vibratory frequency that extends about two and a half feet from the person. This level contains the entire form of the body, the chakras, and the body organs.

If a person is in alignment at this level, the Creator's will and the person's will are one. The daily prayer should be that he/she be aligned with the will of the Creator. He/she will experience a great sense of power and a great sense of connection with everything.

If your life takes on more purpose, more sense of order, and you are able to accomplish more, your fifth level is very strong. You will acquire a greater sense of self worth and you will feel a sense of alignment with all things.

Medical intuitives, people who are able to see inside the body and the energy fields around the body with their Third Eye, see the layered structures of the fifth and sixth level of the electromagnetic field. The fifth level is composed of golden light and looks like oscillating energy points.

The higher mental body is where inspirations and knowledge from the higher self manifest. You can connect with your higher self by putting both feet on the floor, squaring your shoulder, and breathing rhythmically. Inspirations and knowledge can then be absorbed into the lower mental body if the channel between these two bodies has been opened. This is normally achieved through meditation and spiritual practices.

The first level of the aura is the template for the physical energy of the body. But it is the fifth level of the aura that holds the first level in place. How does this work? In order to create, you must first set your intention, and you must create a space to manifest in.

Fourth Level of the Aura

The fourth level of the aura is filled with fluid, bioplasma, containing all of the colors. The energy in the field looks different because it forms beautiful streams of light that begin radiating from the body out to the fourth level. The streams of color come from clouds of color that are more vibrant and robust than the colors of the 2nd level. The lines of energy are the colors in the rainbow and you can see the energy moving up these lines. The chakras in this level are infused with the rose light of love in a person who is truly loving.

The pituitary gland, which governs the lower brain, left eye, ears, nose and nervous system produces golden pulsations of light when a person is in love and strongly connected to another person. A person who can see auras will describe the meeting of two good friends as the bioplasmic fluids from both people moving out and connecting with each other. The kind of relationship between the people will determine the colors of the fluid. For example, I ask my audience if they have ever attended a party where they know that two people are having an illicit affair, even though they have no visible proof. When questioned, the people in the audience said that they could feel the sexual energy flowing between the two people. Those who see auras see the orange bioplasmic fluid of the second chakra and all the colors of the fourth chakra connecting between these two people. Most people don't know how they know, but seventy five percent of the audience say they do know.

The fourth level of the aura represents our feelings about each other. It goes way beyond that. Connections that we have with plants, animals, other people, inanimate objects of all kinds, and even out into the universe, the sun, stars, planets are connected through the fourth level.

Anytime you feel exhausted, bloated, in pain or discomfort, with basically a sense of heaviness or low energy, you need to check your fourth level and think about how energy equals low vibration. An aura seer would view thick, dark energy.

Locate your fourth auric level with your pendulum and ask questions in that energy field. First, you will want to ask about your relationships with other people to discover who you are having challenges with. You probably already know this, but it helps you see the effects of these conflicts.

The fourth level acts as a bridge between the first three auric levels (level one: physical, level two: emotional, level three: mental) and the three levels of our spiritual world.

Third Level of the Aura

When I am speaking I can always tell which members of my audience are mentally turned on because their third auric level is lemon yellow and filled with delicate high vibrating thin lines of energy that are associated with thoughts and mental processes. Like the first level, the third level is a structured body and the more you concentrate, the larger it becomes around the whole body. The mental level is strongest around the head and shoulders.

Thought Forms

Remember all the aspects of energy–thoughts are energy, energy carries information, and energy can be transferred. Thought forms are as real and viable as the chair you are sitting on. They can be described as "spaces of reality" or "belief systems" that we have heard about so much. Every definite thought produces two effects: first, a radiating vibration: second, a floating form. Those who can see thought forms describe positive thought forms as appearing like a spray of a waterfall as the sunlight strikes it, raised to the highest of color and delicacy. People create conceptions or misconceptions of reality. You may not even be aware of the thought forms you are creating. Depending upon how much energy you put into them, they will be as strong as you make them. Like all forms of energy, they are high vibration or low vibration. Are some of the following thought forms creating your reality? All men are after just one thing, only children are selfish, everyone from some country is evil, women are just looking for someone to take care of them...on and on.

As mentioned before, thought forms radiate different colors, which make them observable. They are energetic, which means they can be sent to people and places. The kind of thought forms you are sending out depends on the intensity you are giving them and how you are defining them. In order to achieve health, happiness, and success in life, you need to be clear and definite about your thoughts. Your emotions when added to your thoughts give them color, intensity and power.

Here are some basic facts about thought forms:

Thought forms do not carry information, they carry the character of the thought form.

Clearness and definiteness of the thought form produce a more powerful vibration.

The higher the level or vibration of the thought form, the more powerful it is. For instance, thought forms based on truth and love and directed by a strong will are the most powerful kind of thought forms. Most people send out what are called thought-desire forms, which are not high levels of thought.

A friend of mine named Leah owned a pawnshop and then closed it, but she kept a lot of the merchandise in boxes at her house. She kept complaining that the energy at her house was negative and she couldn't get rid of it. I told her that she needed to get rid of the pawned merchandise because people who pawned items were in a very negative state at the time they pawned and their energy went into the items. For instance, the items may have been stolen, the person might be an alcoholic or on drugs or in a bad state financially. You can be assured that no one pawns things for a good reason. If you buy items from a pawnshop you must clear them by holding your hands on the item and sending in love energy.

How Long Do Thought Forms Last?

The life of a thought form depends upon: 1) the initial intensity, 2) the amount of continued energy it is given by the originator of the thought or by others, 3) the length of time the person holds the thought. If a person broods or sustains the same thought form, it will gain tremendous power within the person. Many times we become encased in our own thought forms and then when we look at the world through these thought forms, our perceptions are tainted.

The Astral Body by A.E. Powell says, “Man is continually peopling his current in space with a world of his own, crowded with the offspring of his fancies, desires, impulses and passions.” These thought forms remain in his aura, increasing in number and intensity, until certain kinds of them dominate his mental and emotional life so that the man rather answers to their impulses than decides anew: thus are habits, the outer expression of his stored-up force, created and thus his character is created.

Thought forms can attach to you if you are not protected. This is how mass consciousness or mass thinking forms. Thought forms can enter your aura but you do not have to hold on to them. When a mob of people form, each person develops a mob mentality or thinking and doing the same way because the positive or negative thought forms enter their auric field. The thought form grows strong in another person’s field because they add their own energy to it. **If the thoughts were not already in the person, these new thought forms would have no way to link up to him.** Thought forms sneak into auric fields and attach to major or minor chakra centers, giving or taking energy.

You probably know when someone is thinking about you. The good/bad news is that when you send out a thought or someone sends you a thought, a cord is sent out that works its way into your energy field or their energy field if both parties are at the same vibration. We really need to be careful whom we are connecting to and where are we sending our thoughts and energy. Once a cord is established, it becomes a two-way energy exchange route. If you are an overly open person or overly sensitive, you do not know how to put up barriers and boundaries to other people’s low vibrations. If you become depressed and start thinking negatively, ask yourself who have you been hanging around with in both the physical sense and the mental or emotional sense. When I was younger I would get negative letters from my mother and be depressed for a couple of weeks after I read them. When I grew older I learned to clear myself of the negative beliefs she had taught me as a child. Now the negative comments go right through my auric field because there is nothing to attach to.

Thought Forms Are Created In The Third Level Of The Aura

Let’s look more deeply at how thought forms are created in different colors on the third level. The color of the thought form depends on the emotion connected to them. For example, we talk about being blue or in the pink, being so mad we see red, and being green with envy. Thought forms have a nucleus that radiates a level of vibration depending upon the density of the substance that is attracted to it.

Remember the cartoon character who always had a black cloud over his head. Guess what his thoughts were about. You can literally choose to have positive or negative thought forms around you by habitually thinking of what it is that you want. People get into negative cycles of thinking and they begin to see everything from that point of view...much of which may not be true. We get into habitual thinking patterns and then we start attracting similar thoughts and feelings. In the worse case, the person finds someone on the same level of negative thinking and they fuel each other.

My friend Red Morris looked at my energy field while I was writing this book and she did a drawing that showed several thought forms around me. They weren't bad, but I was making this book harder than it should have been because I was "going around the block" looking for information instead of relying on intuitive information. When I stopped doing research, new insights and new information came to me from Universal Mind.

When you read the information on mind energy in this book, you will want to come back and check your clarity and balanced energy on this level. In order to develop your intuitive abilities, you must first have a clear mind. You control your thought forms through meditation and visualization. There are several good books on visualization that will give you some exercises and techniques. Thousands of people have had success with Silva Mind Control and Transcendental Meditation.

Thought Forms As Energy Vampires

We do not become perfect when we pass over; we retain our personality traits. You may have relatives or friends who have passed over who are still energy drainers. My friend Julie had severe back pain and had been doing several things to relieve it. She just had a two hour massage the day I visited her. She felt great, but when she got into her car the pain returned. I found that she had three cords from an aunt and uncle attached to her root chakra. I used a pendulum to locate the cords and to tell me where to cut the cords. I sent the cords back to the aunt and uncle and the other ends back into Julie's field. The Bible refers to the cords that bind us.

Thought forms can come from a person, idea or concept. The media produces a lot of thought forms that people take in without investigating. Many of us are holding on to old thoughts forms that no longer serve us. I recommend that you think about where you got the old thought form and that you clear it out so that you have space for newer higher vibrating thought forms. Be really conscious of your thoughts for at least the next seven days. You may find that you want to say goodbye to some friends who are filling you with negative thought forms. You may find that you need to raise your own thought forms before you send them out. Thoughts are built by the energy we put into them, so stop giving negativity energy.

If you have books, pictures or possessions around your house that carry negative memories, you need to get rid of them. Be careful of taking in other people's clothing or furniture, especially antiques, because they carry their energy. If you have a chronic illness check out your possessions.

Julie was driving through the mountains of Tennessee and she began feeling a space filled with negative, fearful thought forms. She mentioned the exact location to her brother who lived in the state and knew the area. He said that people like to sky dive at that location and several had accidentally died and left their fearful thoughts. You know this feeling if you have ever visited a concentration camp, battlefield, or military post. You can feel the spirits and energy of souls who did not go to the Light and are still hanging around.

Second Level of the Aura

This level and the first level follow the outline of the physical body. This level and the energy into it appear to be cloudlike or balloon-shaped fluid in continuous motion. You can look at the GDV images and see how these balloon shaped balls of emotional energy look like when someone releases them or they are strongly holding on to feelings. You need to be careful that the released emotional energy does not attach to you. Traumatic events of any kind will create huge blobs of emotional energy that cause your aura to be unbalanced. Arguments can create blobs that interact with the other person in the argument and they can spread to other innocent people sharing the space, such as children. Look at the GDV images of Sandra and you will see the draining effects of arguments.

When our emotional energy is negatively charged our emotions cloud logical and rational thinking. Look at the GDV images in the center of the book and when you see highly charged emotions, represented by the pink color, you notice that they displace our physical, mental, and spiritual energies. Charged emotions can have the most powerful effect on our auric field as they push and squeeze the other auric levels causing stagnation. I would say that learning to feel your emotions and then making the right healthy choice about how to release them is the most important thing you can do for this energy field.

Again, the chakras are contained in this level and they follow the colors of the chakras in the physical body: red, orange, yellow, green, blue, indigo, white. The second level contains all the colors of the rainbow that represent all of the emotional feelings that we have. Have a depressed day and you will have dark colors. Feel anger and you will have dark red, cutting energy. When you are having negative thoughts, use your pendulum in your second level and measure your energy according to Dr. Hawkins in *Power Versus Force.* Thoughts of hatred, anger, and revenge will lower your vibration tremendously. These energies will stay blocked in your field and cause you health problems later on. On a day that you feel love for yourself and very comfortable being who you are, measure your vibration and compare the results.

First Level of the Aura

The body nearest to the physical body is the etheric or energy body. The etheric body is structured just like the physical body so you can see all the organs and other parts of the body. Almost everyone can see the light of the first auric level around a person even if they can't see the structure of the body. This level contains the chakras and *nadis*, which are energy channels.

If you want to see the etheric, have someone stand in front of a dark or a light wall and they will be able to see white light around the body. The white light is created by tiny energy lines that look the lines on a TV screen, but they are sparkling and connected like a web. The scintillating energy lines are in constant motion so you will see it quickly move down and out the arms and legs for instance. When I demonstrate the physical level I take about five deep breaths so the audience can see my etheric energy increase. Usually this level extends only about two inches from the body. The clearer the light in this level, the better your health.

Contrary to what you probably think, the etheric level is created before the physical level. What is called an energy matrix or structured lines of force, shapes and anchors the tissues of the body.

Most of us feel pain or pleasure prior to feeling it in the physical body by feeling it in the first auric level. You have five nonphysical senses that operate at this level just like they do in the physical body. Someone with prickly or bristled negative energy is felt at this level. You will feel very relaxed and comfortable if you gently move your hands in this level and smooth out your energies. You will read about the auric weave, energy fluff, and auric facelift in Chapter Ten.

How To Measure The Aura

To measure the seventh level of a person's aura, hold your pendulum as instructed about eight feet away from the person.. Ask the pendulum to indicate "yes" when you reach the seventh level. You can actually feel when you have moved into that vibration because the energy will be a very high, finer frequency. The energy beyond the 7th level is too fine or subtle for most of us to feel or see. You will have to nudge the pendulum into the seventh level because the golden lines of energy are interwoven. The lines form all the physical components of your body. The first level of the aura is a template for the body's physical energy. The seventh level represents the physical body on a spiritual level.

You can use your hands to feel how the edge of the seventh level is thicker and stronger because it protects you from foreign and unhealthy energies. If you look above the head of a person, you will see a funnel of white light that extends through all the auric levels. The white light is the divine mind of the Creator. This is one way that we stay connected to the Creator. The width of the funnel varies depending upon how "open" you are to receive all the divine love and mind the Creator has to offer.

The golden threads connect you to everything in the universe. Some people can see this golden grid; others receive information through them intuitively. It is through these golden lines you can receive the highest level of creativity, a better understanding of the Creator.

Energy Leaks

When we're healthy, our energy systems are balanced and the rate of vibration, in both our physical and non-physical bodies, is high. If the relationship between the body, emotions, mind and spirit breaks down, however, our vibrational energy becomes unbalanced and our overall equilibrium is disturbed.

At these times, the body is more susceptible to disease from both external and internal sources. We become less resistant to those external forces that bombard us daily and internally, our level of health can be more easily affected in a negative way by our state of mind, beliefs and thought patterns.

In the first instance, imbalances reveal themselves at an emotional level, usually as an energy blockage. These blockages may cause a slowing in the vibrations of a cell, organ, system or energetic body and result in disease or illness. If we ignore these blockages or fail to deal with them effectively, they will eventually show themselves as more serious physical symptoms. The basic premise of vibrational medicine, then, is that our emotions are responsible for our disease and we are each wholly responsible for the state of our own health.

It is important to your energy level that you live in places that are compatible with your auric field. I hear people talk about being invigorated by cold weather while my activity slows down. Some people want to live in the low humidity, tree barren areas while others thrive in green, mountainous areas. Last year I spoke at three hospitals in New York City for Nurses Week. Some of my friends travel there to be reenergized while I felt pulled down by the accumulation of dead energy. The pollution of all the cars, overhead railways affected my breathing and clouded my auric field.

Healing Energy Leaks

Here are some procedures if you want to help a person stop an energy leak. Ask permission to work with the person. Set your intention to heal the energy leak. Place your hands palms down on the person's back and move them back and forth. Seal this extra energy with the palm of your hand for a minute. Use your pendulum and ask which color(s) you should send into the person's body. You will always be told to send pink loving light energy from the heart. If there is a wound or an infection, you will probably send in green light for healing or blue light to remove the heat. Gold light will cleanse and purify the area.

Energy Streams

Streams of energy distribute energy throughout the aura appearing as brilliant and glowing, symmetrically or meandering. The second layer of the auric field is the astral or emotional layer. If the person is feeling very enlightened and spiritual, a purple region will appear. The third layer of the aura is the mental layer and it appears yellow. Where the two colors border each other there are often streams of high energy. Those who are sensitive to the feel of energy get a tingling sensation when they run their hands through the auric field. Sensitives can also feel blockages that cause a loss of energy and if the blockage remains illness will occur.

You may have leaks, breaks, or voids in your energy field. Voids are non-functional and inactive areas. Look at the GDV camera images and you can see the empty spaces and breaks in the energy fields. You can actually feel the flow of cool air with your hand, or when using a pendulum, it will go counterclockwise.

On the emotional level, Dr. Slate in *Aura Energy* says that when energy leaks appear in the aura's inner levels, they are often associated with feelings of emptiness. They can represent unfulfilled strivings, discouragement, and loss of hope. Extensive voids are often found in the auras of people who experience identity diffusion, depersonalization, and detachment from others. Leaks are the result of trauma, cuts, injuries, giving birth, or surgery. When I point out to a person about their GDV images and show them the energy leaks, they already know about the old incisions and injuries, even though they are several years old, and that they are still bothering them.

Sometimes these leaks occur at what appears to be points of darkness. As it has been noted, illness occurs where there is weakness in the aura. Ann has tinnitus, ringing in the ear, in her left ear that several of healers have not been able to cure as yet. Julie, a medical intuitive first saw gray energy flowing from

Ann's left ear, and she asked her if the name John meant anything to her. Knowing that she had never told Julie of her mistake in lending a man named John several thousand dollars, she remorsefully said, "Unfortunately I do." They agreed that the tinnitus occurred at a weak area in Ann's body and would not be healed until she released her feelings of anger around the issue.

Energy Clusters

Sensitives can also feel warm and vibrant energy in clusters. Those who see auras see clusters as bright, colorful, symmetrical, and interconnected networks of energy that appear in the sixth and seventh layers of the aura. They appear after meditation or invoking energy to enter your field when you need empowerment. When I do energy healing, observers report that they see clusters of white and green light flowing where I am sending the energy.

Whenever you feel the need for more power, energy or healing, you can envision energy streaming into a funnel above your head, entering your crown chakra, going to the pineal gland and then flowing to wherever you intend it go.

Points Of Light

Just as the Universal Energy Field is composed of points of light, we have points of light seen in energy clusters, more likely in the upper part of the aura. They especially appear when you are doing meditation and seeking spiritual enlightenment. Points of light are also indicative of past-life experiences.

My friend Julie was speaking before a group and working with a woman named Bonnie who had felt abandoned all her life. After Bonnie's parents died, she went to live with her grandparents who died when she was a teenager. Bonnie's shoulders were rounded in fear and she seemed heavy because her energy was lifeless. As Julie worked with her she saw Bonnie in a past life as a Civil War soldier dying from a sword piercing his heart and left abandoned on the field. When Julie began telling what she saw, Bonnie actually began shivering as she began to relive the experience. Points of light hovered at the wound perhaps to remind the woman that we are never alone and that angels are around us. At the end of the session, Bonnie was able to release her feelings of loneliness. She became warmer, the sense of weight on her back was lifted so that her posture straightened. She was much lighter on all different levels than when she arrived.

When I teach people how to see auras, I then ask them to look behind my right side and tell me what they see. Time after time people describe James, as tall slender figure wearing a robe and looking much like St. Francis of Assisi. However, the figure is the Apostle James. When I speak his name, clusters of lights brighten the people report. In each of the occasions I was with people who were in no way connected to the other people I knew. Nor did I give them any hints about who was in my auric field. Since then, friends who are more adept at seeing guides and spirits who have "passed over" and are available to help us, have described several angels and guides around me. Their energy is at a much higher vibration than ours so if you can't see them, you can locate them by using a pendulum. After saying my prayer, I ask the pendulum if it would help me find my angels or guides by moving either clockwise or back and forth toward me when I go into their energy field. You can actually feel the difference when you start moving pendulum into this high vibration.

You Can Determine The Size Of A Person's Aura Using A Pendulum

Step back about 6-12 feet from the person you are measuring. Most people's auras are about twelve feet in circumference, but you may have a person with a very strong aura that measures several more feet. Hold your pendulum between your thumb and index finger and ask the pendulum to motion yes when you get to the seventh level of the aura. The information on the pendulum discusses how to determine which directions the pendulum will move for "yes" and "no". Feel the finer vibration of the energy in the seventh level. As you move forward, you will notice that there is a change in vibration, and it is harder to move the pendulum when you get to the sixth level of the aura because the energy is denser. You will feel as if you have to push the pendulum into the different levels of the aura as the energy is in a lower vibration as you come to each level. You can use anything to mark the different auric levels and then determine the overall size of the aura.

The important thing to remember is that while we speak of measuring an aura this does not mean that your aura is not a part of the universal energy field. Just as the millions of cells in your body each have positive and negative charges that create an auric field and the combination of these cells makes up your auric field, so each person, each plant, all matter is a speck of frozen light in the universal energy field. You can take out a drop of water from the ocean, and it still has the same properties of the ocean, though it appears to be separate. You cannot take a drop of energy from the universal energy field because there is nothing outside of the universe.

An Exercise To Measure Your Aura

All the energy that forms your aura is in constant movement producing change in its form. However, you can still get a pretty accurate idea about its size and the size of each of the levels.

Get a partner to go with you to a place that has concrete so you can draw on it with colored chalk. Take a yardstick so you can measure the size of your aura later on. Mark a circle around your feet where you are standing. Draw an outline of your shoes so that you stand it the exact same place later. Don't move out of this place. The partner should find the beginning of your seventh level auric field as already explained, but use the colored chalk to draw short lines in an oval shape. After the partner has gone around the circle they can connect the lines. Do the same procedure with each of the auric levels. Now look at the seven circles and see the shape of your aura. Is it egg shaped or are there parts that are out of alignment?

Measure the width of each of the auric levels. The following sizes are approximations. Level one- 3" Level two- 6"-8" usually unless you are emotionally charged about something and then the energy can go out a couple of feet or even more and throw the other auric levels out of balance. These two auric bodies follow the exact outline of your body whereas all the following auric bodies will be egg shaped. I find that the emotional body is the most easily changed and misshapened of all the bodies. This is the reason we really need to learn how to control our emotions. Level three-the mental body is the next largest auric body besides the seventh level. It is about 2 feet. Level four-the relationship level and Level five are both about 10". Level seven is about 3-3 1/2 feet wide.

If you want to change the size of the auric bodies you can do something appropriate to that body. For instance, to change the size of the first level you can do some deep breathing or run around the block and then measure again. A few minutes of deep breathing and meditation will calm emotional outbursts in the emotional body. If your emotional body is consistently misshapened, you should see a body worker regularly to release the emotional memories in your soft tissue, or a Rolfer to release the memories held in the connective tissue.

Dr. Ida Rolf is the founder of Rolfing or Structural Integration. Dr. Rolf developed a system based on the fact that the body's connective tissues hold not only the memory of traumas in our bodies but also the responses to the emotion related to the trauma. The result is that we have a chronic psychological state that shapes the connective tissue. A result of traumas is that the body is thrown out of alignment with its natural gravitational alignment. It would be worthwhile for anyone who does not feel that they are "peak performers" in any aspect of their life to research this information further.

Mary asked me to do some healing work on a hump about the size of half a grapefruit on the upper left side of her back. Blocked energy had collected in her back muscles at this location. Muscles move because we produce thoughts that send electrical impulses through nerves and cells. A muscle can atrophy because of a physical trauma such as an injury in an accident or wreck. Because cells have the ability to remember, they hold on to traumatic experiences. They also hold on to emotional feelings and memories connected to the trauma. The hump was located at the backside of her heart;

Subtle Energy Called The Aura

I knew intuitively that Mary held onto some feelings of anger toward one or more people.

If she had been sending loving thoughts, the energy would have stayed in flow. When we send thoughts of any kind to someone, we create an energetic connection between us. If we do this over a long period of time, a cord connects us. I asked the healing angels around us to help me know where to place my hands to cut the cords. Then I used my right hand to send the cords back to the people they belonged to. I sent Mary's cords back into her body. Lastly, I moved my right hand counter clockwise to pull the blocked energy out of Mary's muscle. To do this, I used my mind energy to direct the blocked energy to collect in the palm of my hand and then I pulled the energy out of the muscles and finally sent it back into the universe. When I closed my eyes I could see the very thick, taffy like energy being pulled from her body. Mary could feel the energy leaving. After pulling the energy several times, the hump was gone from her back.

Energy Principle: Intention sets the results.

References

Collinge, William, Subtle Energy, Warner Books, New York, NY, pp.2-3.

9. Meridians And Acupressure Points

If you are not familiar with alternative/complementary medicine you may think that meridians are just some imaginary lines that go around the earth. However, your body has twelve primary meridians, also called pathways or channels that pass through the internal organs in a never-ending circle. **They connect every molecule in the body so that they are also are interconnected.** The yoga philosophy calls these channels *nadis.* They bring nutrients to every cell and remove toxic wastes. They are transmission lines that branch into every part of the organism. The horizontal meridians are called luo. They branch and rebranch reaching every cell in the body. They also branch out to the surfaces and interiors of every organ, and to the millions of individual cells or their organelles.

The flow of energy through the meridians of the body determines our energy and health. When the flow is smooth, balanced, and unobstructed, we are healthy and high-energy. Pain and disease are the result of a disturbance in the flow. People who have developed their sensitivity to energy in the body can scan a person and tell if the person's energy is too fast or too slow, too hot or too cold, too rough or too static, or too moist or too dry.

Scanning The Body For Hot Or Cold Energy

Ever had knots in your stomach, complained that your energies are scrambled, wondered why your hands, legs and feet feel cold, or what causes you to get a fever? In Figure 2 you can see an example of scrambled energy and why you feel so mixed up in that state. Your hands, legs and feet feel cold of course because of poor circulation, not just of blood but also of energy. Only recently doctors have discovered that fevers, as long as they don't get too high, are the body's excellent way to fight off infection and foreign bodies. Your immunity to disease depends upon your energy.

You can look at a person's pale or blue skin especially in their face, around the cheeks, under the eyes, their lips, gums, and tongue and know that they have cold energy. Even their fingers, fingernails, toes, and toenails will be blue and cold. When the kidneys and bladder are not well, they produce a cold energy that can travel into the bones. Cold energy is also heavy. This is the reason our legs and lower internal organs become chilled. The pulse is slow and weak. As a healer I find that moving cold energy takes longer than moving warm energy, but both types are able to be moved to a new location or out of the body. This is called chasing energy.

An ill heart also produces a hot, burning energy that can surface as a red rash. People with wet, sticky hands should check out their spleen, stomach, or pancreas because they are producing a damp energy. If you have itchy skin or rashes, you need to have someone check your lungs because they are producing sick energy. An ill liver also creates itchy energy, but it has a more stinging quality.

The reason fevers are most noticeable in the head, neck, and upper part of the body is because heat rises when it is being generated in the internal organs and other tissues and spaces in the body. Layers of hot and cold energy can get trapped in the body. Toxins trapped in the liver, heart, and blood produce excessive heat.

An energy practitioner will scan the patient's body with their hands to sense hot and cold energy. They will also scan each level of the subtle bodies of the aura or electromagnetic field sensing hot and cold energy. By knowing which level the blockage is in, they can determine if it is a physical, emotional, mental, or spiritual problem.

If you are not sensitive to subtle energy, you can use a pendulum to find blocked energy. Hold the pendulum where the meridian starts and move the pendulum to trace it. Ask the pendulum to signal you a yes where it finds blocked energy. Or you may make an agreement that it will circle counterclockwise when it finds blocked energy. This is where you want to use different methods to unblock the energy.

In order to increase your energy you have to know how and where the energy is flowing. Secondly, you have to know how to release blocked energy. Negative energy stored in the body can be released by tapping the body's meridians for emotional release or any of several different kinds of massage therapy. You need to look at and feel where your body is storing blocked, negative energy. This book will give some simple and quick exercises to help you release the negative energy and help you be open to receive positive energy flow.

The twelve meridians are: lung meridian, colon meridian, stomach meridian, spleen meridian, heart meridian, large intestine meridian, urinary bladder meridian, kidney meridian, small intestine meridian, triple warmer meridian, gall bladder meridian, and liver meridian. There are also the governing meridian and the central meridian.

Six pairs of the meridians run over the arms and onto the torso of the body. They are the large intestine, small intestine, heart, triple warmer (the abdominal cavity which maintains internal heat,) and the lungs. Six pairs run up and down the legs and onto the trunk of the body. They are the gall bladder, urinary bladder, kidney, liver, stomach, spleen and pancreas.

Meridians And Acupressure Points

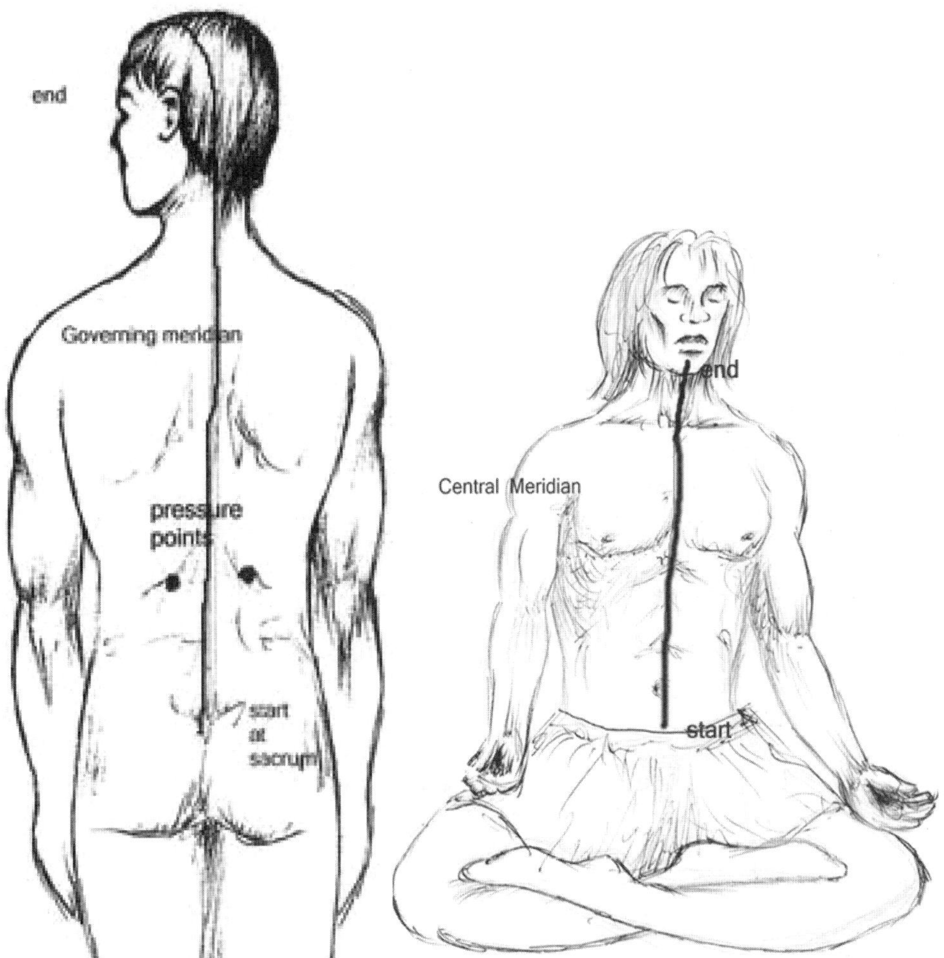

The governing meridian ends below the nose

The Governing meridian, also called the Governing vessel, links the spinal column, brain and nervous system. The points along this meridian are important because they alleviate stiffness of the spine, irritability, fever, and muscle spasms of the back. The Governing Meridian begins at the base of the spine (coccyx) and goes up the spine to where the neck meets it. Since you probably can't draw the energy up your back with your hand, unless you have been doing your yoga for years, you will need to visualize bright gold light traveling up the meridian. It works.

The Central meridian, also called the Conception Vessel, is linked to the digestive and reproductive systems and flows up the front of the body. Pressure on the acupressure points along this meridian works on coughs, asthma, and urinary-genital problems.

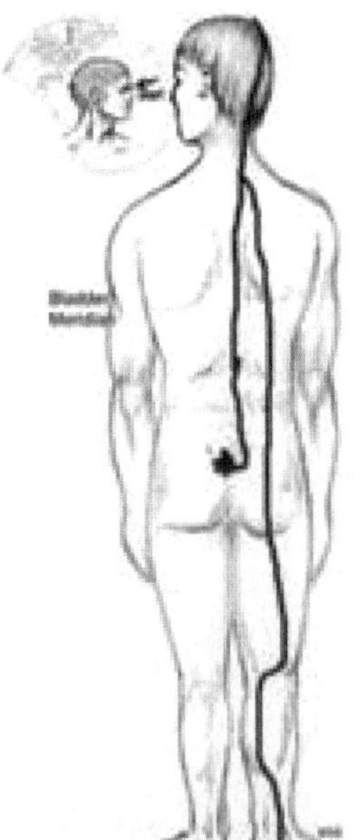

Tracing The Circulation-Sex Meridian

Tracing the Circulation-Sex Meridian
From the nipple, down the middle of the inside of the arm to the end of the middle finger

Tracing The Bladder Meridian
Go from the corner of the eye, over the head and down the back along the inside to the buttocks. Skip back to the shoulder, down the outer line, down the back of the leg to the end of the little toe.

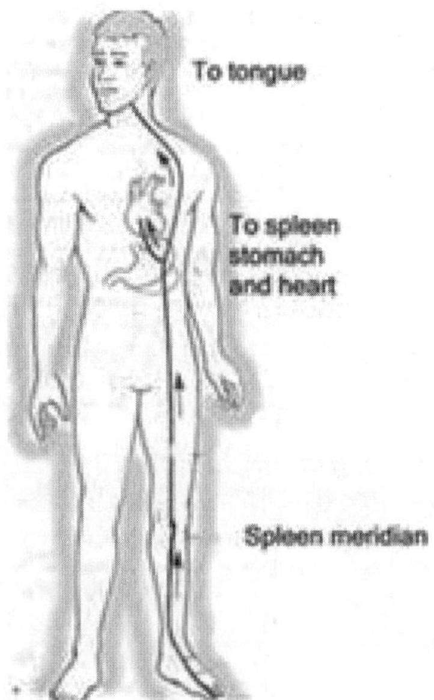

Tracing The Spleen Meridian
From the big toe, up the inside of the leg, front of the abdomen to the side of the chest

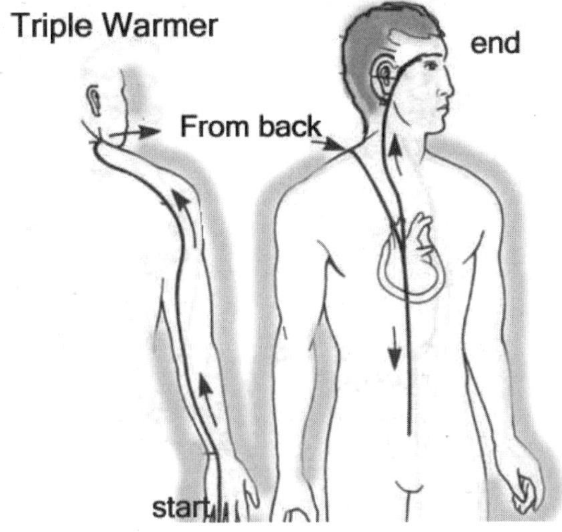

Tracing The Large Intestine Meridian
Begin at the end of the index finger, up the outside of the back of the hand and arm to the nose

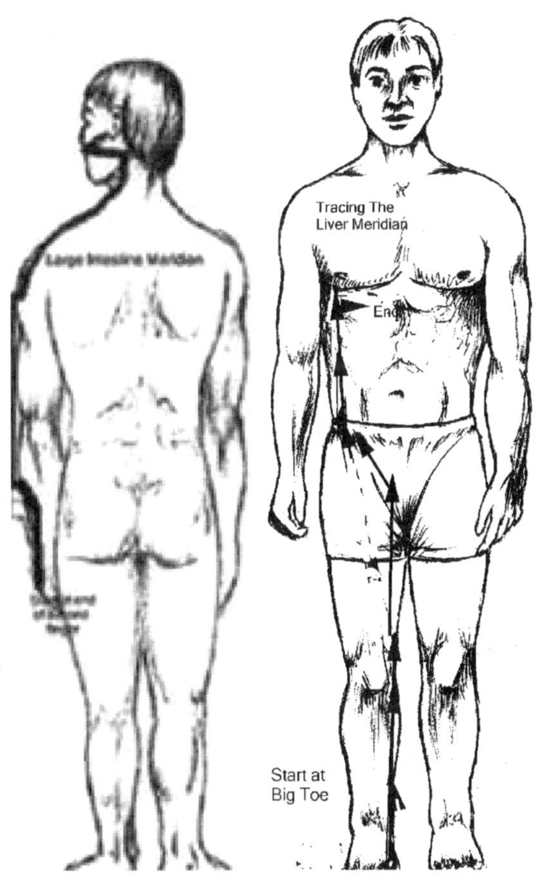

Tracing The Liver Meridian
Start inside big toe, up inside leg to hip bone, backward on hip, up around the waist and forward to rib cage

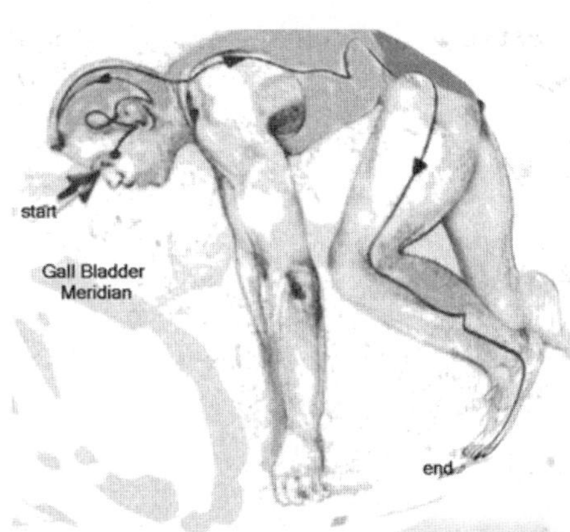

From the corner of the eye, loop around the side of the forehead, behind the ear, back to the forehead, down the back of the head and shoulder, under the arm, down the side of the chest and outside of the leg to the end of the 4th toe

Tracing The Gall Bladder Meridian

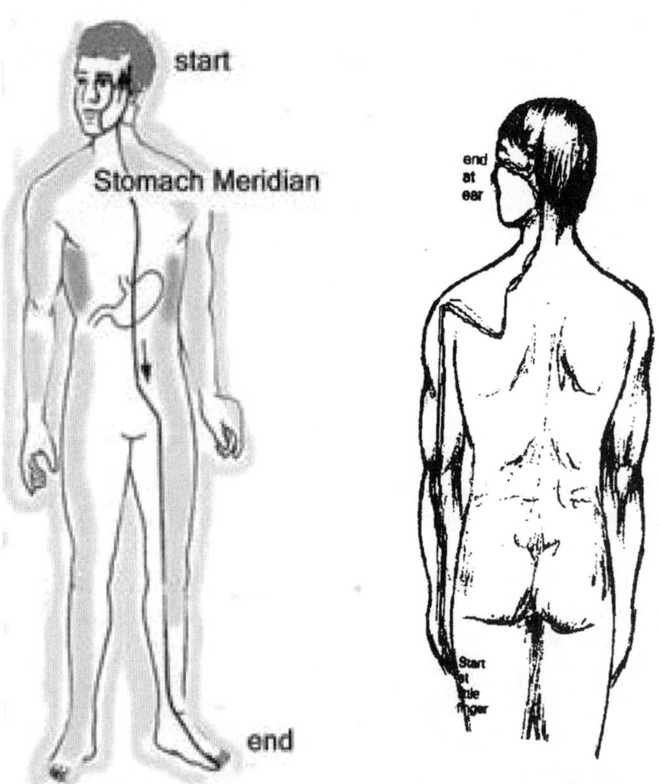

Small Intestine Meridian

Tracing The Stomach Meridian

From below the eye, around the cheek to the forehead, over the eye, down the jaw and the front of the neck, across the collar bone, down the chest and abdomen, across the front of the hip, down the outside of the front of the leg to the end of the second toe.

Tracing The Small Intestine Begin at the little finger, go straight up the outside of the arm to the shoulder. Go down to the scapula, over to the cheekbone, and back to the opening of the ear.

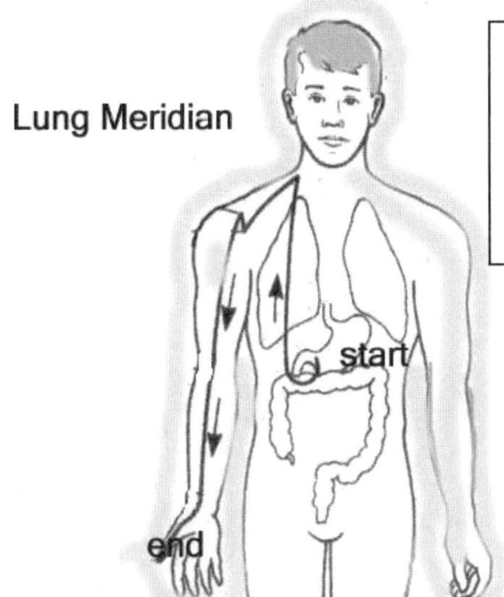

Tracing the Lung Meridian
From the chest, down the outside of the front of the arm to the thumb

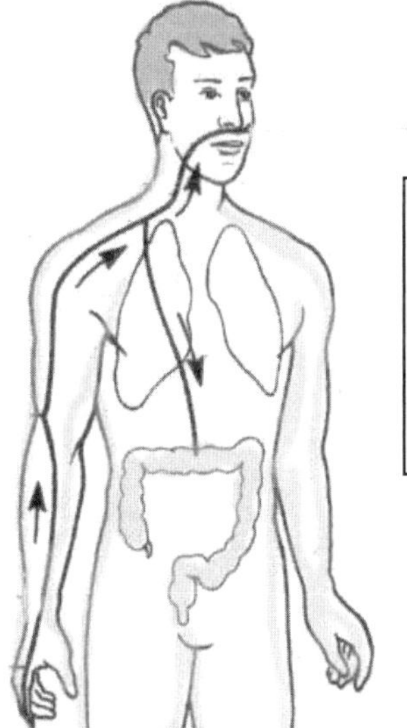

Tracing the Colon Meridian
Begin at the index finger, move up the forearm, through the middle of the elbow, up the upper arm, up the chin ending under the nose

Colon Meridian

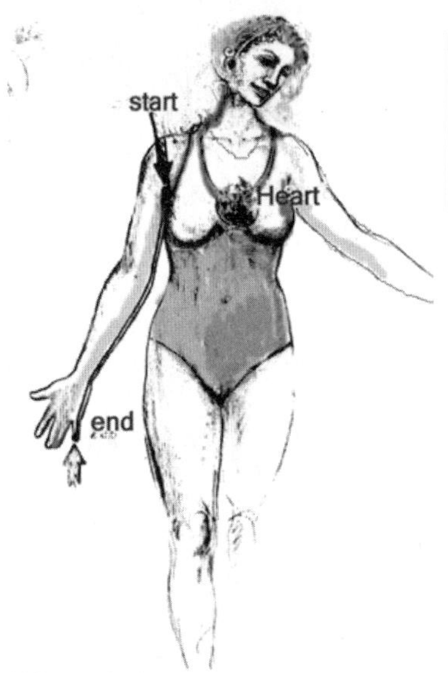

Tracing The Heart Meridian Trace in the downward direction, from the armpit, down the inside of the arm to the end of the little finger

Tracing the Heart Meridian

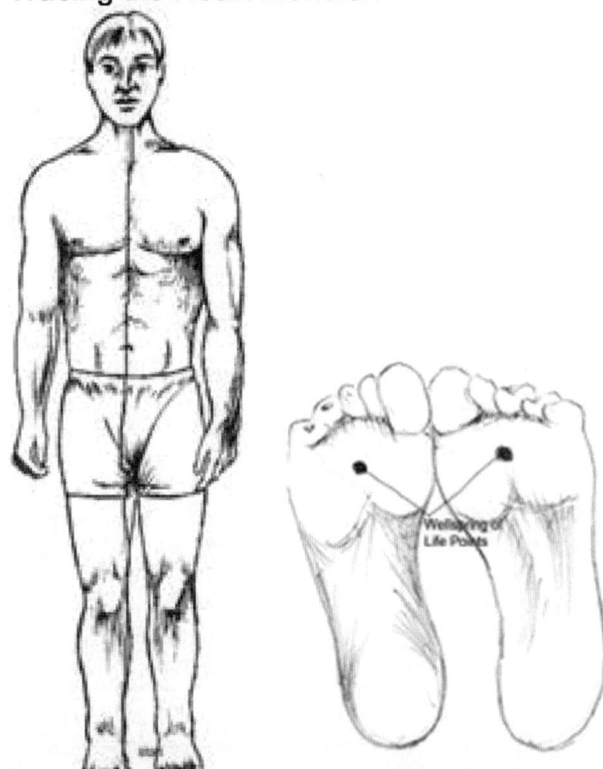

Tracing the Kidney Meridian

From the ball of the foot up the inside of the leg, abdomen and chest to the knob on the collar bone. **To trace the meridian, begin at the wellspring point on the bottom of the foot.**

Meridians And Acupressure Points

Kidney Meridian: **The kidneys are considered to be the storehouse for energy. The energy in the kidneys affects your bones, is connected to your brain, and the other vital organs enabling you to be more creative and alive. A blocked kidney or kidney meridian will affect your urinary system and your sexual energy.** Do you want to be healthy and energetic? Then take a few minutes each day to scan your meridians.

What are acupressure or Shiatsu points

Meridians have pressure points where energy is gathered or focused and are places of high electrical conductivity. Pressure points are also called energy points, reflex points, and acupressure and Shiatsu points depending upon what modality is used. The energy at these points can be stimulated, calmed, or released if it is blocked. Conductivity is greater at these points because they are close to the surface of the skin. On the other hand, tension concentrates around these points causing stagnant energy and inhibited circulation. If you are pressing one of these points to reduce pain, use the left hand because the energy of the left hand is negative and has sedating, soothing, and cleansing effects. Use your right hand for a strengthening effect if you want to send energized healing forces to slow, stagnant, and clogged areas in the body.

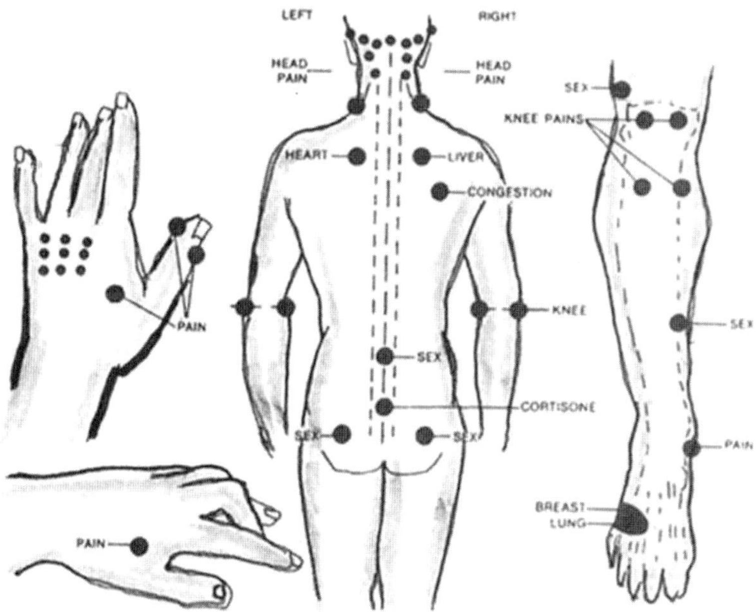

By stimulating these pressure points you cause them to release endorphins, natural pain inhibiting chemicals.

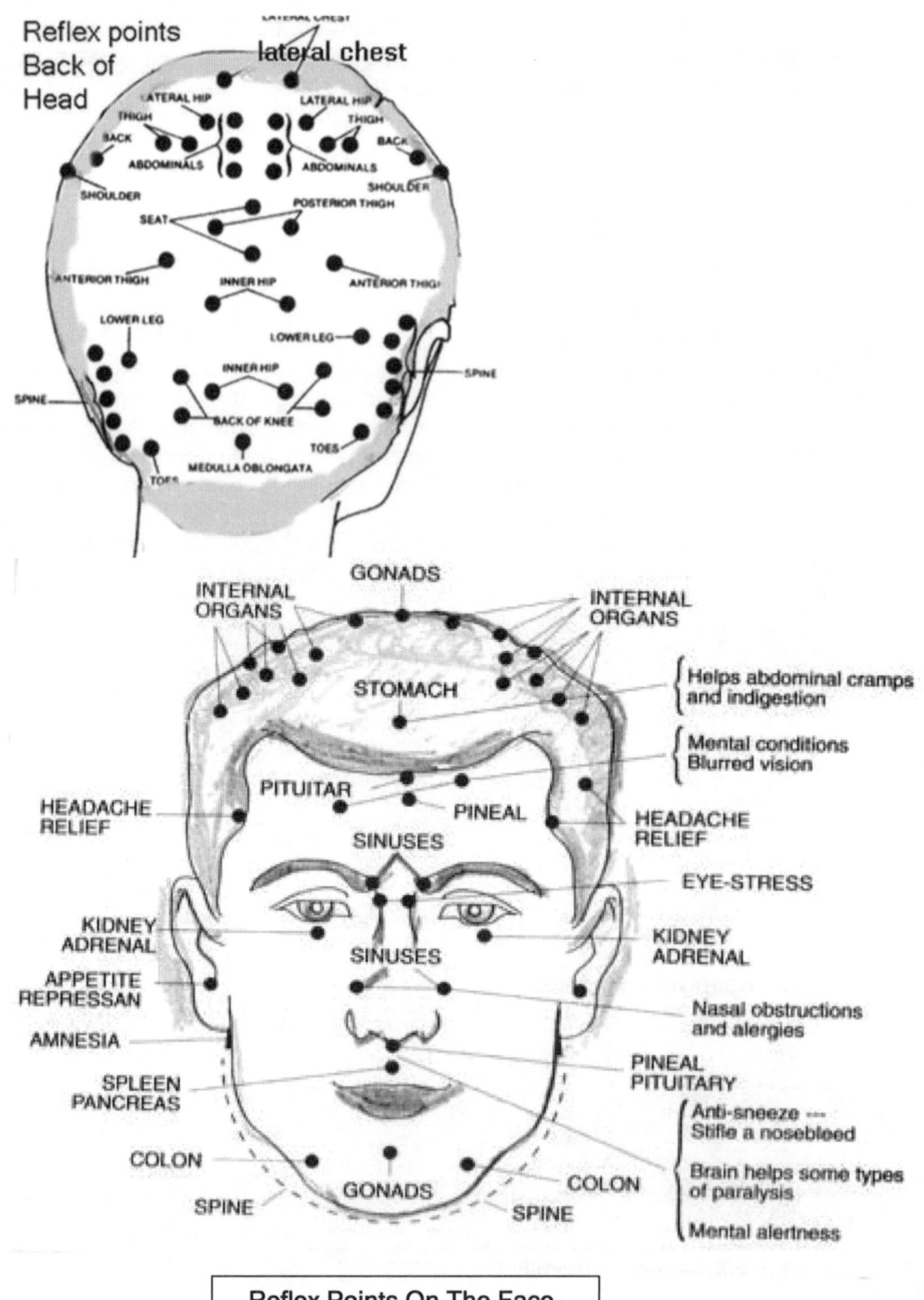

Reflex Points On The Face

Meridians And Acupressure Points

Over **10,000 studies** are published in Chinese medical journals every year about pressure points. Some of the benefits of using pressure points are pain relief, increased energy, muscle relaxation, strength, harmony and emotional balance. When you read all the benefits you can receive from simply pressing the energy points on your body, you will know why it is worth the time and energy to study their locations.

Symptoms of energy imbalance: low sex drive, asthma, throat pain, dryness of the tongue, breathlessness, edema, weakness of the legs, low back pain, and diarrhea.

Many experts say that 70% of our health problems are related to stress and tension. By learning to apply gentle pressure on these points you can balance your energies, release tension and get your blood and Life Energy flowing. The meridians on the front of the body have a yin nature; the meridians on the back of the body have a yang nature. The 12 meridians are divided into pairs-the meridians on the right and left sides of the body are identical pathways and are mirror images of each other.

How Pressure Point Therapy Can Increase Your Energy And Improve Your Health

- Relieves respiratory and digestive problems.
- Improves patients with irregular heartbeats.
- Regulates the nervous system and circulatory system.
- Causes the brain to release endorphins.
- Improves blood and oxygen circulation through muscular relaxation, removes toxins.

Lifting The Sky

1. Stand relaxed and upright.
2. Breathe easily.
3. Keep your mind free.
4. Hold your arms straight down. Hold your hands at right angles and the fingers pointing towards each other.
5. See illustration for feet position.
6. Figure 2 Look up at the hands while they are above you.
7. Repeat the exercise 10-20 times.

Benefits: Physical disorders: headaches, toothaches, coughs, sore throats, fever, stomachaches, diarrhea, dysmenorrhea, muscle pain, sprains, and minor burns
Addictions: food, alcohol
Severe ailments: tuberculosis, hypertension, heart problems, hepatitis, myomas, cysts, migraine, arthritis, and epilepsy

Emotional and mental disorders: stress, tension, anxiety, depression, phobias, manias, paranoia, schizophrenia, obsessive behaviors, and other related ailments

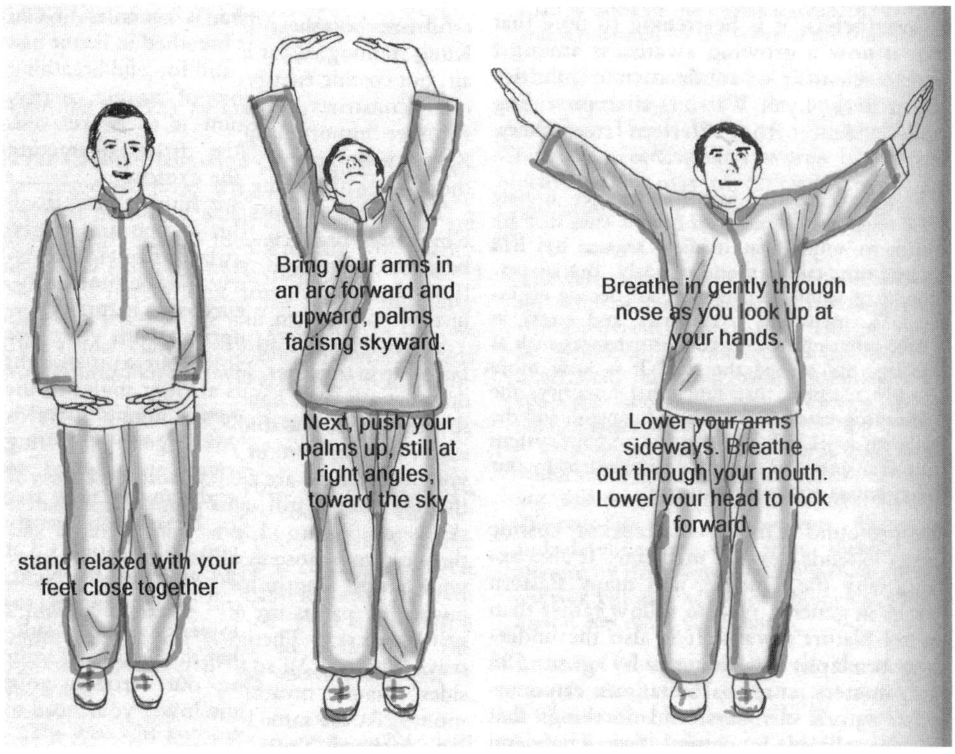

Ten Major Pressure Points

Bubbling Springs: Press on the first point on the Kidney Meridian. The kidneys are the storehouse of the body's energy and each organ depends on this energy for their health and vitality. Each of your kidneys has about one million filtration systems and together the two kidneys filter about 360 gallons of blood every day.

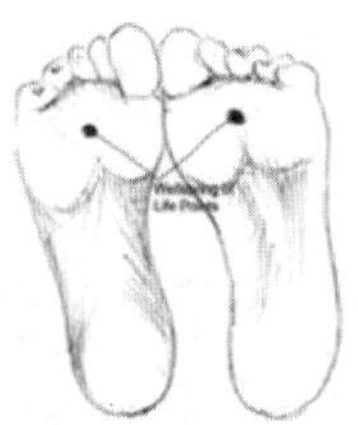

Points are called Well Springs of Life

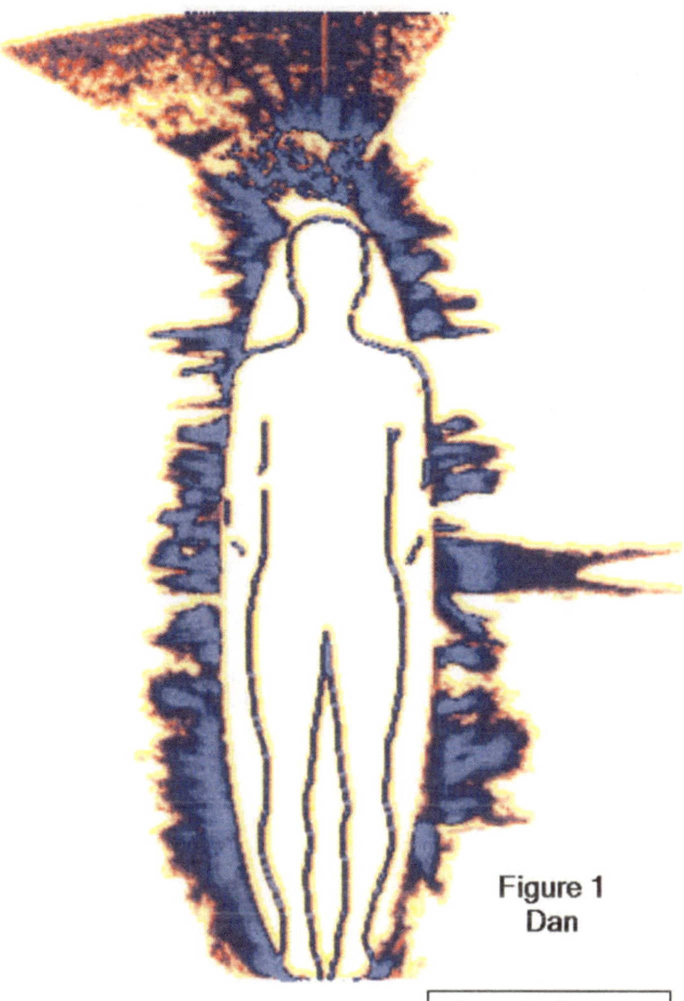

Figure 1
Dan

Blue- physical
Pink- emotional
Purple- mental
Yellow- spiritual

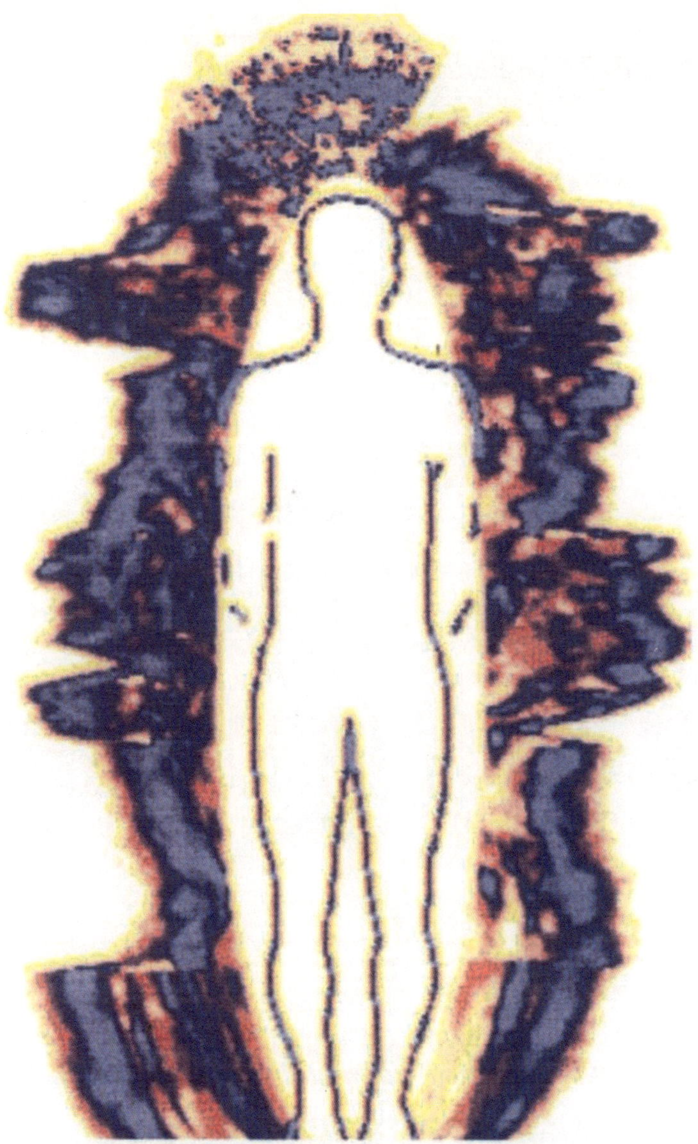

Figure 2 Veronica with scrambled energy
Blue- physical
Pink- emotional
Purple- mental
Yellow- spiritual

Figure 3 Amada 3 months after her stepbrother was killed
Blue- physical
Pink- emotional
Purple- mental
Yellow- spiritual

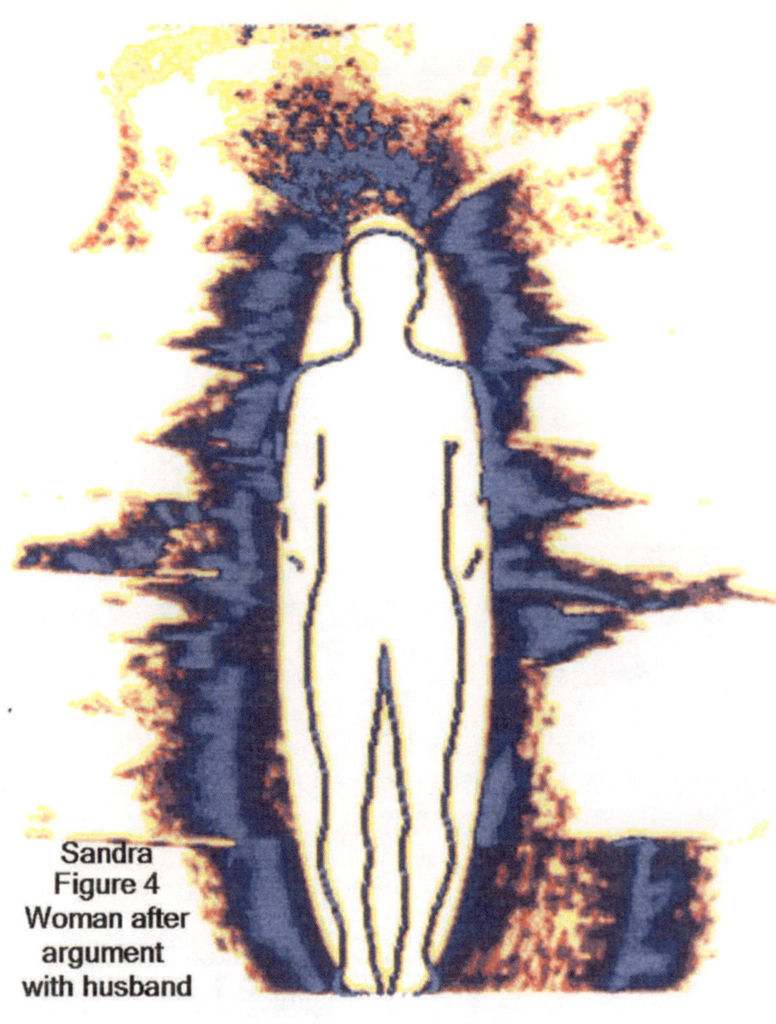

Sandra
Figure 4
Woman after argument with husband

Blue- physical
Pink- emotional
Purple- mental
Yellow- spiritual

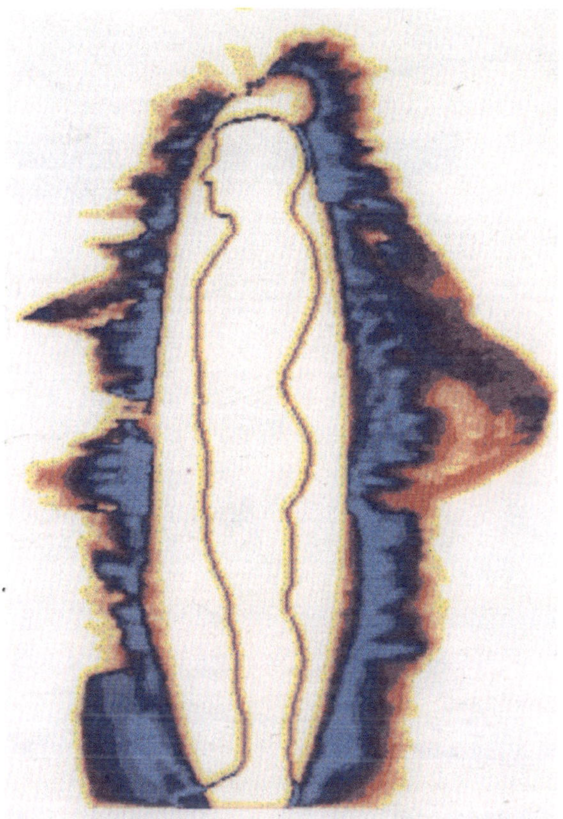

Figure 5 Cindy after EFT
Blue- physical
Pink- emotional
Purple- mental
Yellow- spiritual

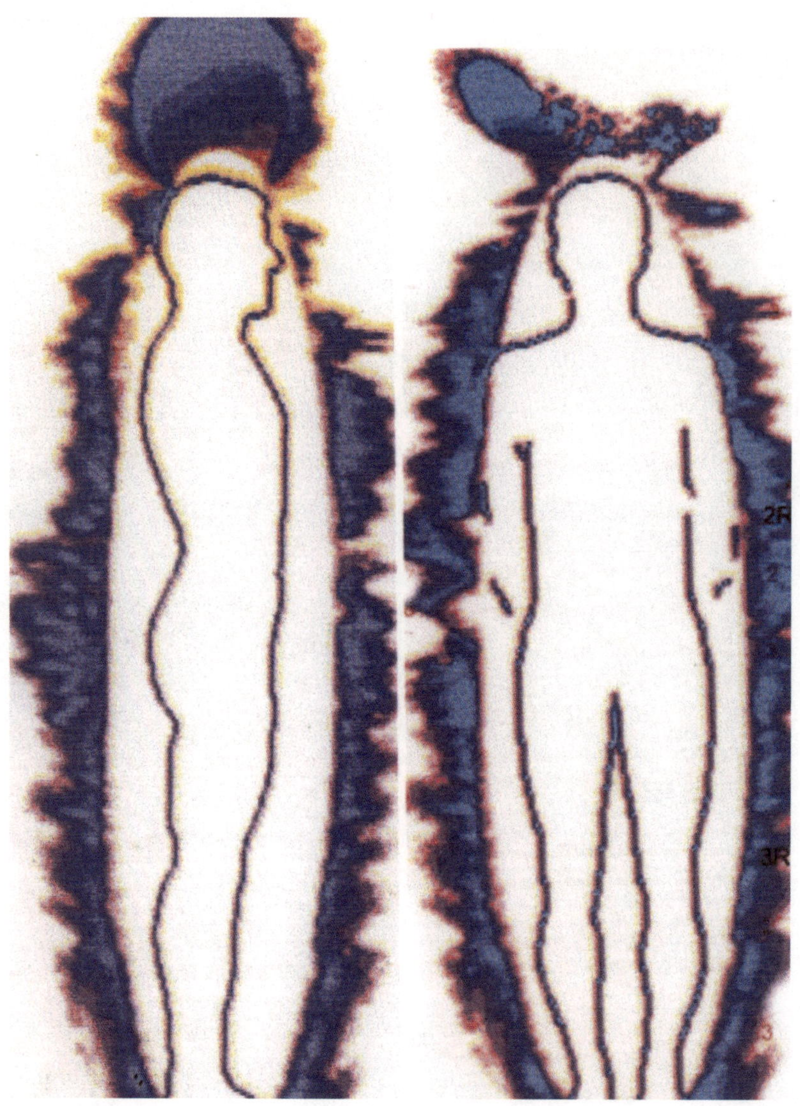

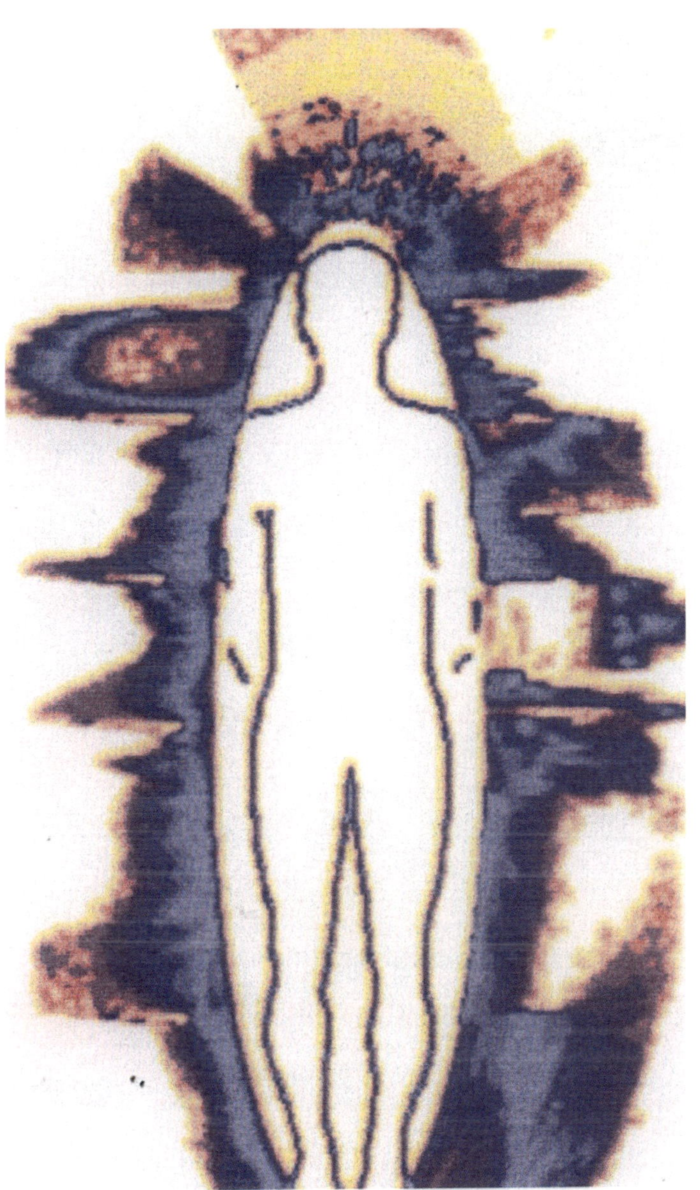

Figure 7 Mya
Blue- physical
Pink- emotional
Purple- mental
Yellow- spiritual

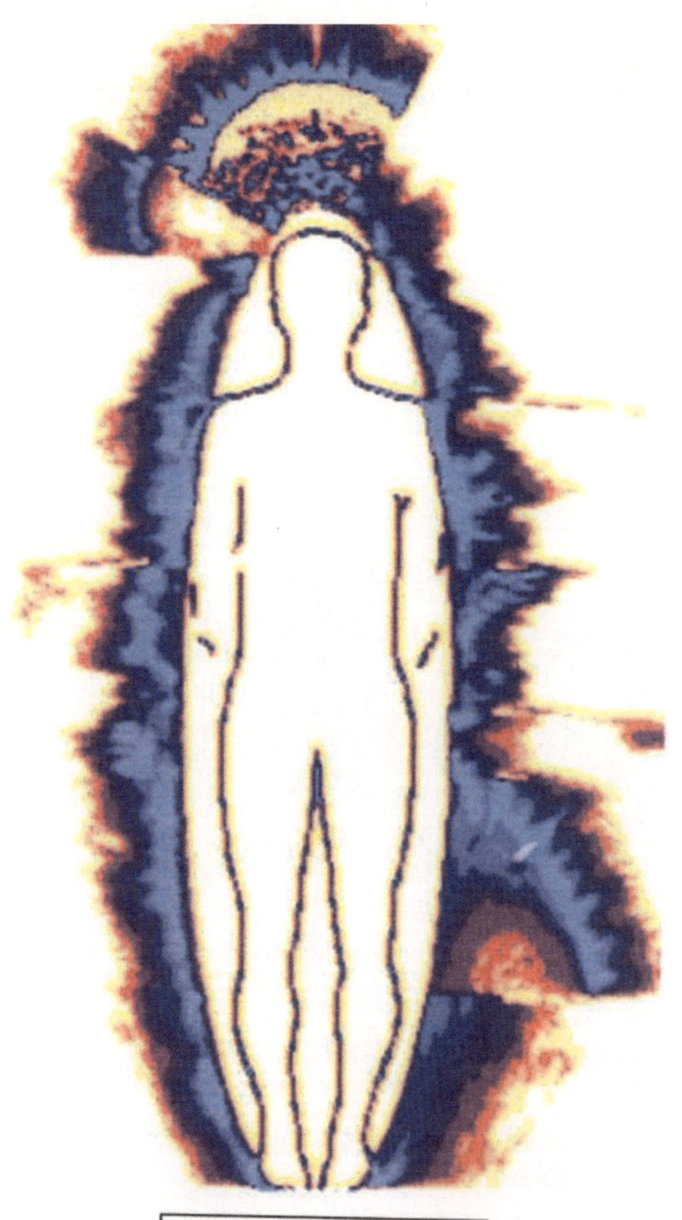

Figure 8 Susan
Blue- physical
Pink- emotional
Purple- mental
Yellow- spiritual

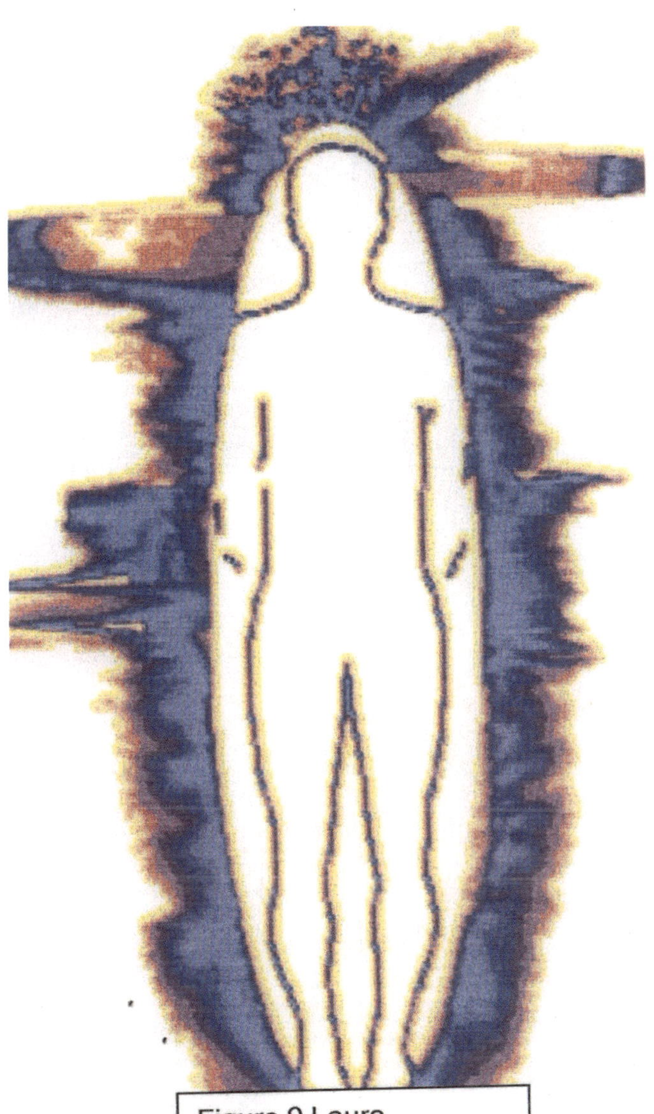

Figure 9 Laura
Blue- physical
Pink- emotional
Purple- mental
Yellow- spiritual

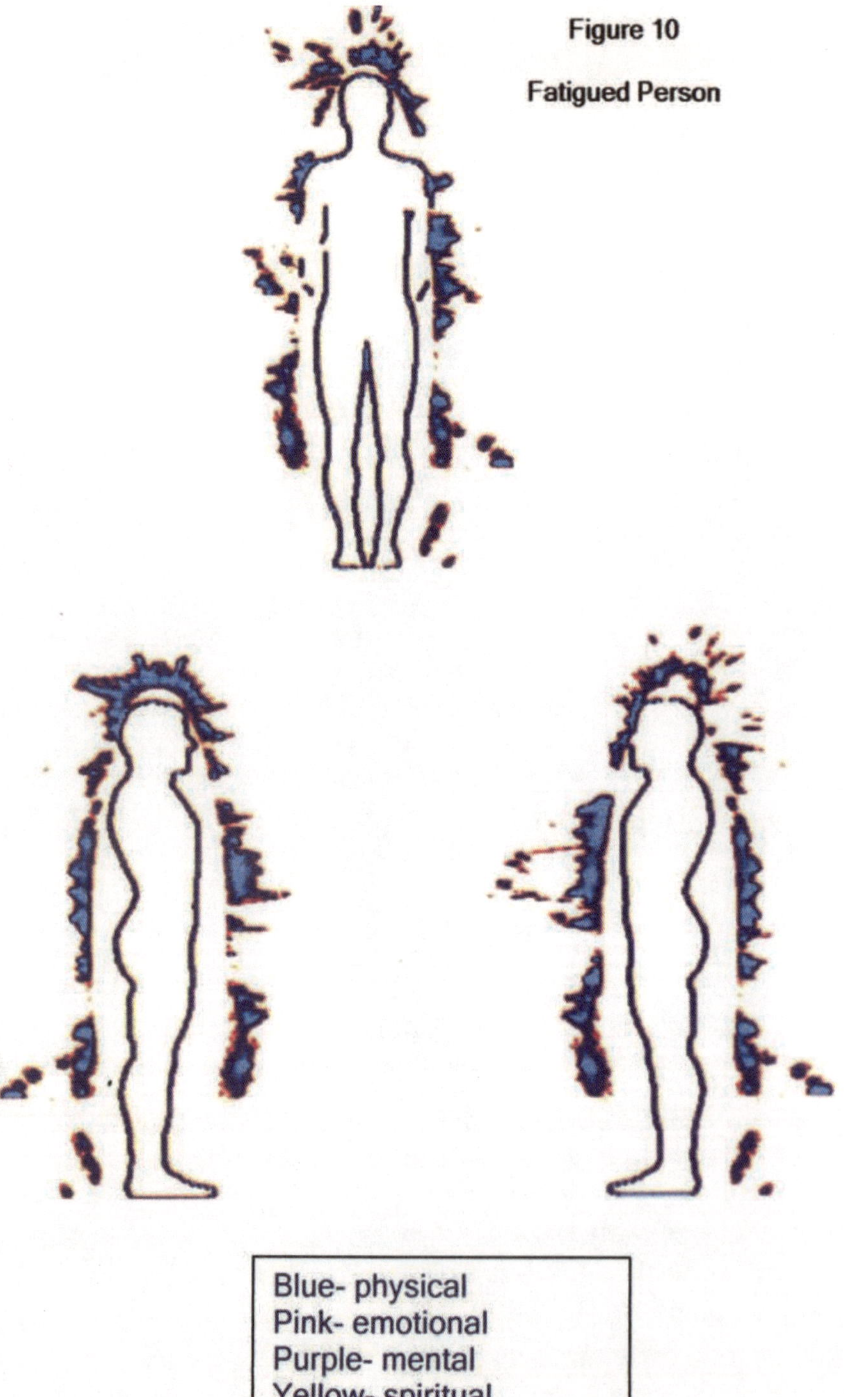

Figure 10

Fatigued Person

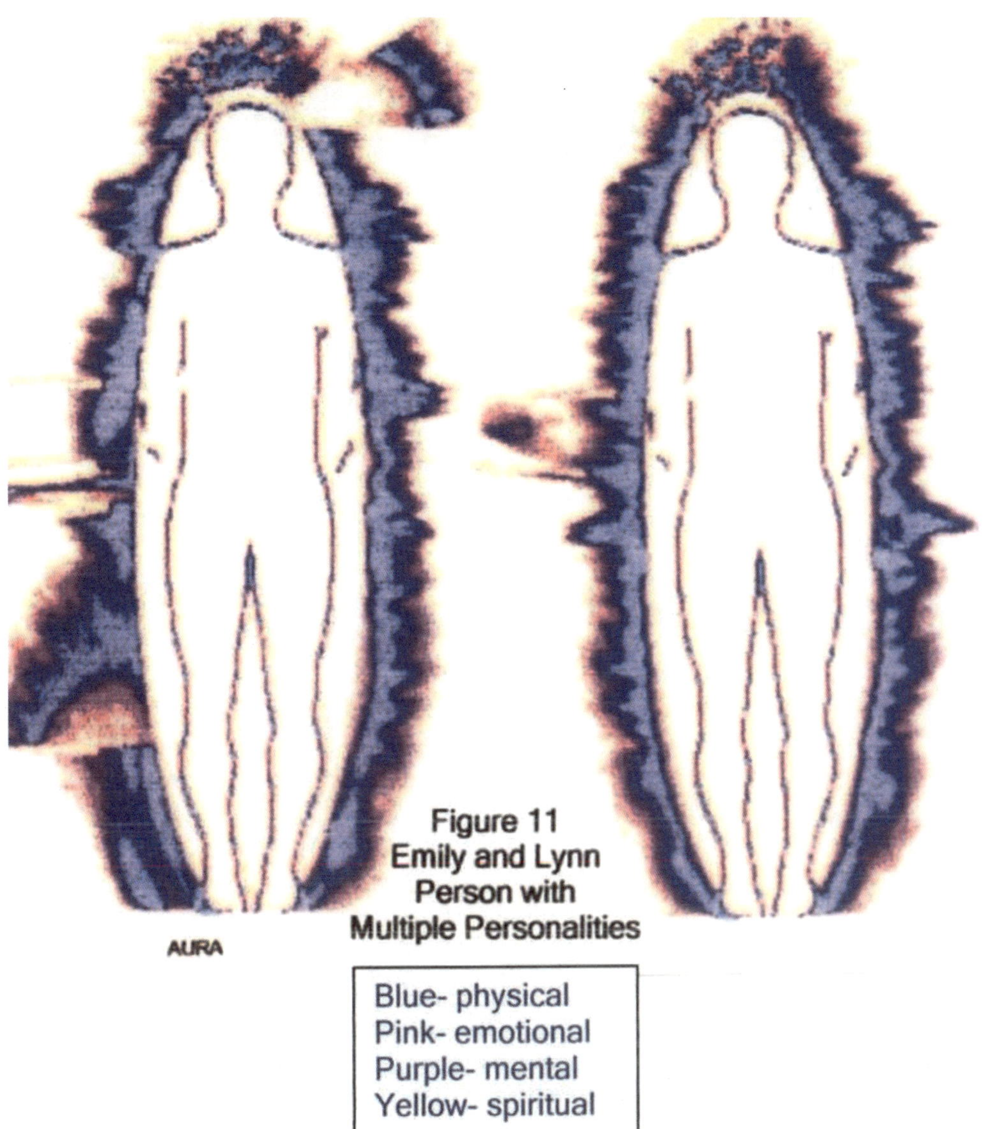

Figure 11
Emily and Lynn
Person with
Multiple Personalities

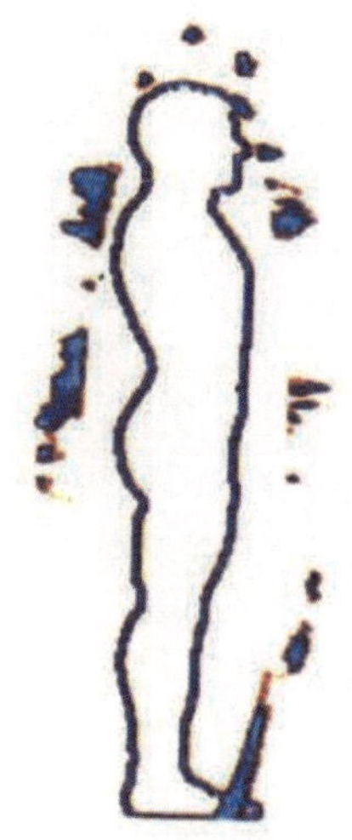

Figure 12 Young man who takes drugs and has disembodied spirits sucking the energy out of him
Blue- physical
Pink- emotional
Purple- mental
Yellow- spiritual

Adjoining Valley (Li 4): This pressure point is a very powerful general pain reliever, relieves headaches, hot flashes, arthritis, allergies and constipation, helps the sinuses and the colon. Take hold of the webbing between your left thumb and index finger. Press toward the bone of the index finger as indicated in the drawing. Hold for one minute, and repeat with the other hand. *(Do not press on this point during pregnancy because it can stimulate premature contractions.)*

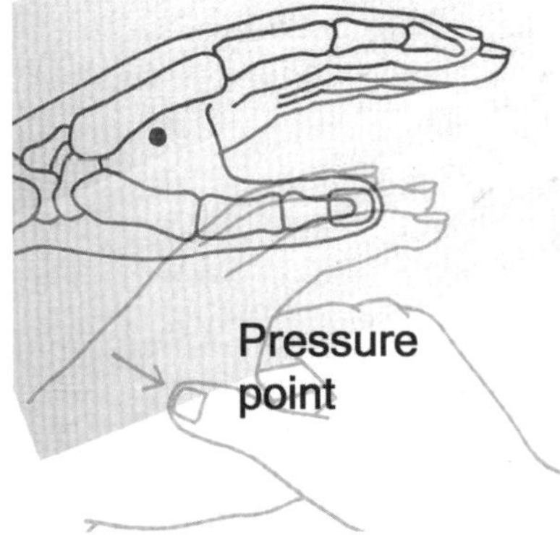

Pool at the Crook (Li 11): Note the location in the drawing below. Hold your arm in front of your cheek, as if you are holding an apple. The point that you will want to hold is at the outside end of the crease at the elbow joint. Press your thumb with firm pressure for about a minute on the right arm and then the left arm. This technique will clear excess heat and dampness from the body and relieve pain in the arm, elbow, and shoulder.

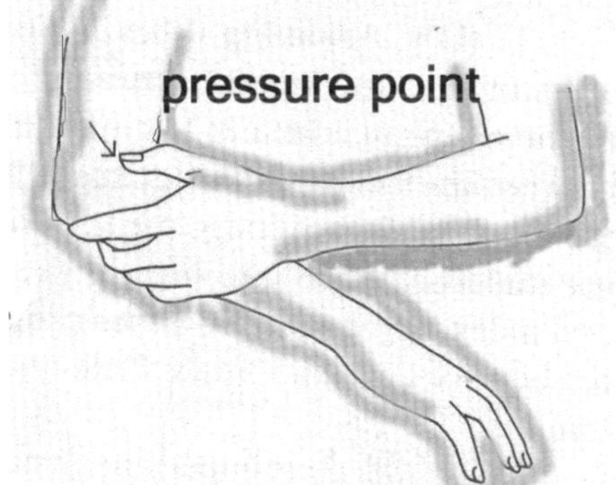

Grey around hands and arms indicates first level of aura (physical).

Three Yin Meeting (Sp 6): Note the location of the pressure point on the drawing, just off the bone, toward the back of the leg. Increase the pressure while you are holding the position for about a minute. Gradually release. This pressure point will increase the yin (feminine energy) of the Spleen, Kidney, and Liver meridians. It moves Liver chi throughout the body. Regulates menstruation, relieves cramps, eases menopause. *Pregnant women should not press on this point.*

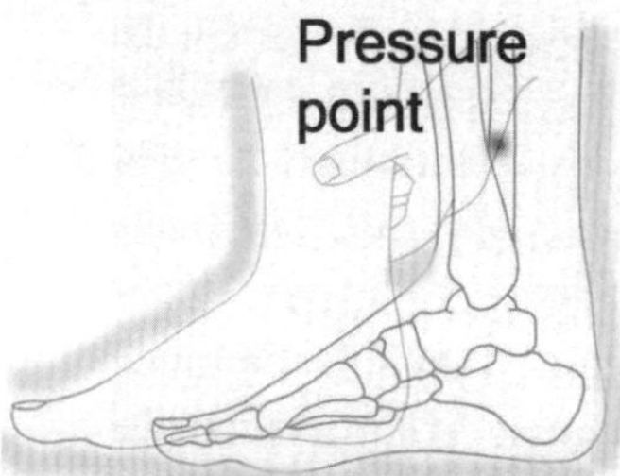

Bigger Rushing Lv3: Note the location using the drawing. You will note a depression when you have found it. Use your index finger to press in the direction of the second toe. Because this point is sensitive, begin with light pressure and increase to moderate or firm for about a minute. **This pressure point prevents blocked chi and is best done on both feet simultaneously.**

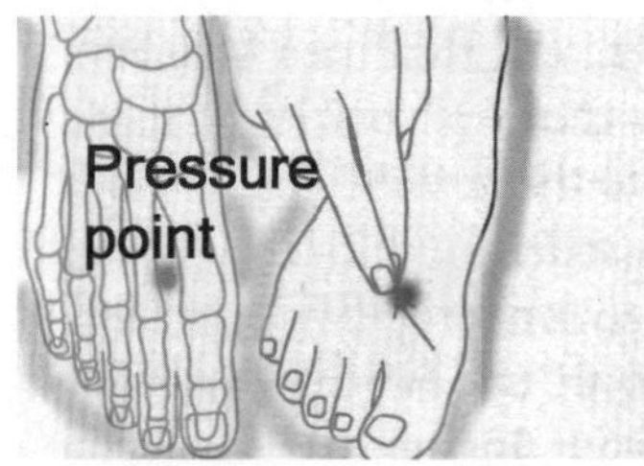

Three Mile Foot: (SP 6) Find the location using the drawing. You will be able to feel the muscle move under your fingers when you flex up and down. Hold with firm pressure for about a minute. **This point is the most powerful point for revitalizing the chi and blood of the entire body.**

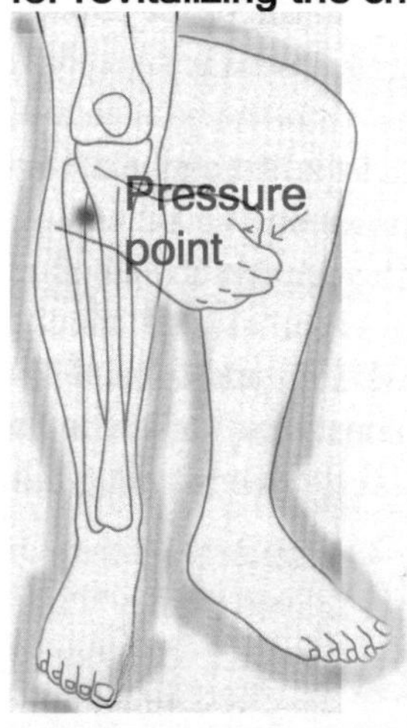

Supreme Stream Kd 3: This pressure point is located in the depression half way between the bone and the back of the ankle as noted in the drawing. Press with firm pressure for about a minute. This is the "source point" for the

Kidney meridian, so it exerts a powerful tonifying effect on the meridian and the entire body

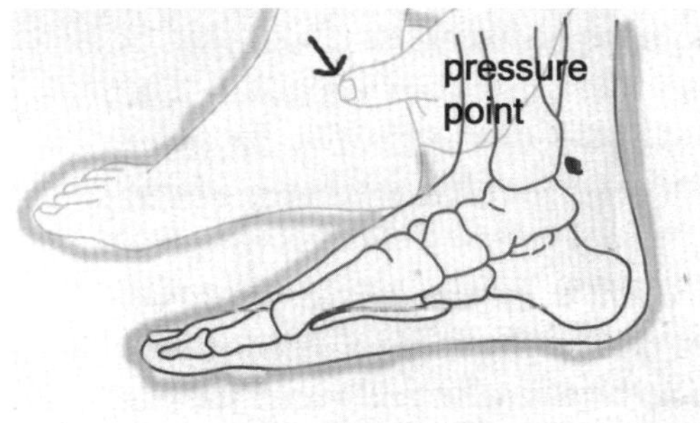

Sea of Blood Sp 10: A lot of blood circulates in the abdominal area of your body to aid in food digestion and circulation. This point helps prevent blood stagnation. And since blood is circulated through the skin so much, this pressure point helps with healing and nourishing the skin. Look at the illustration for the location and press there with the thumb or knuckle of your middle finger.

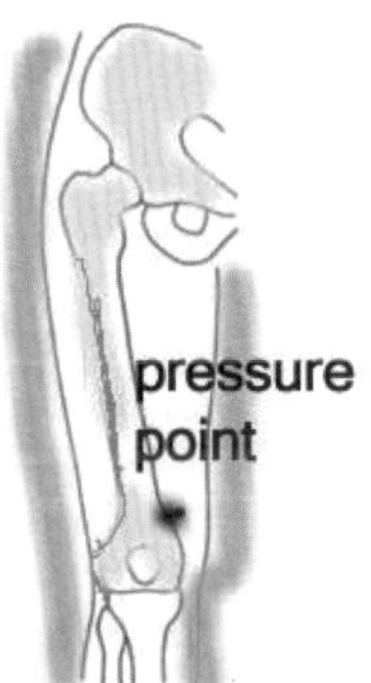

Pressure point is above knee joint.

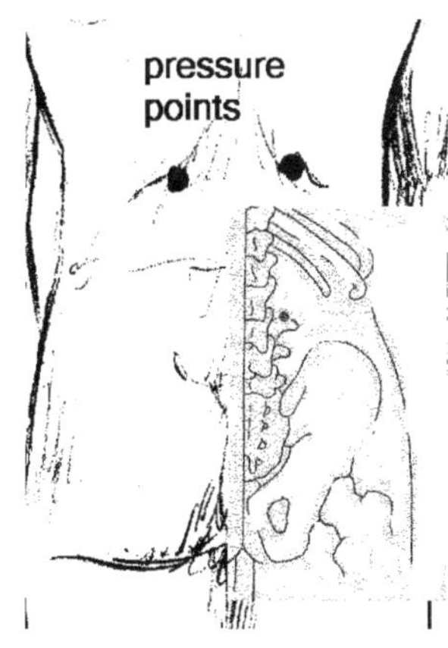

Associated Point of Kidney B 23: To stimulate the point, lie on your back on the floor with two tennis balls behind you. You will stimulate other points on either side of your spine so it is good idea to spend a few minutes pressing the points

Wind Pool Gb 20: Place your thumbs as shown on the illustration. You will know that you have the right location by slowly bending your head forward and then back again because you will feel a depression on either side of the vertebrae in the neck. It is important to breathe deeply as you hold the point for 90 seconds or more. This is such a powerful pressure point because by using it you can regulate the internal movement of energy in your body plus you can relieve headaches, colds, and neck stiffness and pain.

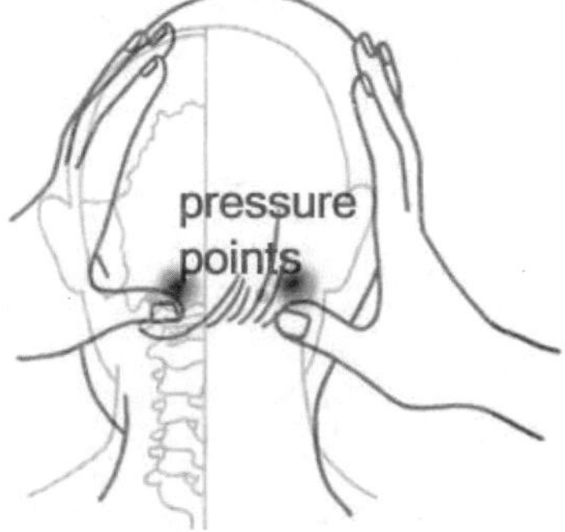

Abundant Splendor St 40: Again look at the illustration to find the exact point to press with your thumb or middle finger. This point will help reduce mucus and congestion.

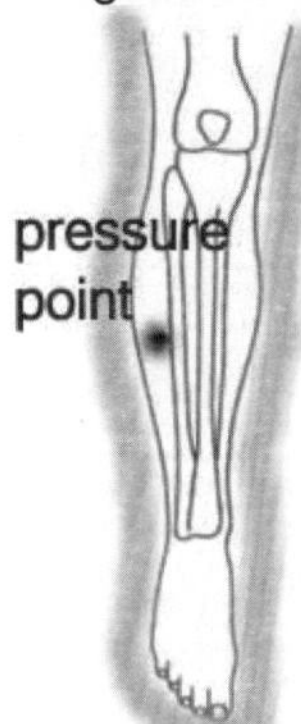

For more information on Pressure Point Therapy I would recommend the book ***Healing with Pressure Point Therapy*** by Jack Forem and Steve Shimer published by Prentice Hall. The book gives an "A" to "Z" guide to around 68 different diseases, a detailed description of Shiatsu, Reflexology, and Acupressure, as well as a list of other books about pressure points.

Healthful Energy Movement

When your body is in a natural flow of energy you are healthy. When there is too much energy, you need to learn how to release it. You also need to know how to send more healing subtle energy inside the body.

Meridians And Acupressure Points

The Energy Release Channel

Energy can be drained through the soles of your feet by simply thinking about sending it from the top of your head, down your torso, then down the legs and out the soles of your feet. Both the hands and feet are the beginning or ending point for most of the meridians. You can trace the meridians and move blocked energy out of your body. You can release energy through shaking your hands and fingers. When you have a lot of blocked energy around the head you get the familiar tension headache and tight neck muscles. The release channel technique is an easy way to get the energy flowing again. In both of these exercises you are working with the subtle energies of the bodies. Subtle energies move rotationally so you will want to see it moving rotationally and move your hand rotationally. You are not working with the physical energy of the body so you will not be draining useful energy.

The Release Channel Technique

A strong emotional state caused by cerebral over-stimulation, low vibrating thoughts of worry, confusion about what to think or do, anxiety, or depression cause blocked energy, especially around the head and neck and heart area. As you see in the drawing, the release channel is located at the right side of the back of the head.

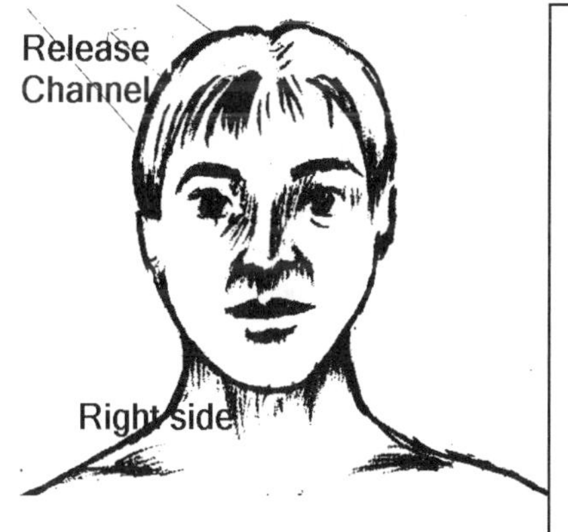

Self-Directed Empowerment Technique: If you are right handed use your right hand on the right side of your head. If you are left-handed use your left hand on the left side of your head. Place your open hand a few inches away from the head, like the one in the illustration, with the palm facing your head. Visualize a pathway opening and see the blocked energy streaming out of your head. I move my hand counter clockwise to remove energy. You may see colors of gray, brown, or black. If you sense energy more than feeling it, the energy will feel very dense. You may see and feel in the energy. In either case, keep your pathway open and hand there until you know there is no more energy to release.

Sometimes released energy creates pain because you are temporarily creating a void that you will soon fill with healing energy. Rest your hand directly on your head and direct the energy with your thoughts to collect in the palm of your hand until the pressure is gone. The energy will feel like taffy as you move your hand away. Place your hand on some inanimate object to drain the energy out of your hand. Again you can do this with your thoughts.

You can do this technique throughout the day, especially if you have a stressful job or experience stressful events and you will go home less tired. If you do it before bedtime, you will sleep much better.

Healing Channel Technique

The healing channel is located on the opposite side of the release channel. If you are right handed it is located on the left side of the head. If you are left handed it is located on the right side of your head. When you visualize the energy entering your body or the person that you are working with, see it as entering the body. I move my hand clockwise to open a pathway.

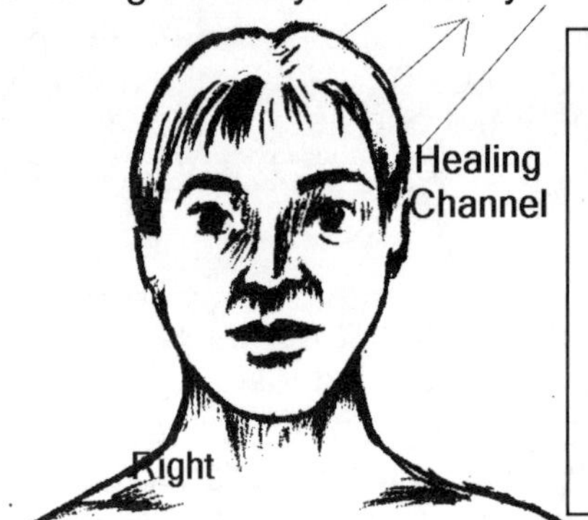

As before, place your open hand, fingers facing the front of your head, a few inches above the area shown in the drawing. Move your hand clockwise for a few minutes and you will probably begin to feel a tingling sensation or heat in your hand. You should say a short prayer about wanting to receive the healing energy.

We can consciously open or close these healing and releasing channels. A tension headache, tense neck muscles, stress, and emotional unbalance are the body's way of getting your attention to deal with what is going on. If you pop a pill to relieve the symptoms you are ignoring the situation. Habitually dealing with excessive energy this way will create long term emotional and physical problems.

Focal Center

The focal center is also called the Third Eye and it is located in the middle of your forehead, equidistant from your eyebrows. This is the area of the sixth chakra and it is the area where we connect with the Divine Mind of God. You can use the focal center to send energy to another person's body. You will send in more powerful energy if you connect the focal center with your heart chakra. It is important for you to first connect to the person by sending them unconditional love from your heart chakra. You won't personally know some people you will be sending energy to, but you still can send them unconditional love because they are children of God.

If you are in conflict with a person, this is the most powerful way to send them unconditional love. Before you begin, **send your thoughts** to the seventh level of your aura–where the energy of the Divine Love of God is located. Then when you send the energy from the focal center and the heart center, you will be sending your own unconditional love and the love of God to the person. You can't get any better than that! You will also receive into your body the great energy that you are sending.

Focal Center Technique

I feel that you become more centered with your eyes closed but you can do the following with your eyes open. Place your open palms side by side a few inches out from your focal center. Keep your hands there until you sense the energy coming from the sixth chakra. It will be a very high vibrating, fine subtle energy. You may see the color purple when your eyes are closed.

If you feel blocked energy expressed as pain or pressure, take one hand and move it counter clockwise to release the energy and then keep your palm on the Third Eye and draw the blocked energy into the palm of your hand. When the pain is gone, remove your hand and release the energy one of the following ways: release it into an inanimate object, vigorously shake your hand, or put your hands in cold water flowing out of a faucet.

Straightening The Spine

The spinal cord in the central nervous system transmits the body's energy. Spinal cord misalignment results from physical, emotional, mental, and spiritual energy imbalances.

Clara was a successful businesswoman I met at a training class. When we stopped for a break I noticed the hump in her back caused by a bent spinal cord. She was delighted when I asked her if she would like for me to straighten her posture. I placed my right hand, the energy sending hand, on her back and my left hand, the receiving hand, in the air to gather and channel in the gold energy circulating in the atmosphere. As the attendees returned to class they stood in amazement, as I did, when we saw Clara grow taller as her spinal cord straightened out. Gold is one of the highest vibrating energies, and it is used to purify stagnant energy from the spine. I suggested that she keep her spine clear by visualizing gold light rising from the coccyx, the base of the spine, and moving up the lumbar, thoracic, and cervical vertebrae and then out the top of the spine where the neck joins. A year later Clara attended another class I taught and she said that her back had remained straight.

10. Health And Energy

When the minds of the people are closed and wisdom is locked out they remain tied to disease. Emperor Juagn Ti (267-297 B.C.)

Synergizing people with high vibrations can influence and change the reality of the world.
Our bodies have all the answers we need to stay high energy and healthy, if we stop and listen to what it is telling us. The body has the desire to be high energy.

In this chapter you will learn what you should do every day to guarantee yourself high energy and how to take charge of your self-health.

Most of us will agree that there is a crisis in health care. In my opinion we must seek forms of treatment other than pharmaceutical drugs because of their negative and long lasting side effects. Many patients are finding that the side effects are worse than the disease or the problem they are supposed to cure. Most pharmaceutical drugs simply mask the symptoms and do not alter or treat the disease. Homeopathy, on the other hand, does not introduce foreign substances into the body. Like other vibrational medicines, it raises the vibration of the patient so that the body can use its own self-healing and self-regenerating powers. Lasers (focused light) are being used in several forms of treatment and surgeries

"I think Vibrational Medicine is the first spiritual science to evolve that unites science and spirituality in a model that really looks at human beings as not just a physical mechanism of flesh and blood, but more like this body, mind spirit complex. Healing involves the correction of disturbances at all these different levels. Vibrational Medicines allow us to not only heal the physical body directly, but to work at the mental and the emotional and the spiritual levels as well." Dr. Richard Gerber

The following is a list of energy healing therapies: Therapeutic Touch, Polarity Therapy, Reiki, Johrei, aura balancing, magnet therapy, Lomi, Lomi, Acupuncture, Star-Powered Healing, toning, tuning forks, crystal bowls, yoga, mantras, chiropractic, massage, ayurveda, homeopathy, acupuncture, Chi Kung, fitness training, nutritional counseling, and the utilization of such nutrients as live foods, herbs, vitamins and minerals, fasting, increasing awareness and expression of cognitive behaviors and emotional patterns, breathing exercises, Applied or Behavioral Kinesiology, the use of colors, sounds and music, meditation, prayer, hypnosis, visualization, positive suggestion, sensory development, dance, Shiatsu, Bio-feedback, and spending time in nature. These modalities affect not only the interior of every cell in the body, but the cell nuclei down to the DNA makeup. Since this book does not discuss all of them, you might want to research them.

As energy fields we are constantly sending and receiving energy. It is my belief that if you understand the properties of energy you can positively affect other people's energies. Before you do any energetic work on any person, however, you must first get their permission. Ask, "Do I have permission to work with you, your guides, the archangels, your guardian angel, and your higher self (soul)"? I believe that at any time you can send unconditional love to a person, but you should not do healing or any other energy work without asking permission first. You have probably never thought of yourself as an energy healer on any level, but if you have ever told a person, "My thoughts and prayers are with you," or "I am sending you love," you are sending that person loving energy.

What we now call "Alternative Medicine" was, until the 1930's and the advent of pharmacology medicine, the main healing practice for centuries. Today Alternative Medicine is also called Vibrational Medicine, Complementary Medicine, and Integrative Medicine. All "Alternative Medicine" will use some form of light, sound, and magnetics, all forms of vibration, in a wide variety of healing modalities. Healing facilitators using light therapy might use different devices like Lumatron ™ Light Therapy or other phototherapy devices. Energy healers will use their thoughts, intentions, and hands to send White Light, one ray or several rays of different colors of light to help a person heal or energize. Spiritual practices have always urged us move toward the Light by raising our vibrations, to be aware of our light bodies.

In a 1990 review of more than 131 controlled scientific studies of healers from around the world, Dr. Daniel Benor found evidence of healing for a wide range of human conditions. These include changes in immune system functioning as well as improvement of skin wound healing, blood pressure, nearsightedness, leukemia, anxiety, asthmas, bronchitis, epilepsy, tension headache, neck and back pain, post-operative pain, self-esteem, heart disease, and relationships.

The Office of Alternative Medicine at the National Institute of Health has designed clinical trials that show the effectiveness of alternatives to conventional treatment. Despite over 300 hundred studies during the past 40 years showing the efficacy of energy healing, they are still ignored or rejected by many scientists.

Diseases And Ailments Treated By Energy Medicine

All of the techniques mentioned in this book recognize that our bodies are physiological prisms with energy flowing in and out at a variable rate and level. The flow of energy is dependent upon our mind, which is encapsulated in the electro-magnetic energy field. When we are attuned, that is balanced, aligned, and aware, we become powerful spirit-mind-body energy beings. We already possess a wisdom that is capable of creating at whatever level we choose, our health, happiness, and success in life through fulfillment of purpose, when we choose to act upon our inner power.

When the body is operating at peak, our energies are dynamic, open, and fluid. Happiness is our natural state; we are hardwired for bliss. Happiness is what we feel when our biochemicals of emotions, the neuropeptides and their receptors, are open and flowing freely throughout the psychosomatic network, integrating and coordinating our systems, organs, and cells in a smooth and rhythmic movement.

Only when our systems get blocked, shut down, and disarrayed do we experience the mood disorders that add up to illness and unhappiness. Unhealed feelings are the accumulation of bruised and broken emotions. Dr. Norman Shealy believes that all illness is caused by depression. Depression is anger turned in on itself, unexpressed, buried below consciousness where it seems to be controlled but slowly implodes. We have been taught to keep our feelings hidden. We are afraid to express them honestly for fear others will be indifferent to our sorrows, or alienated or hurt by our anger. The reason that we have illness is because we felt that it was better to deny our feelings and to suppress them, and to go through the emotions of happiness, pretending to be in control–until one day the bottom falls out and we face a serious illness or depression..

Fortunately, we have an active intelligence within our body that enables us to self-heal. Learning how to monitor our body's internal conversation enables us to intervene in our illness. It is important that we take control of our body's biochemical interactions through meditation, self-talk, prayer, and directed mind energy and that we return to a state of homeostasis (balance). Part of our healing process is learning how to stop being a victim of chronic diseases by controlling our mind energy.

As energy beings we operate under the same rules as the universal energy system because we are a part of the universal energy system. While we are a different (higher) vibration of energy than other forms of matter, we are unified with all energy; we are in constant motion sending energy through space in all directions. The same innate intelligence that runs the world runs our bodies through our nervous system. The spine is the central core of the nervous system. Just as energy is intelligent and it carries information, we are an intelligent system that involves a massive and rapid simultaneous exchange of information in spirit-mind-body.

The body is a holographic reflection of the universe functioning as a psychosomatic (mind/body) network. It operates through the connection of all the body's systems–the respiratory, musculature circulatory, immune, lymphatic, nervous, and digestive systems, organs, the skeleton, endocrine glands–all which form a nonhierarchical web of relationships. Just as the entire universe is connected, every atom, every cell, every system of the body functions in relation to the whole. All of the systems mentioned above communicate with one another via electrical and chemical messengers. Every second a massive information exchange is occurring in our body.

The information that is exchanged becomes manifest in our emotions that literally transform mind into matter. This information transcends time and space going beyond limits of matter and energy. When emotions are expressed and biochemicals that are the substrate of emotion are flowing freely, we are made whole. All of the techniques listed are just different methods of allowing us to become clear channels in order to become one with God.

When stored or blocked emotions are released through touch or other physical methods, such as massage, there is a clearing of our internal pathways. We experience more energy. When emotions are repressed, denied, not allowed to be whatever they may be, our energy matrix or you might to call it, our network pathways, get blocked, stopping the flow of the vital feel-good, unifying chemicals that run both our biology and our behavior.

When I speak people from the audience always come up and tell me of people who have had spontaneous healings and of people who were told by the doctors that they would not live...and they did. A friend of mine named Johnny said doctors told him that his mother, who had just suffered a stroke, would not live another three days. Johnny gathered all his brothers and sisters around her bed and told them to hold hands around her body and send energy. I asked him how he knew to do that and he said he was just led to do it. His mother is alive several months later and now able to walk again.

About a year ago I was teaching a class on the Gas Discharge Camera, a Kirlian photography camera. Look it up in the glossary for more information. When I did the images of a student called Beth, they showed blocked energy in her right shoulder. She noted that she had constant pain in that shoulder. I asked her if she would like for me to remove the blocked energy. She said yes and during the class break I began pulling the blocked energy out of her shoulder by placing my right hand above the area and moving it counter clockwise several times. I asked her to visualize with me all the blocked energy collecting in the palm of my hand. When I closed my eyes, as I moved my hand away from her body, I could see the energy being pulled out like thick taffy. As I pulled my hand away she could feel the energy leaving her body. After pulling out the stale energy several times, I sent in new healing energy.

The next day she told a co-worker about how much better she felt since the energy healing. The co-worker said that it was just in her head, although the healing lasted for several months. Beth relayed the story when she called to make an appointment a year later because the pain was starting to come back. We discussed the co-worker's skepticism, and how her response was due to ignorance about energy. I hope that this book will present information about energy so logically, so scientifically based, and in a simple to understand language that it will change the minds of many disbelievers.

Medical Intuitives

You may have seen on the nightly news that doctors now have a camera that is so tiny it can move through the body snapping thousands of images for diagnosis. Did you ever think that this was possible? Do you believe that it is true? Probably. Especially since they have pictures to prove it. But if I tell you that there are people called medical intuitives who are able to see inside the body and they get images or pictures like the tiny camera, will you believe me? The intuitive receives the images from the vibration put out from whatever they are tuning into. Each organ of the body produces a different vibration, as does every other part of the body. In the same way a sonogram records the vibrations of a baby or a tumor, the medical intuitive is aware of disease through vibrations.

We haven't figured out how to get medical intuitives to produce a picture yet, but there are doctors who use the intuitives to help diagnose patients accurately. Medical intuitives "see" inside the body differently. Some say that they sense see; they vaguely see an image, but they know intuitively. Others say they literally see any part or parts of the body. When they look at a person's liver, for instance, they look to see if it has the normal color, they look inside the liver for anything that should not be there–deposits and toxins. Other intuitives feel the energy of an organ by putting their hands over the organ. Organs feel warm or cool, moist or a bit dryer. Each organ has a specific vibration and feel.

Medical intuitive Carolyn Myss, author of *The Anatomy of the Spirit,* worked for several years with neurosurgeon Norman Shealy detecting illnesses in patients. A patient's name and date of birth were given to Myss, who had no previous contact with the patient. Myss would psychically "enter" the patient's body and systematically examine the health of each organ system. On one sample of fifty patients, Myss' clairvoyant diagnosis matched Dr. Shealy's medical diagnosis in 93% of the diseases identified. Myss' statements were specific, such as "left testicle malignant, spread to left kidney", "venereal herpes," and "schizophrenia".

Secrets of Energy

Recently, a morning news show reported on a device, invented by a doctor at Emory Hospital in Atlanta, that produces constant sounds and reduces the unbearable ringing noise in people's ears caused by tinnitus. The news reporter and the medical doctor on the news show made the not so brilliant statement, "It sounds like snake oil," though they admitted that the device has an 80% cure rate. Obviously they do not understand energy. The noise producing device (vibration) tells the brain to turn off the noise (vibration.) You would think that reporters would know that vibrations, whether they come in the form of sound, light, smells, energy in any form are being used in so many forms of medicine today that they wouldn't doubt all of the vibrational modalities. Can you imagine what doctors said when Dr. Koch started doing small pox vaccinations? How could putting a small amount of smallpox virus into your body keep you from dying of the small pox disease? The reason that we still get vaccinations for various diseases now is because they work.

Within the last few years many of us began accepting the fact that we are multi-dimensional mind/body/spirit beings. Though too many doctors still want to hold on to the belief that illness is only caused by viruses, bacteria, and toxins, most of us know that emotions such as fear, hate, and revenge and psychological factors create most of the mental and physical disease in the body or weaken it so that it is overpowered by the viruses, bacteria, and toxins.

A Brief History Of Electrotherapy

Electrotherapy began to be used widely at the end of the 1800's as a result of the technical development of batteries and other devices producing electric energy. By 1894, over 10,000 physicians were using electrotherapy in their practices regularly.

The Carnegie Foundation set up a commission to study medical education and standards of medical practice. One of the reasons for the commission was the excessive use of electrotherapy and charlatans. As a result, medical education and licensure of physicians changed and the requirement that medical therapies were required to be based upon sound scientific principles was introduced. At that time how energy medicine worked could not be proven. It has not been until recently, that scientific instruments were invented that showed the effects attributed to electromagnetic healing devices.

Dr. Bruce Lipton wrote in an article for *Bridges*, the following: Currently in the medical sciences, the emphasis on pharmacology permeates the training of physicians and in fact, our entire society. This situation produces an additional difficulty for the introduction of electromagnetic technology since physicians are not likely to be as well versed in biophysics as they are in biochemistry. Since an understanding of biophysics, which includes an introduction to the basic mechanisms by which electromagnetic devices most probably function, is not part of current medical education, physicians have no practical knowledge of how EM fields impact biological systems.

This chapter is going to look at how our structure (posture), chemical makeup (hormones), psychological (emotions), and spiritual level create our state of health. It is important that you find a doctor who not only looks at your structure, neurological, lymphatic, vascular, and cerebrospinal functions, but who knows about the effects of nutrition and the functioning of the meridian system. And just as importantly, find a doctor who understands that your energy is the force in your spirit. The old paradigms, that the body is a biological machine whose parts age and wear down, and need to be replaced or simply treated with drugs, no longer serves us. The body is now seen as pure energy. Each year doctors are utilizing the healing benefits of light and sound, the two new health paradigms.

"In the world of vibrational medicine, illness is thought to be caused not only by germs, chemical toxins and physical trauma-but also by chronic dysfunctional emotional-energy patterns and unhealthy ways of relating to ourselves and other people. Rather than relying on drugs and scalpels to treat illnesses, the vibrational approach employs different forms of energy to bring about healing changes in the mind, body, and spirit of the sick."
Vibrational Medicine, Dr. Richard Gerber

Dr. Richard Gerber practices internal medicine and is one of the leading researchers and practitioners of vibrational medicine. He is highly respected for his 25 years of progressive research into alternative methods of diagnosis and healing. In ***Vibrational Medicine,*** Dr. Gerber states that the term holistic implies not only a balance between the aspects of body and mind but also between the multidimensional forces of spirit. He says, "For truly, it is the endowing power of spirit that moves, inspires, and breathes life into that vehicle we perceive as the physical body. A system of medicine that denies or ignores its existence will be incomplete, because it leaves out the most fundamental quality of human existence–the spiritual dimension. [1]Gerber

Today's New Medical Devices

Today's energy-producing technologies create magnetic fields that are used to heal injuries to soft tissues: nerves, tendons, skin, and muscle. Magnetic fields can treat both soft and hard tissue simultaneously.

The following list, based on research by Sisken & Walker comes from James Oschman's book, *Energy Medicine, The Scientific Basis* giving the effects of electric and magnetic fields on soft tissues.

- ✦ Enhancement of capillary formation
- ✦ Decreased necrosis
- ✦ Reduced swelling
- ✦ Faster functional recovery
- ✦ Reduction in depth, area, and pain in skin wounds
- ✦ Reduced muscle loss after ligament surgery (10 Hz optimum)
- ✦ Increased tensile strength of ligaments
- ✦ Acceleration of nerve regeneration and functional recovery [2] Oschman

Because of the new devices, doctors and Integrative Health Practitioners are learning more of the mysterious workings of the human mind, body, and human consciousness. Let's look at how these new diagnostic imaging systems such as the electron microscope, the CAT scanner, and the MRI. Work. As our vision of light has extended to understanding not only inorganic physical matter but also the behavior of organic living matter from a subtle energy perspective, we are creating the foundation for a new medicine and a new psychology of human beings.

The MRI: Physicist Zang-Hee Cho at the University of California, Irvine, stimulated an acupuncture point on the toe, which was not connected to the circulatory of nervous system, and the MRI showed that the point affected the blood flow in areas of the brain. **The electrical stimulation was carried to the brain via a meridian.** [3]Cho

The body's tissues are fed by oxygen, glucose, and chemical nutrients, and just as importantly, by higher vibrational energies which give us life and creative expression. We are extraordinarily effective at detecting signals from our environment. Our bodies have large numbers of sensing molecules packed tightly in crystalline structures. Doctors can apply low frequency electric and magnetic fields to stimulate repair of bone fractures and damaged nerves, skin, and vascular tissue. Pulsed electromagnetic field (PEMF) therapy is a device used in leg and arm fractures that produces a magnetic field that induces currents to flow in nearby tissues. Diathermy uses electromagnetic waves in the application of electric currents to produce heat in the deeper tissues of the body. Heat producing electrodes are strapped to specific parts of the body. Hard X-rays are used to destroy cells of the physical body. They are used in the treatment of malignant cancerous tumors.

Health And Energy

Our crystalline bone structure, in general, acts as an antenna for all incoming and internal vibratory energy and information, including direct thought from energy. Look at the posture and walk of a person you know to have a closed mind. Their closed minded attitudes have caused the fissures in their skull to grow closed. They are hardly able to move their necks because they have been uptight for so long, and their shoulders have moved up their necks. Even their walk is so stiff they walk "hard" and have a Frankenstein gait.

Our bone structure resonates with all levels of nutrient energy, which it receives directly from music, singing, or chanting. For this reason it is so important that you monitor all the sounds that enter your body. As the chakras take in energy from your electromagnetic field and the electromagnetic fields of your environment, they step down the incoming virtual energy that has entered the system through the seven subtle bodies. Just as the seven levels of your auric field protect you from outside atmospheric energies, your chakras protect you from receiving energy that is vibrating too high for your physical body.

Sound And Color Healing

Light and sound are the primordial energies from which life evolved–the essence of nothingness into some-thingness. We, too, are an expression of this energy–light, color, sound. Color and sound are vibration and they affect all other vibrations. The human body is energy/vibration. Sound produces measurable vibratory feelings throughout the body, depending upon the frequency and amplitude of the sound used. This is the reason you don't eat dinner where they are playing hard rock music. There has been a wide variety of sound healing developments over the last ten to twenty years. Certain sounds have a healing influence upon the body because they influence the geometric patterns and organization of cells and living systems. Sounds also affect the auric field and its seven levels

Color healing has been documented to cure back pain, high blood pressure, addictions such as food and alcohol plus scores of other diseases. It also cures patients with traumas, phobias, and obsessive behaviors.

The body is a "self-repairing" living entity. When using my ***Star Powered Healing,*** I always ask Universal Mind what colors should be sent to different parts of the body because each organ, tissue, muscle will need different frequencies. For instance, the red and orange frequency should never be sent above the waist because their frequencies are too slow. Healing can use several colors.

Researcher Theo Gimbel discovered that blue light reduces blood pressure, eases asthmatic attacks, helps insomnia and creates a state of relaxation and peace. Conversely red raises blood pressure and creates over-activity, which is helpful in anaemia. Orange lifts depression. Green light dissolves virgin cell structure and is beneficial in healing cancer. Turquoise helps strengthen the immune system and reduce inflammation; therefore it is good for infections. Yellow dissolves calcium deposits in the joints so it is good for arthritis. You can do the same thing for yourself by using your mind to send color to your body.

Pranic Healing Is Color Healing

Pranic healing uses prana–vital life force energy–also brings in energy from the air and the ground. The basis of the healing is that diseased energy appears first in the subtle energy body. What affects the energy body affects the physical body and vice versa. If you want to know more about Pranic Healing, read *The Ancient Art and Science of Pranic Healing, Advanced Pranic Healing, Pranic Psychotherapy, The Ancient Art and Science of Pranic Crystal Healing, Meditations on Soul Realizations, Practical Self Defense for Home and Office and Universal* and *Kubbalistic Meditation on the Lord's Prayer* by Grand Master Choa Kok Sui, the modern founder of Pranic Healing. You can also get more information from the Institute for Inner Studies and The World Pranic Healing Foundation.

Patti Conklin, a medical intuitive living in Atlanta, was born with the "gift" of being able to see differently than most people. She tells the story of her mother's best friend visiting their home when she was three years old. Patti says she saw sperm fertilizing the woman's egg. She blurted out as a three-year old would, "You are pregnant, but you will die in nine months!" At that point she said, her mother backhanded her across the room, but in nine months the best friend gave birth and died in the process.

Patti told another story where God, whom she calls Father, told her to go visit a mental hospital for three days, not because she has mental problems, but because they would be able to test how her mind works. The condensed version is that doctors ran tests that revealed that her body and mind vibrate at such a high rate that she is able to see inside the human body and to see illness. She is also able to see the causes of illness that originate in the subtle bodies. Patti sees everything differently than most people. She sees other people, and other objects of matter, as constantly moving energy. This causes her daily problems such as when she is driving. To drive safely, she must sense how the drivers around her are going to react even before they do. Patti always drives in the left lane, she says, because it gives her one less person to keep track of. She cannot drive without a car in front of her because she everything in her vision is always moving energy and there is no person to act as a guidepost. She has problems walking up stairs because they usually are the same color so she doesn't know when one step begins or ends.

Several people operate in the world differently than most of us. Some people see letters of the alphabet as having different colors. For example, an "e" will always appear as red. Other people hear music from the radio but it comes with different colors or smells. Patti relates to people differently. She recalled talking on the phone to a medical doctor who had spinal cancer that had metastasized. He asked her to diagnosis the origin of the cancer, which she did correctly. However, she connected to the man through his voice and when he spoke it made her very sick. We may connect with people visually, vibrationally, or through smell. Patti connects with people through each of these modalities. Patti is affiliated with Millennium Health originated by an outstanding Atlanta surgeon, Dr. Susan Kolb. Patti says that in order to heal we must raise the frequency of our vibration.

Sound And Healing

Watch any musical concert and you see the effect music has upon people and their emotions. This is the reason it is so very important to monitor the sounds we allow to come into our body. Intricate musical tone studies done by the Shanghai Chinese Traditional Orchestra resulted in a series of six tapes, collectively known as Yi Ching Music for Health. Yi Ching music is actually a healing music based on the Five Element Theory of Chinese medicine. These are particular songs or musical compositions associated with each of the five elements. To use the healing compositions for a particular illness, one would analyze the illness in terms of classical Chinese medicine. For instance, in Five Element Theory, the liver meridian and organ are associated with the element wood. To assist in healing an individual who has a liver disease, such as hepatitis, you would utilize "Wood Music" to help balance the element wood in the body. The wood music may stimulate balanced flow of energy in the liver meridians that feed nutritional Qi (energy) to the liver organ.

Healing with musical compositions based on the energy systems of ancient Chinese medicine is one of the many varied approaches to healing with sound. It is a unique example of ancient healing principles merging with new vibrational concepts to provide yet another sound healing system. Perhaps future research will verify the particular healing benefits of each sonic healing technology, alone, or in combination with other vibrational healing modalities. Paul Hubbert's **Holographic Sound Healing technology-healing the body through the chakras with sound** is a powerful ancient/new sound healing system which should be utilized as an important part of vibrational healing modalities.

The Art and Science of Sound Therapy

Sound therapy is an ancient healing art recognized today for it's sound science! In Egypt the hieroglyphic for music was also that for joy and well-being. In the Old Testament, David played his harp and lifted King Saul's depression. The Essenes documented that they used sacred words for healing. In Hellenistic culture, flute-playing eased the pain of sciatica and gout. We can choose to believe that these remedies are superstition and legend, or we can look further into the science that underlies such mystery.

Scientists are choosing to look deeply into these vibratory phenomena. Sound therapy as such is emerging as a viable tool for recovery from and prevention of illness. Research supporting the integration of music and sound to promote emotional and physical healing is widespread.

Sound therapy has been proven to reduce stress, which is a major factor in depression, hypertension, heart disease, cancer, ulcers and stroke. By reducing stress hormones, elevating mood, enhancing the release of the body's natural pain killers (endorphins), easing muscle tension, lowering blood pressure, increasing immune system function and lymphatic circulation, promoting relaxation and creativity, defusing strong emotions and focusing our attention into the present moment, healing sound has the power to transform our lives.

The basic tenets of healing with sound are the scientific principles of resonance, entrainment, and frequency. Scientists have come to believe that everything is made up of energy defined by differing vibratory rates or frequencies. These frequencies can be identified through various methods including calculating the relationship between an element and it's wave number in the periodic table, applying the deBroglie formula which combines Einstein's E=mc2 with the formula for photosynthesis, calculating the inversely proportional relationship between time and frequency, or observing the action of particles and waves. And of course we can identify audible frequencies with our hearing.

Resonance is defined as the frequency at which a substance most naturally vibrates. Sympathetic resonance occurs when one vibration matches another, amplifying and strengthening that vibratory field. Forced resonance or entrainment occurs when one vibration is able to change another provided the latter has the ability to resonate at a variety of frequencies.

As oscillating systems of energy, we humans resonate at many frequencies and easily respond to both resonance and entrainment for better or for worse. Our fast-paced life-styles exist within frantic frequencies with which we desperately synchronize. If we take the time to allow resonance with healthier sounds, we will discover a powerful preventative against disease and illness. In addition, entrainment with appropriate frequencies can help overcome compromised health.

There are numerous sound therapies that have been developed from the pioneering research of leading scientists, doctors and musicians. The research of Dr. Hans Jenny inspired Dr. Peter Guy Manners to develop the first bioresonance "frequency generator" therapy, cymatherapy. This therapy involves an electro-magnetic unit with an applicator that delivers frequency commutations for relief of many physical and emotional conditions. Each commutation consists of five frequencies and produces an audible sound as well as a physical vibration.

Vibro-acoustics engineered into chairs, beds and domes were developed from the bioresonance research as well. A visceral resonance is experienced as sound is transmitted through bones and tissue.

Dr. Alfred Tomatis, ENT specialist, created the first neurodevelopmental listening programs, which inspired a profusion of auditory integration and psycho-acoustic therapies. He specifically combined the filtered high frequencies of Gregorian chant, Mozart's music and the mother's voice to produce therapeutic listening programs designed to supplement patterns of development, which were disrupted during important phases of a child's development. He proved that the sounds heard by the ear charge the brain's neo-cortex with electrical impulses necessary for brain cell growth.

Don Campbell expanded upon Dr. Tomatis' research popularizing "The Mozart Effect". His books and CDs brought to public awareness the role that music and sound can play in a child's development. He promotes the importance of balanced and beautiful frequencies for stress relief, whole brain stimulation and whole health.

Dr. Jeffrey Thompson extended The Monroe Institute's brain research with his own research and became one of the first to interlace music with brain wave frequencies. In his musical CDs, underlying pulses of sound entrain the listener to various brain wave states for specific functions such as active thinking or deep meditation.

It may be surprising to some that familiar medical tools such as ultrasound, lithotripsy and acoustic haemostasis are actually frequency-based procedures! Many doctors are now venturing beyond these standard medical procedures to embrace alternative sound healing techniques.

Dr. Mitchell Gaynor, while director of the Strang-Cornell Cancer Prevention Center wrote "Sounds of Healing" documenting his successful integration of quartz crystal bowl therapy into his oncology practice. In group and private sessions for patients with life-threatening illness and chronic disease he has found that toning and playing crystal and Tibetan bowls have been beneficial both for psychospiritual development and physiologic entrainment.

Quartz crystal bowls produce sine waves, which stimulate neuro-immune responses through resonance with the body's crystalline properties. Tibetan bowls, seven-metal bowls forged by Tibetan monks, create hemi-sync and binaural beat frequencies that promote deep relaxation through brain wave entrainment. And toning, a vocal technique of producing elongated vowel and consonant sounds on a deep relaxed breath, is a term coined by Laurel Elizabeth Keyes in the 1960's which she describes as "...an ancient method of healing...the idea is simply to restore people to their harmonic patterns." The physical benefits of toning are powerful. Toning regulates breathing and improves oxygen supply. It stimulates deep-lying tissues, nerve cells, the endocrine glands and the flow of cerebrospinal fluid.

Dr. John Beaulieu created Biosonic Repatterning®, a tuning fork therapy, which is directly influenced by Pythagoras' proofs of the interrelationship between nature's mathematical ratios and sound's harmonics. Tuning forks are applied to the vertebrae and meridians as well as sounded in the energy field to help the body entrain with these natural, healthy ratios.
Jonathan Goldman and Steven Halpern have also taken their cue from ancient sound healing practice incorporating toning, overtoning, Tibetan bowls and chant into their beautiful healing music.

Dr. Helen Bonny developed GIM, Guided Imagery and Music, a therapy that recognizes and utilizes music as a catalyst for one's emotions. Scientific research now points to specific chemicals produced in the body that creates these emotions as a result of listening to music.

As research and clinical documentation continues, scientists are gaining a profound respect for the mystery of healing with music and sound. From the sacred mantras to the science of cymatherapy, healing sound spans the centuries with powerful prescriptions!

The Art and Science of Sound Therapy was written by Candace Ketch. She trained as a classical flutist at the University of Georgia and New England Conservatory of Music. She trained as a sound therapist with sound healer, Wayne Perry, in LA and with Dr. John Beaulieu, ND, PhD in NY, learning the art of toning, vocal harmonics, voice analysis and scanning, as well as the theory and use of tuning forks, the bija mantras, five element music and movement, and voice energetics. Her CD, "as Above so Below–a healing journey through the elements" features flutes, synthesizer and crystal bowls. It is available at specialty stores and through www.SonicAngelMusic.com. Candace is a sound therapist, polarity practitioner, and a Usui/Karuna Reiki master.

According to Renee Brodie, "Sound is an energy form generated by a vibrating body. Depending on its frequency, the human body will react to and perceive this energy in different ways. If the pitch is below the audible level and the amplitude is high, we may feel it although we do not hear it. If it is within the audible range, we will hear it and classify it according to our knowledge of sound. If the pitch is ultrasonic-above the audible range-we will not hear it but may experience unpleasant bodily reactions to what is known as White Sound."

Brodie, author of ***The Healing Tones of Crystal Bowls***, says in her web site that sound brings about states of emotional feeling. The web side quotes Brodie as saying, "When you create harmonics of sound, it reminds your body of something. It reminds your body of Light, of deep Cosmic love and other worlds. Your body comes into joy and sometimes overwhelmingly into sadness. It seeks and accesses a frequency that it has been longing for, of which the sound has reminded it. As you allow your sound to play your body, you discover a frequency that you have sought. This frequency is connected to the evolution of the helixes within your body. Sound is a vehicle or conduit to connect you to the higher chakras outside your body because you do not have a way of accessing them logically. You must access all frequencies and chakra centers by feelings, and sound will connect you with feeling, which will allow you to understand the information.

Barbara Marciniak in her book, ***Bringers of Dawn-Teachings from the Pleiadians,*** says, as a registered acupuncturist of BC, she has always been searching for alternative healing technologies she could integrate with her Traditional Chinese medical modalities. Sound healing is definitely a very powerful healing modality as discovered by a fellow French acupuncturist and musician, Fabian Maman. Dr. Carolyn Shreeve's Journal of Alternative & Complementary Medicine article called *"How Far is Sound & Colour Therapy Medicine of the Future?"* noted, " Maman also teaches his patients to sing the curative note, rather like a chant or a mantra. He has synthesized aspects of his knowledge of sound with the use of movement, meditation and color into a complete healing system. Movement (he uses Qi Gong) regenerates the life force in the meridians. This he believes links us to cosmic energy and when practiced with our fundamental sound, starts up vibrations within the individual's morphogenetic field.

Fabien Maman says that color links us to the energy of the planets. It can be used to "clarify the astral (emotional) plane," and that sound, because it surrounds vibrating particles and increases their spin, facilitates their expansion and widens our field of consciousness. Maman's research with cancer and sound may turn out to be one of the most significant and exciting discoveries of this century.

Maman's particular contribution has been to discover that certain specific sound frequencies transmitted to acupuncture points by Tuning Forks are as effective as needles in treating patients. His interest was further stimulated by his meeting with the French physicist and musician, Joel Sternheimer. Sternheimer has discovered that elementary particles vibrate at frequencies in accordance with musical laws; he views the material world as an aspect of music. Maman and Sternheimer are working together to successfully investigate the harmonic and melodic equivalents of living matter. They claimed they have found that all meridian lines, acupuncture points, tissues and organs have their own individual "musical note". Moreover, they are in constant state of flux, affected by such factors as the seasons, time of day and night and so on, and therefore have constantly changing sound equivalents.

A particular achievement of the pair has been the transposition of the characteristic vibratory resonance of certain key molecules into their lower frequency musical equivalents. The effect of this is to slow down the vibrational rate of the molecules concerned. Maman contends that this process has enormously important therapeutic implications in that it can be used both to stimulate healthy human cells and to harmonize and heal sick ones. He also emphasizes the adverse effects of environmental noise, which should be significantly reduced if the human organism is to reach its potential of vitality and well-being. In his clinical research, with the biologist Helene Grimaud and others, he discovered that blood cells, subjected to a chromatic scale of sound frequencies, became colored and altered their shape according to the particular frequency employed. The note A (440 hertz) changed them to Pink, C made them longer, E made them round, and D produced considerable color variety.

When cancer cells were subjected likewise to a chromatic scale, their intracellular components started to lose definition as the scale ascended, and generally disintegrated between A (440 hertz) and B. Individual cells have "personal" qualities related to the overall condition of the person from whom they are taken. This partly accounts for the fact that when sound is used therapeutically, cure is achieved in some cases and not in others. Maman determines the level at which energy is depleted-physical, etheric, astral, mental, psychic or spiritual-and decides which sound frequency to use through pulse examination, the use of instinct and by listening to the patient's voice. Just as the correct note is therapeutic, so inappropriate ones can cause damage. Sounds are therefore highly specific in each case, and are applied through tuning forks to acupuncture points or chakras, or by means of headphones." Renee Brodie, author of *Crystal Bowl Therapy and Holographic Sound Healing!* and *The Healing Tones of Crystal Bowls.*

Polarity Therapy

"Polarity" refers to the universal pulsation of expansion/ contraction or repulsion/attraction known as Yang and Yin in Oriental therapies. Similarly, Polarity integrates the "Three Principles and Five Chakras" of Ayurvedic tradition, and has been called the modern manifestation of ancient Hermetic

Philosophy. At the same time Polarity Therapy also enjoys rich ties to modern science, which has confirmed its essential theme of energetic relationship as the basis of all phenomena.

Basically one has to imagine the field of the fine magnetic substance in the body in a three dimensional way. The front left of the body is positive and the front right of the body is negative. If one imagines a system of lines from left to right, this system would be spread over the width axis. The positive force would be strongest on the outside of the left side, and the negative force would be strongest on the outside of the right side, this system would be spread over the width axis. Towards the middle it becomes weaker, and the one cancels out the other. The third axis, the length axis, runs down from the head to the toes, and is magnetically the weakest. The head is positive, the feet are negative. The latest scientific research reveals that individual cells have a positive and negative polarity.

Polarity Therapy was further developed by Randolph Stone, DO, DC, ND (1890-1981), who conducted a thorough investigation of energy in the healing arts over the course of his 60-year medical career. He found that the Human Energy Field is affected by touch, diet, movement, sound, attitudes, relationships, life experience, trauma and environmental factors. As a result, Polarity has strong, mutually supportive connections to many other holistic health systems.

The Application of Polarity Therapy

In the Polarity model, health is experienced when energy systems function in their natural state; energy flows smoothly without significant blockage or fixation. When energy is unbalanced, blocked or fixed due to stress or other factors, pain and disease arise. Blockages generally manifest in sequence from the subtle to the dense levels of the field. Polarity Therapy seeks to find the blockages and release energy to normal flow patterns, and to maintain the Energy Field in an open, flexible condition.

Reflexology

We all would love to have someone massage our feet every night–right! If that doesn't happen you should massage your feet as often as your can because it will improve your health and energy immensely by activating sluggish glands and organs. The feet contain about 7,2000 nerve endings that are connected through the spinal cord and brain and all areas of the body. Reflexology breaks up tiny mineral deposits called "crystals" that settle in the body, especially in the feet, plus it removes toxins and allows the energy to flow.

Reflexologists focus primarily on the feet but also they can work on the hands, ears, and the entire body. It is a good idea to walk barefoot as much as possible where it is safe because your feet will contact with the energies of the earth. Sounds woo, woo? Read any science book and you will discover that the earth's core is liquid iron boiling at 9,000 degrees and is the source of the earth's powerful magnetic field. Now that's powerful energy. All this hot energy is just a few hundred feet below the earth's crust as shown by volcanoes. Remember, we can move energy with our thoughts. You can actually move earth energy up through the soles of your feet.

You can learn to be your own reflexologist because you only need to practice using your thumb like an inchworm. You will need to have a short thumbnail or it won't work or feel good. Also, you do not need to memorize the locations of the various parts of the body in the illustration below. You can move your thumb like an inch worm horizontally, and then vertically, across and then up and down your foot to be essentially covering the whole body. If you are aware that certain organs are not functioning properly, you can concentrate on them. If you feel a hardness in an area, then you know you should continue to massage in that location until it becomes softer.

If you want more information about reflexology read *Better Health with Foot Reflexology,* by Dwight Byers who is also director of the International Institute of Reflexology in St. Petersburg, Florida. There are 25,000 reflexologists worldwide. *Healing With Pressure Point Therapy* by Jack Forem and Steve Shimer is an excellent book teaching how to massage away more than 100 common ailments

Use Your Energy To Help Others Heal And Be Healed

Everyone has the ability to send energy; so everyone has the ability to be a healer. There are so many healing techniques you can do to prevent illnesses, to take the place of synthetic drugs with harmful side effects, and to help you heal after surgery so that you can be responsible for your health and energy levels.

You can use a pendulum to find the exact location where a person is losing energy or having pain by following the pendulum directions. One thing to remember, the location of the pain may not be the source of the energy loss. For instance, if the left side of the body is losing energy, the right side of the body compensates and may feel the pain.

Here are some directions about how to hold your hands and fingers if you are an energy healer and/or want to send someone energy. Place your hands on either side of the body as close as you can get to the place of energy loss. If it is an awkward place, you actually can place your hands somewhere else on the body and still get results since the body will direct the energy where it needs to go.

For small areas on the body or to concentrate the energy, you can put your fingers together. This helps you get to the center of the place that needs healing.

Specific Techniques Before You Begin Facilitating Energy Movement:
The energy facilitator should:
Be centered and still
Set your intention for the highest and best
Call upon the healing angels, the archangels, the guides and, the higher self of both the healer and the person seeking healing. Review the information in Chapter 2. The palm of the right hand is positive and stimulates energy, which has a strengthening effect.

References

Cho, Zang-Hee. "*New Findings of the Correlation Between Acupoints and Corresponding Brain Cortices Using Functional MRI"* in 1998 in *Proceedings of the National Academy of Science,* v. 95, pp. 2670-2673.

Gerber, Richard, MD, *Vibrational Medicine, Bear and Company.2001, p. 419.*

Oschman, James, *Energy Medicine, The Scientific Bas*is, Churchill, Livingstone, Edinburgh, 2001, p. 76.

11. The Living Matrix And Posture

The living matrix is all the connective tissue in the body. It is constantly changing its shape and ability to move, signal processing and set up of signals. In order for the body to utilize the most energy, the posture has to be strain free and totally stable in its alignment. Any misalignment will require other parts of the posture to adjust, compensate and expend extra energy. Connective tissue holds the body in form. It connects the bones of the skeleton and all of the muscles. It keeps all the organs in their proper location. Any misalignment or blockages in your connective tissue results in energy loss. Since the connective tissue of the body is all connected, you can see that your overall energy will be compromised by any misalignment in your body.

The living matrix system remarkably contains two non-physical aspects of us–our memories and attitudes. The section on cells discussed how different kinds of cells–blood, skin, organ, brain, and nerve cells–hold memories and attitudes. The nervous system also holds memories and attitudes. The electromagnetic energy produced by the cells creates millions of energy fields that radiate throughout the body that reflect the energetic level of our memories and attitudes.

What Different Forms Of Energy Radiate Through The Living Matrix?

The living matrix absorbs energy and then it can send that energy as a signal as a solitary pulse or in waves of energy. Because of the connection of all of the parts of the living matrix, touching one part of the living matrix instantaneously affects the whole. Thus the living matrix becomes an excitable medium with waves of energy propagating throughout the system. Almost all the body's membranes and tissues are activated by the waves of energy.

You should go back and review the section, You Are A Totally Crystalline Being in Chapter 4 so that you understand this more in depth discussion of the living matrix.

Electrons: The living matrix is a crystalline substance; therefore, certain electrons move from atom to atom or molecule to molecule conveying information.
Holes: When electrons and protons migrate through the semi-conducting protein fabric in the body, a hole is created
Phonons: energy of sound
Photons: energy of light

Your Posture Shows Your Energy Loss

People have a walk that is totally unique to them. It is a result of their living matrix (all the different kinds of connective tissue) and the skeletal structure that is formed by their health, the foods eaten, memories and traumas, and expressed and repressed feelings. We inherit our physical makeup genetically. But how our physical bodies develop depends on our childhood circumstances.

In between therapeutic massages, we need to daily massage ourselves. Massage therapy can release stored energy if the person getting the massage is willing to release it. You can tap several times or massage yourself on the stored energy location to release stored energy. If you put your hand over the location and move the energy to the end of the meridian you can then send it out of the body.

After you read this chapter you will begin to look at peoples' bodies and know so much more about them. For instance, the ridges of skull of a person who is rigid in their thinking will actually grow together. You can look at a person's stiff posture and walk and get insights into how he/she stiffens the body any time a new thought or idea is introduced. Ida Rolf, one of the first body workers, saw that the human body adheres to the rules of gravity. Each part of the body and the ways it functions is supported by the parts and functions below it. Anyone wanting to extend their range and efficiency of motion, balance, timing, flexibility, resilience, and precision needs to monitor their posture and receive frequent hand-on bodywork and do movement therapies.

The outline of the body below shows key places to look and see where a person is either losing energy or energy is not flowing at all and is being stored. Get a partner and take turns doing posture analysis. Begin in the head area and put a check that indicates which side is lower and losing energy.

Posture Check	**Higher**	**Lower**
Right eyebrow		left eyebrow
Right eye		left eye
Right ear		left ear

Possible muscle weakness: neck muscles, sacrospinalis, psoas, rhomboids, gluteus medius, and upper trapezius

Right nostril		left nostril

Check out and see if your nose is out of alignment and is pointed to the right or the left

Right corner of lip		left corner of lip

Does the face slant left or right?

Is the head centered in the middle of the shoulders
Head twisted to the right head twisted to the left
Possible muscle weakness: Abdominals, rohomboids, trapezius, and sacrospinalis
Right shoulder left shoulder
Possible muscle weakness: neck muscles, latissimus dorsi, gluteus medius, upper trapezius, and deltoids
Right shoulder twisted left shoulder twisted
Possible muscle weakness: levator scapulae
Right elbow left elbow
Right hand/fingers left hand/fingers
(If you have trouble determining if one hand is lower than the other, ask the person to relax their fingers and to stand with their back facing you. You can see which hand hangs lower much better.)
Hands turned differently
Possible muscle weakness: teres minor
Hand held away from the body
Possible muscle weakness: Gluteus medius
Swayback or stomach hanging out:
Possible muscle weakness: abdominals, psoas, piriformis
Back curved out or belly curved in
Possible muscle weakness: sacrospinalis, psoas
Right hip left hip
Possible muscle weakness: adductors, gluteus medius, and psoas
Do the knees touch?
Knocked knees:
Possible muscle weakness: sartorius, gracilis
Knees hyerextended or pushed back too far
Possible muscle weakness: gastrocnemius, quadriceps, and popliteus
Body leans forward: person is giving away their energy and trying to push in on other people's space
Body leans backward: person is avoiding the energy of others, perhaps because they feel that it is coming on too strongly
Possible muscle weakness: soleus
Bowed legs: Gluteus medius, adductors, and fascia lata
Ankle turned in or flat feet
Possible muscle weakness: Anterior tibial, psoas
Foot turned in-pigeon toed
Possible muscle weakness: psoas
Foot turned out
Possible muscle weakness: psoas, abbucors, gracilis, hamstrings, and peroneus
Ankle bowed out: Possible muscle weakness: peroneus
Is the hole in the ear in alignment with the middle of the shoulder?
From a side view, start a line in front of the anklebone and pass it through the side of the knee, the center of the thigh, the center of the upper arm, and the

center of the neck and ear. The natural way to hold the forearm is forward with the elbow slightly bent, the thumb in and the hand against the thigh.

To check out a person's alignment, have them stand so that you get a side view. Start with a line beginning in the center of the ear, go down the middle of the neck, the center of the upper arm, the center of the side of the knee, the center of the thigh, and the finally the center of the ankle bone.

Look at the top of the waistband or the belt and see if one side is higher, or lower.

When a person is balanced, the weight of the body will rest toward the back of the foot, with the hips directly over the heels. Is the person balanced?

Look at the person from the side. Does their head lean forward? Is there a hump in their back? Is the lower back swayed?

Look at the person from the back. It helps if they have back pockets because you can see if one side is lower. The pelvic bone gets out of alignment and tilts forward so that buttocks are tucked in.

Look at the person's back to see if the head is centered on the shoulders. A line beginning in the middle of the feet should go straight up the spine and in the middle of the neck and head. Is it straighter?

Are the feet pointed directly in front of them, or are they pointed inward or outward?

Does one foot feel more grounded than the other? Is one foot out further?

How Can You Balance And Align Your Posture For Increased Energy?

Self-Directed Empowerment Technique: Stand or sit with your shoulders square and straight to achieve balance and centeredness. It is in this position of power that you control the energy around you.

The body can actually become twisted to the point that the head, shoulder, waist, and hips point in different directions. I was doing posture analysis on a new client, a tall thin blonde who had her own decorating business. When I first looked at her I thought she had not heard the instructions to stand facing me. Her body below her neck was directed toward the right. She did not notice that even her feet were pointed to the right. I realized that she had a severe case of scoliosis so I placed my hands on her back and became consciously aware of breathing from my diaphragm. I visualized and set my intention that her spine straighten. The body wants to be balanced and in a state of homeostasis so her spine straightened out and turned back to normal. The second time I looked, her whole body was facing me.

Many times people have one hip higher than the other. This is an alignment problem that can be corrected with energy medicine, but not if one leg is truly longer than the other. *Here are the directions.*

1. Get down on one knee so that you can see if the hips are level. Sometimes I find it easier to check from the back, especially if the

person is wearing clothing with pockets because one pocket will be higher. Another way to determine if there is a an alignment problem is to put your fingertips on the top of the hip bone (ileum) in the front of the person's body and press down gently.

2. Gently place the palms of your hands on the crest of the ileum on the higher side and start sending energy. Inhale through your mouth by taking one long breath in. Exhale to the count of four. You can breathe this way for a few minutes, but stop if you feel dizzy.
3. Follow the same procedure on the backside of the ileum. Hipbones can move in all sorts of different directions, and it is amazing what sending energy can do to align the posture.

Getting Your Head On Straight

Many doctors will tell you that you cannot move the occipital ridge, which is located at the base of the skull at the back of the head. It sits on the top of the neck bones. Sending energy by following the directions below enables you to move the cranial bones of the occipital ridge and help people realign their spines.

1. The person you are working with needs to be seated. Look at the picture and you can easily find the occipital ridge. Place your thumbs in the little ridges on the sides as pictured-equally distant from the center. Place your thumbs on top of the hair and even press up on the hair.
2. Move your body so that your eyes are level with the occipital ridge and your thumbs.
3. Place your thumbs at the base of the occipital ridge and the rest of your fingertips while breathing deeply from the diaphragm. While it only takes seconds to move the cranial bones, you might want to continue sending energy a bit longer.

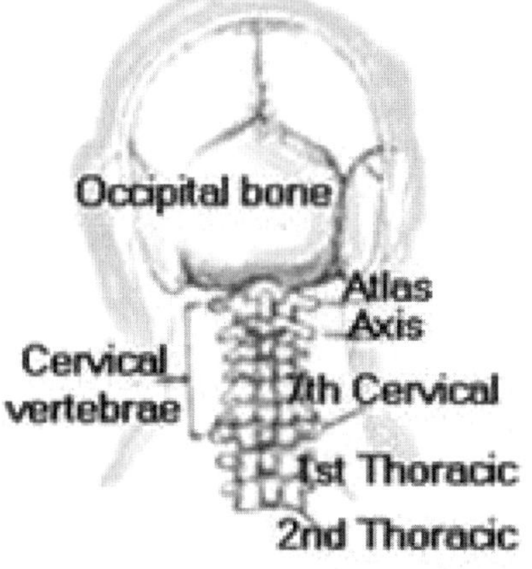

The occipital ridge is where the occipital bone and the neck meet.

Accessing Information From A Person's Aura

You can access information about another person by connecting with the seven levels of their aura. First you need to get into a theta state by totally relaxing your body and then lifting your eyes so that you can stare at a spot on the upper part of the wall. Go through each of the seven levels and say to yourself, "I am processing information on this level." Next, move either or both your eyes and tongue back and forth. This causes the left and right side of the brain to function together. If you are processing on the physical level, you will feel how the physical level feels. If there are hot places along the spine, for instance, you will know that the spine is out of alignment. If you are processing in the emotional level, the will actually feel the other person's emotions at that time. I have felt people's emotional state as being shrunken, fear based, or confused. Each of these states has a different feeling. Go through each of the levels for more information.

The following illustrations deal with what body psychotherapists call certain physical and psychological types in people. Of course, our parents pass down our genetic makeup, but what happened to us during childhood is as equal a determiner of our physical and psychological structure. When trauma occurs children block the energy flow first in their auric fields that then translates down into the physical body. Trauma can begin in the womb.

For those who believe in past life experiences, you will see that because of our past life experiences, we developed specific belief systems. I have a client who has very negative energy. She is also very fear based and judgmental. In many of her past lives she experienced torture and traumatic deaths. The result of the tension and stress caused by fear has created many health problems.

Bioenergetics describes the five major character structures as: the schizoid, the oral, the displaced or psychopathic, the masochistic, and the rigid character. You will come to see that these words have different meanings than the Freudian terms you are used to. You may find a little bit of yourself in some of the character structures. What I am hoping is that you understand is that each of these character structures is blocking a person and their energy from being who they truly are.

Fear causes us to feel unsafe. Different fears create different character defenses. When an event occurs which causes fear, a person reacts with an energetic defense that in turn creates weakness in the auric field and physical body. You will notice in some of the illustrations that the chakras are out of alignment in the body. The effect is reduced and distorted energy.

The Living Matrix And Posture

This book will only discuss a few of the character structures. Barbara Brennen discusses in detail all of the different character structures in her book *Light Emerging.* Her other excellent book is *Hands of Light.*

The illustration above is an example of how thought forms can be sent from one person to another. The woman is sending the man splurges of energy that will stay in his energy field if there are energetic thoughts on the same level of vibration. Notice how the woman is sending energy directly at the man's heart and solar plexus. His chakras are open and receiving the negative energy. Cords are attached to the energy and the man will be influenced by the thoughts of the woman until she installs protection. Now this is important. A cord will not enter your system unless you have a similar vibration to it. Slow frequency energies (thoughts of fear, greed, revenge, hate) can only attach themselves to other slow frequency vibrations. Remember when you were a kid and you had a bottle of bubble stuff? Thoughts are floating in the air from everyone. If they resonate with you, good or bad, they attach to you and they stick around like they were held with superglue.

The Rigid Upright Person:

The rigid upright pulled back person pulls back their body while standing. This action causes the front of the body wall to extend and stretch at the same time that the muscles of the spine are pulled back. The result is that the lumbar and cervical curves increase causing the muscles to shorten. The stance pulls back yet the man appears ready to go forward. We describe this person as being tightly strung like an arrow in a drawn bow ready to attack. By following the directions above you can put yourself into the pulled back person's emotional state and feel their fear. When the rigid upright person pulls back in fear, the muscles at the base of the head shorten in the back. The chest and diaphragm pull up. You can see the change in their walk as the muscles contract in the buttocks, the quadriceps, the thighs and calves. Fear based people have stomach and spinal problems. All of this contraction actually affects the contents of the brain by changing the intercranial pressure. As you can see in the illustration, the rigid person is off balance, which is also reflected in the shape of the man's aura.

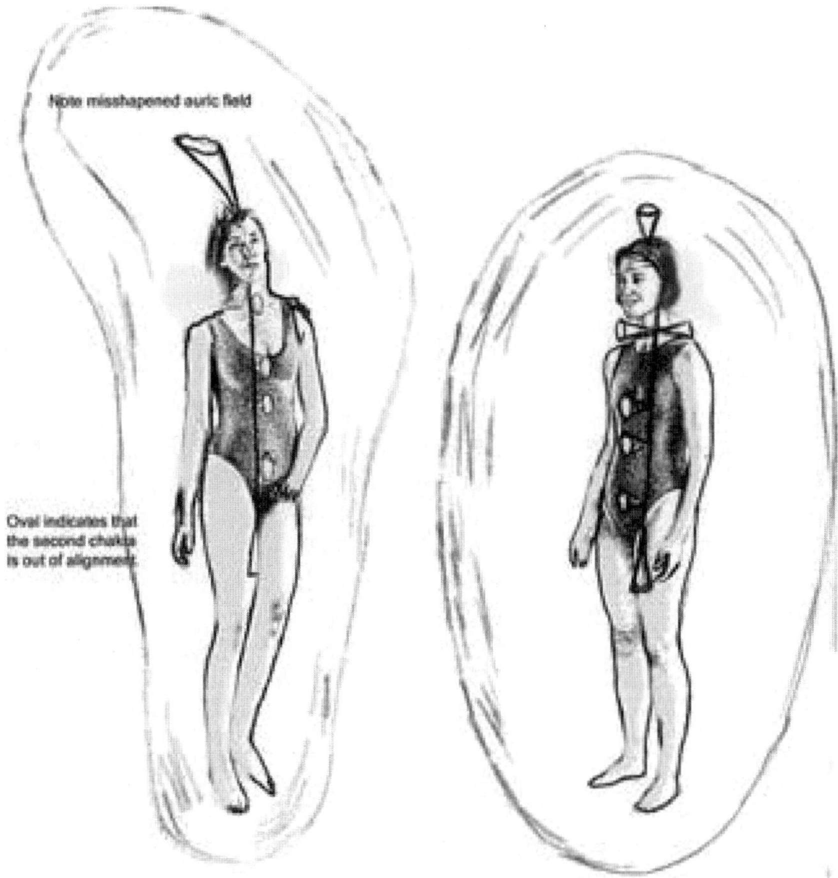

The Schizoid Character

Susan, who will be discussed in Chapter 12 because she has chronic fatigue, is a perfect example of a schizoid character. She does not want to live in her body in this lifetime because she experienced many lives in physical pain and death by torture in past lives. Schizoid characters have problems connecting with other people. Abusive parents are examples of schizoids.

When I looked at Susan's aura, it was behind her. Her seventh level never developed a strong boundary. Like other schizoids, she has a twisted body and a very sensitive body. She has lots of allergies and a weak immune system. Susan has a withdrawn and vacant look in her eyes. There is no sense of external or internal power. She acts as if she wants to heal her chronic fatigue, but she uses it to pull the energy out of other people.

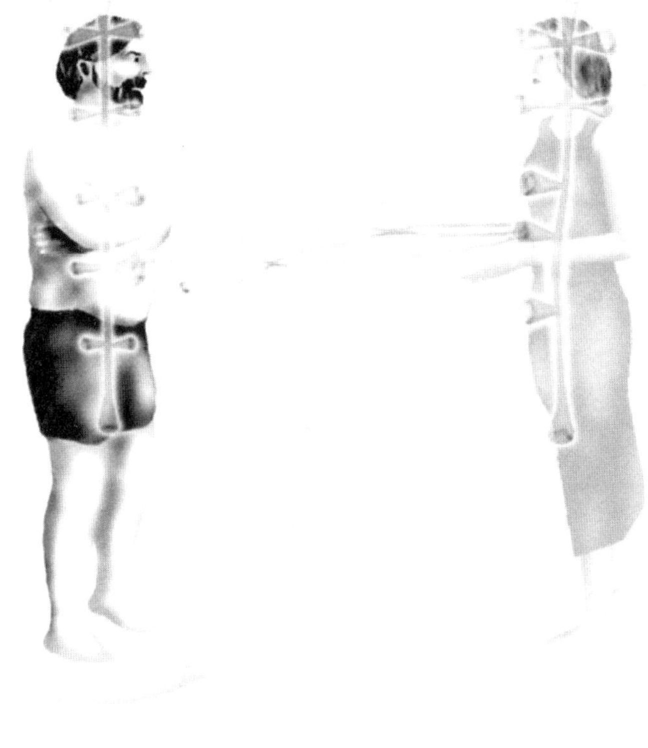

Masochistic Defense and Pull Reaction

The masochistic character is a person who does not like to be controlled or having their space invaded. Don't apply other meanings to this word in this situation. I feel that I have experienced several lives as a masochistic person. They are people who have suffered imprisonment, slavery, or political control or religious control. I know that I was a slave in Charleston, South Carolina. In another lifetime, I was a woman who healed people and I was accused of being a witch and killed. In another lifetime I helped out runaway slaves on the Underground Railroad. I must have been chained up several times because in this lifetime I feel choked by necklaces and bracelets. This also accounts for my need to express myself. I don't think the following description of a masochistic applies to me.

Many masochistic people fear claiming their freedom and they are strapped in dependent situations blaming others for their circumstances. They were born into families who totally dominated them, even to the extent of their self-expression. On the one hand their parents loved them, on the other hand their parents reached into their auric fields to keep them hooked in. The child was not permitted to have his/her own feelings–just be an expression of the parents.

Look at the next illustration and you will see that the man has created a massive physical body to keep controllers out. Finally, the masochistic person has to cut the cords from the parents if they ever want to act independent. If you have ever dated or married a masochistic person, you know how hard it is to communicate with them. They have retreated within so long they have trouble expressing themselves.

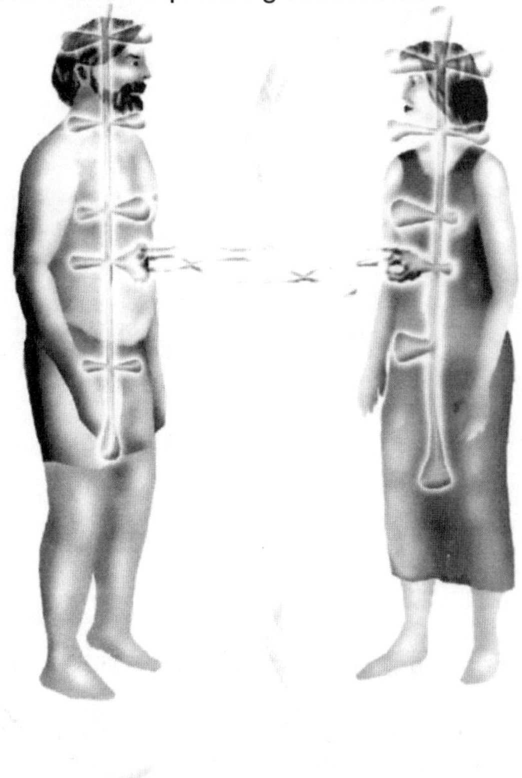

Masochistic Defense Allow or Denial Reaction

The next illustration shows what it looks like when someone stops a masochistic person. If you find yourself in the defensive mode, ground your self in the earth by imaging a root coming from your root chakra and going all the way into the earth. Bring up the energy of the earth into your second chakra. Begin to feel connected with everything around you so that lots of energy will flow into your field.

Concentrate on yourself more than the other person by letting go of the other person and connecting with your own star core. Remember, where you place your attention is where your energy will follow. Let yourself be free to express your ideas in your own time frame and how you want.

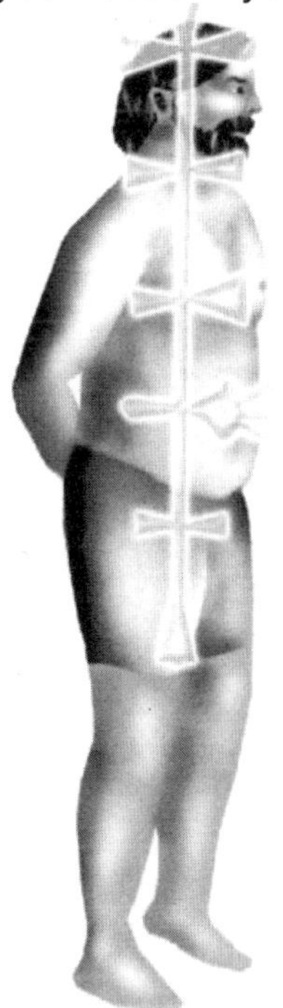

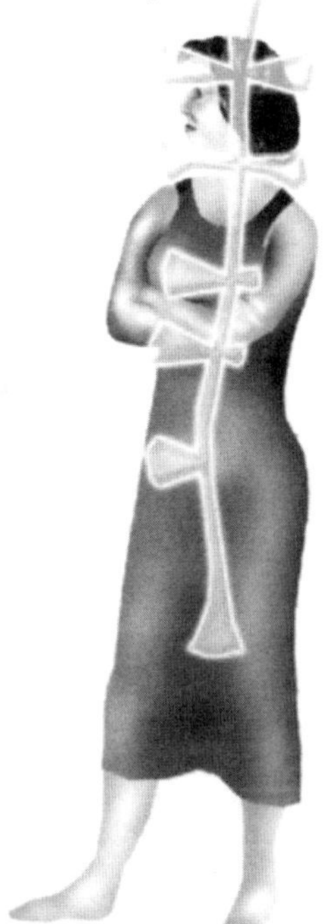

Masochistic Defense and Stop Reaction

The Rigid Person

People form rigid character structures because as a child he/she was rejected by the parent of the opposite sex. As a child he/she may have been sexually abused or not given love. In response, the child learns to control all their feelings-even the good ones. As an adult, the person continues to hold in his/her feelings because they fear releasing their childhood feelings of rejection. We've all met the manipulator who tries to manipulate us into giving what he/she wants instead of simply asking.

You can look at the rigid person's posture, head held high, backbone stiff with pride. Being in relationship with this kind of person is hard because they want you to love them, but they are uncommitted to loving in return. The partner complains that the person has no feelings. They are the perfect example of the armored person.

When I am at an exposition using my GDV camera, a few people tell me that they have too much energy. What they don't realize about their hyperactivity is that they are not using their energy to fulfill their purpose. While the other levels of the aura may be bright and integrated, the 6th level, called the celestial level, is not strong because it is not open to receiving unconditional love. This person operates from his mind and will rather than from his heart. The person needs to open the chakras in the front of his/her body and develop their spirituality.

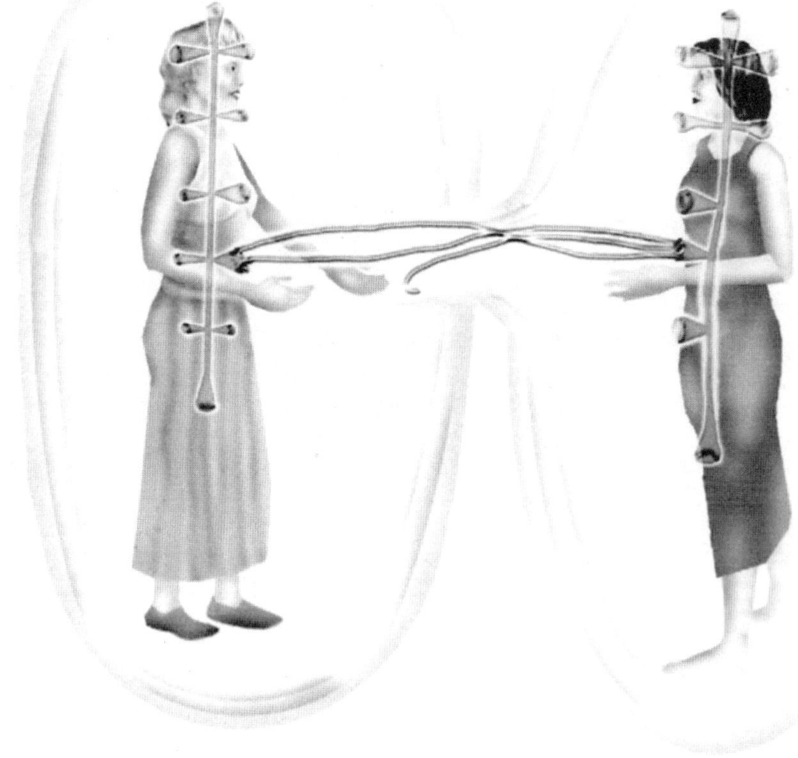

Rigid Defense and Pull Reaction

The Rigid Upright Pulled Up Person

We've all met the uptight person. From the pelvic area to the heart area they are pulled up. Because they are off-balance, they must brace themselves against falling backward. This causes the biceps, hamstrings, and abdominal muscles to contract strongly. The contractions pull the pelvis forward and the floating ribs move down through the abdominal muscles causing the chest to descend. It's like wearing a too tight belt. Because the diaphragm is locked, the abdominal area the stomach has to move up. To brace the head, the muscles at the top of the head contract, which forces the muscles in the head to compress and squeeze toward the center. Holding this erectness is hard and inhibiting to natural energy flow.

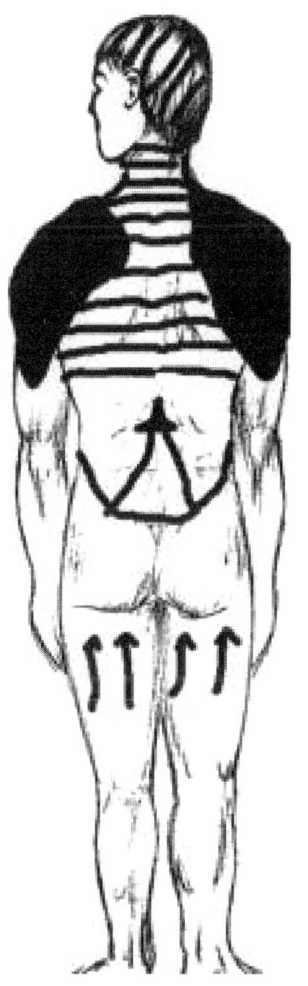

The rigid, controlled person has certain areas that are over-expanded. The dark areas in the illustration show a person very rigid in the shoulder area. The white areas show where the energy is flowing. The black and white areas denote areas where the energy flows on and off. When the shoulder muscles are rigid the arms hang at the side with little movement. The abdominal and pelvic areas contract. Pressure pulls the buttocks back and the calves down. The pubic area contracts for self-protection.
The following is a good example of the mind/body connection. A person not open to receiving new information develops a mind that is overactive and inhibited. The body of the rigid person creates pressure that is directed toward the head. You've seen people who operate from the cerebral part of their brain. The head and thorax are pulled upward. This type of person is over reactive.

Energy Foods

By now you know that our bodies operate on a subtle electromagnetic current. Every cell–blood cells, skin cells, to name a few, and the cells of all your different organs– heart, brain, liver, etc. emit and create a field of electrical current which is the way that they communicate with each other. Our bodies break down the food that we eat into small nutrient particles called colloids, that are the carried through our cells by an electrical charge. Fast foods and processed foods have low energy frequencies and do not meet the body's electrical needs. It actually takes electrical nerve energy from the body's digestive system to break down these foods.

The elements of every substance ingested as food–protein, fats, sugars, vitamins, minerals, etc.–has a maximum wavelength, or color absorption and emission characteristic specific for its identity and function.

Energy Clearing

Magnetic Unruffle

If you have ever watched a healer, you have probably seen this standard procedure for doing energy release. The multitude of reasons for doing the magnetic ruffle are: chronic pain, trauma, anesthesia, breathing polluted air or other harmful environmental substances, systemic disease, pollution due to smoking or recreational drugs, and long term and short term prescription use. Also, in addition to having massage and doing energy psychology methods, magnetic unruffle is a way to release emotional blocked energy caused by fear, anger, worry, tension and anxiety.

Be sure that you clear the whole body from head to toe because you don't want to move stale energy and deposit it in lower torso of the body or the legs if you begin at the top. I was working on a friend named Margy whose doctor thought she might have to have kneecap surgery. Moving the stale energy helped release the swelling so the doctor said if her knees kept improving, she wouldn't need surgery. Thankfully my friend feels the energy movement in her body because the last time I worked with her I stopped moving the energy at her hips and she said she could feel it stuck there. I moved it out of the top of her head.

Procedure: The person being worked with should recline on their back. The person moving the energy should hold their hands about 12 inches above the person. The fingers should be spread and relaxed and curled. The curled fingers help with the raking effect of moving blocked energy. Move the hands from the top of the body to the toes in one smooth continuous sweep. You will learn to feel when you have removed all the stale energy, but it takes only about 30 seconds per stroke. It make take about 15 minutes to do the whole body. Remember the power of setting your intention and that thoughts are energy? You can direct the hands to act like magnets by pulling out the energy. This is the reason that people who move energy shake their hands at the end of a movement. After each stroke the energy will move more and more easily although new layers of energy will surface until you are finished.

The Living Matrix And Posture

Stress And Energy

Ever wonder why you can't act rationally during stress? Well, catecholamines suppress activity in the front part of our brain where we usually concentrate and think rationally. This enables you to act quickly without inhibition if you are in danger. Your lungs take in more oxygen, your heart starts pumping 300 % faster, and your spleen discharges more red and white blood cells to carry more oxygen.

Here's what happens in other parts of your body. Your immune system distributes white blood cells to either the skin, the bone marrow, or the lymph nodes. It knows the exact locations where to go. The skin gets white, cool, clammy and sweaty because blood is flowing away to support the heart and muscle tissues. All this activity is occasionally okay, but when we are under constant stress, it has debilitating effects.

There are well-known chemical messengers called neurotransmitters. You are probably familiar with the messengers dopamine, norepinephine, and epinephrine. They leap across the tiny gaps, or synapses, between brain cells. If the receptors of the receiving cell permit, the neurotransmitters are available to either fire or shut down, depending on the message received. The amygdala is an area in the brain that the catecholamines trigger when there is stress. The hippocampus, another area of the brain, stores emotionally loaded experiences in a long-term memory bank.

A person chooses whether to be frightened and in a nervous state, thereby increasing the heart rate, or a person can choose to meditate and achieve a peaceful state. When stressful challenges appear we can choose to be calm, contented and relaxed. The hypothalamus gland makes the decision whether we will be in a peaceful or agitated state. That decision is based on the amount of light energy the hypothalamus is receiving through the eyes as it coordinates and regulates the body's life-sustaining functions. L. Lohmeier, in an article called "*Let the Sun Shine In*," noted that **approximately a hundred bodily functions have been identified with having daily rhythms that need regular exposure to the sun's day/night cycle to function correctly.**

Energy Wells

Rooms in houses or offices can have energy wells, places where the energy is strongest. You can find energy wells by using your pendulum to survey the room asking it to say "yes" or "move clockwise" when you come to the energy well. People who are sensitive to energy can feel the high vibration of the well by holding up their hands and moving around the room. You should use energy wells as places for healing, meditation, renewing and revitalizing. Several of my friends have been able to locate my room's energy wells without my telling them the location.

Energy Vampires

While doing healing sessions at a church I used my GDV camera to do analysis of each person's energy levels. Very attractive and well educated parents brought their eleven-year old son. He appeared very healthy and active, but his first GDV images showed that he had no energy. Thinking that he had not followed my instructions, we repeated the procedure with the same shocking results. After I took the third images and they appeared the same, I worriedly told the parents that some disembodied spirit was sucking out the boy's energy. To my shock, the mother said, "Oh, we knew that. My husband's father was an alcoholic who died of lung cancer because he was a chain smoker. We felt his spirit around all the time and saw it several times shortly after his death. I believe that when my son was born his grandfather entered into my son's auric field and he has been taking my son's energy ever since. I wondered if it would show up on the GDV camera."

After doing some research I found ways to remove disembodied spirits, spirits of people who have passed on but have not gone to the Light, using the world's oldest stone, obsidian. This stone is a lustrous volcanic glass stone good for grounding (feeling connected to the earth) and as a protection from physical and emotional harm. It provides a shield against negativity, transforming negative vibrations around you. Obsidian is used in shamanic rituals and by energy healers to remove disembodied spirits. I removed the grandfather's spirit and sent it to the Light.

Tim was a young man in his mid twenties with dark circles under his eyes when I met him. Though he was currently unemployed, he had the least energy of anyone I have ever met. Tim is very open about his homosexuality, has a very slight build, and a very soft voice and manner. At some time in his life he became vulnerable to disembodied spirits who entered his auric field and who were literally sucking the life energy out of him. You could feel his lack of energy the moment he walked into the room. Tim was so disassociated with himself that he was unaware that he had no energy and barely reacted when he saw his GDV images. He did not ask what he could do about his situation.

How Pain Takes The Body's Energy

The body's best device for getting your attention is to make you feel pain. You already know that when you are in pain neither your body nor your mind functions properly. Unfortunately, many of us wait until we are in severe pain before we will listen to our bodies.

Blocked energy often causes pain. The next time you have a tennis elbow, swollen ankle, or migraine, move your hand counter clockwise above where you feel the pain. Set your intention that the blocked energy will be sent to the palm of your hand. As you move your hand counter clockwise you will pull the blocked energy out of your body. I close my eyes and I see with my Third eye streams of energy being pulled from my body. You can also feel blocked energy. In the beginning you will feel the resistance and as you continue you will move the energy more easily. When you have removed all the blocked energy, send in white light energy.

How To Cleanse Out Blocked Energy

The Hopi Technique comes from the Native American Hopi tribe. You can determine the exact location of the blocked energy by holding a pendulum over the spine. Follow the directions for holding the pendulum correctly. The pendulum will either go counter clockwise for blocked energy or right and left depending on what agreement you have made.

1. Place your index, middle, and ring fingers on either side of the spine. Rest your hands together to keep the energy frequency running evenly. The person you are working with may feel some pressure as you point your fingers down the sides of the spine.
2. Let the energy flow from your fingers where there is stagnant energy or you may want to go down the entire spine. It is okay if your hands and fingers vibrate. Keep your fingers positioned until there is a smooth and balanced flow.
3. Place both thumbs on one side of the spine closest to you and all the fingers of both hands on the opposite side of the spine. An energetic ring is formed.
4. Deep breathing by the client will help them experience inner sensations and emotions. Remember, all the components of the body hold memories of pain, traumas, and accidents. The energy will intensify and pulsate.

   Encourage the person you are working with to breath rhythmically with you at a slower pace. When the spine feels balanced, pull the hands up quickly to break through the many layers of the energy field.
5. Placing your hand over the spinal area will reseal the energy field.

Remember to always intentionally set a shield around you so that released blocked energy does not come in your auric field. You should also let cold water rinse your arms and hands.

My second surgery for cancer taught me about pain. Several nerves had to be cut in the groin area that caused lumps of fluid to form in my legs. Two months after surgery I spent a week in the hospital because the lumps of fluid were causing pain. After a week I went home because none of the doctor's procedures worked and I still had pain. By the way, none of the doctors, nurses, or the people running the tests ever touched my legs. A friend, who had very strong hands and a bottle of pear smelling lotion, massaged the lumps and my pain away. The doctor did not know the benefits of massage for moving blocked energy in the body.

This has been the year to knock down walls at my house. In order to make an 8 foot opening between my kitchen and dining room, Davin, the carpenter, and I hammered an 8 foot piece of 10 x 2 board to support the load bearing wall. We didn't have time to nail it in before it popped out. On its way down the board hit the nearby ladder, which in turn hit the inside of my leg just above the knee. I immediately began to feel heat and pain. To release the pain and avoid bruising, I started massaging my leg with my left hand and moving my right hand counter clockwise to release the energy. Amazingly, I had no bruising or pain later on.

Acupuncture is now an acceptable form of energy work because the public started going to acupuncturists and because of a 1997 published consensus statement made by the National Institute of Health that noted opioid peptides are often released during acupuncture treatments. Acupuncture is used for post-operative conditions and in pain relief for menstrual cramps, tennis elbow, fibromyalgia, and low back pain. Acupuncture, like other vibrational medicine modalities, can be helpful with headaches, addictions, carpal tunnel syndrome, asthma, and rehabilitations from stroke and accident injuries.

References

Gordon, Richard, Quantum Touch, North Atlantic Books, Berkeley, California, 2002.

Oschman, J. 2001 *Energy Medicine: The Scientific Basis,* Churchhill Livingston, London p 76.

Sisken B F, Walker UJ 1995 Therapeutic aspects of electromagnetic fields for soft tissue healing. In: Blank M (ed) Electromagnetic fields biological interactions and mechanisms. Advances in Chemistry Series 250. American Chemical Society, Washington D.C. p 277-285.

Walker M 1994. The healing powers of QiGong (Chi King) in four parts. Townsend Letter for Doctors, January, February/March, April and May issues.

12. Human Performance and Energy

The Plan for More Energy, Happiness, Health, And Success

- Connect with the Universe
- Connect with the Creator
- Connect with high-energy people
- Fill your space with living, air purifying plants
- Connect with nature, communicate and draw energy from plants
- Listen to relaxing harmonious music
- Fill your atmosphere with energy increasing aromas
- Be conscious of the colors you are wearing, the colors in your home
- Repolarize your nervous system by walking on bare grass.
- Surround yourself and wear minerals, gems, crystals, and coral to balance and harmonize your energies

Athletic, artistic, and intellectual performance is enhanced when all the body's communication channels are open and balanced. James Oschman Ph.D. *Energy Medicine, The Scientific Basis*

The Power Of The Hormones To Create Illness or Health

The Healing Secrets of the Ages, by Catherine Ponder says that the state of a person's health is strongly affected by the state of his glands because the nerve-gland areas in the body are also centers of vital mind powers. Learning to control and understand these twelve "cosmic centers" releases tremendous power into the mind and body. Ponder states that the mind power of STRENGTH is located between the adrenal glands and the loins at the small of the back.

Did you know that the adrenals are the fighters for the body and are closely connected to the sympathetic nervous system? They react strongly to unhealthy mental and emotional situations, and if they were removed you would die. Adrenaline is injected into the heart of dying patients to revive them. Ponder also says meditating upon strength will create mind and body changes. Releasing the word radiates an energy that actually contracts and expands the body's cells. Strength, she notes, is developed through sustained effort.

CHR, corticotrophin-releasing hormone, produced by the hypothalamus, is sent out by the brain to provoke responses by the adrenals, the immune system, and endocrine system. ANF also affects the pineal gland, the body's light meter and producer of melatonin, the thalamus and the pituitary gland–where much of our learning, memory, and emotions take place.

The adrenal glands produce some of your body's most essential hormones, including cortisol–too much is the response to stress, and too little creates chronic fatigue. The adrenals of my friend Susan are producing too much cortisone caused by excessive emotional demands. Susan is single, fifty something and has suffered chronic fatigue for thirty-one years. She is hardly able to work as an interior decorator because she has no energy and frequently suffers from pain, infections due to a weak immune system, and frequent migraine headaches. Of course, this creates financial problems. Doctors have yet to find one physical reason for Susan to be constantly tired, and terribly underweight. None of them has bothered to ask about her life history.

Susan was a very sensitive child of a mother who preferred her son to her daughter. To keep from being constantly hurt, Susan tried to suppress her hurt feelings, and those thousands of hurt moments became stuck in her meridians. The result is that Susan is now anorexic, and emotionally devastated.

Susan had an unhappy childhood overpowered by a domineering mother who was jealous of her strikingly tall, beautiful red-haired daughter. Her mother cut her hair short and dressed her very feminine daughter, who loved lacy dresses and Mary Jane shoes, in tailored clothes and brown saddle oxfords. To survive her mother's verbal abuse, Susan shut down her feelings as a child and this armor remains today shutting down her energy. Even though Susan argued with her mother during her teenage years, she always felt powerless because she didn't want to create problems for her passive father.

Raised in the South and taught to be an obedient, good little girl, Susan made the mistake of marrying a man who threatened to commit suicide if she didn't marry him. Her mother refused to let her call off the wedding saying that it would be embarrassing because the invitations had already been sent out. Susan decided to stay in her victim role. Her husband later divorced her, remarried, and then died of cancer.

After so many years of chronic fatigue, Susan is suffering from depression and anxiety, which in turn is causing sleep deprivation. She has migraine headaches and she takes huge amounts of medication to stop the pain that then causes her to be sick for several days. All the medications she takes cause her to lose her appetite. Susan has spent years going to doctors who have run every kind of blood test they can only to determine that they cannot find any cause for the chronic fatigue. Visits to psychiatrists have resulted in more medications that make her sicker when she takes them. Susan cries frequently because she believes friends and family blame her for her illness and they suggest various reasons that she has chosen to be sick.

I used a pendulum to determine Susan's vibrational level according to the book *Power Versus Force* by David Hawkins and she registered below 200. The majority of people on the earth unfortunately vibrate around 185 which means that they live in fear, worry, and doubt. When we store negative words, memories, and feelings in our brain cells and the other cells in our bodies, it stops the flow of energy in the meridians. Meridians are connected to the organs in the body and they are the channels through which our energy travels.

I have known Susan for over three years and, unfortunately, I think she is the perfect example of a person not taking responsibility for her healing. For example, I have told her that meditation stops migraines for many people. She says she wants to learn how to meditate but never does. I've told her that you can create your own system for stilling your mind with meditation by walking in nature, sitting by whatever kind of water you prefer, or sitting in the tub. Do whatever works for you, but make time to listen to your Creator. Susan is anorexic but she claims her thinness in inherited. Though she has some food allergies, there are still plenty of foods she can eat, but she doesn't. She is having to take shots for Vitamin B that is readily available in several foods. Susan's conversations dwell mostly on her being a victim. She repeats the episodes, remembering the conversations verbatim. As she retells the stories she is reliving the emotions. The truth is that her body is listening too and storing the words and events. Susan will never heal as long as she is playing the victim role and shutting down the energy flow in her body.

The image taken by the GDV camera, Figure 8, shows Susan in the process of releasing negative memories and feelings. Remember that the order of the subtle bodies of energy is: first level, physical (etheric), second level, emotional (astral), third level, mental, fourth level, relationships and a bridge between the physical, emotional, and mental levels and the three spiritual levels, level five, the Will of God, level six, the Mind of God, and level seven, the Love of God. The GDV camera only shows the first three levels and groups the levels 5-7 as the spiritual level.

The outline of Susan's body is a frontal view. Note that all of the energy being released above her head on the right side is a repeat of the layers closer to her body. Pink emotional energy is attached to the right side of her head and is so strong that it is pushing the physical, mental, and spiritual energy extremely out. The energy on the rest of the right side of the body is in even flow. Compare that to the left side of the body that contains several outbursts of energy. See the energy stored around the heart and in the stomach (solar plexus) area. In the second chakra, located in the hip area, is our power center in dealing with relationships and work. You will see a blob of pink emotional energy attached by a thin cord. Susan was in the process of releasing negative emotions surrounding her mother after I taught her EFT.

Our legs are powerful indicators of what has gone on and what is going on in our lives. Our memories as a baby are held in the cells and muscles of the feet. Early childhood is held in the ankle area; our teenage years' memories are held in area below the knees. The present traumas and emotions are held in the thighs and upper parts of our legs. The blue being released represents all the physical energy Susan has held bottled up. The dark purple represents her mental thoughts. There is even more dark purple in her childhood and teenage years when Susan stuffed down her memories of anger and fights with her mother. All of the pink color represents all of the bottled up emotions Susan is now releasing.

Laura is a good example of someone who became energetically out of balance. She is in her forties and had to quit her job with an advertising firm and be on worker's compensation. You can see her GDV images, Figure 9. Look at all the pink emotional energy above her head and surrounding her subtle body energy. Laura said that from the moment she arrived at work until she left she felt extreme stress. "The company pushed and pushed you to work, work, work. It was killing me" she said angrily. "I am so angry at them." Now look at Laura's GDV images, especially in the heart area, and you will see how she is holding on to a big glob of hate filled emotional energy directed toward her company. Part of her healing process will require that she release that emotion because it is depleting her energy and causing her chronic fatigue. About a year ago Laura's boyfriend broke up with her and she went into deep depression for several months. Instead of accepting the breakup and giving up trying to control the outcome, Laura became physically and emotionally sick.

She asked me and Julie, an intuitive who is able to see, via the Third Eye, inside a person's body, to help her heal. Before we began the healing we prayed for help from the healing angels. Julie was brought to tears as she saw dozens of angels entering the room through a portal. Archangel Raphael, the healer, and several other magnificent angels helped us.

Julie said that Laura's bones were very cloudy. Laura said that there was infection in her right elbow and in both knees. Julie and I worked on each of these locations by putting our hands on top of each other to increase the healing power. We began sending in white, green, pink, gold, silver, and platinum light to purify the infection and heal the bones. We stopped when Julie said that the bones appeared clear. Julie looked at Laura's right knee and saw her in another past life experience as a rider wearing a red jacket and hat and black leather gloves. She was very aggressively engaged in the hunt of a fox. When we worked on the left knee, Julie saw Laura as a very aggressive knight dressed in full armor. She prayed that Laura, as a knight in a past life, would give up her aggressive behavior.

How To Have More Mental, Physical, Emotional, And Spiritual Energy Techniques And Exercises

Energize The Whole Body

Many exercises and yoga exercises activate all the major energy pathways. Getting in and out of Hatha yoga positions presses and massages many acupressure points. When you do yoga you have the benefit of the weight of your body working for you. Also, your internal organs and glands are massaged as you bend and stretch. Yoga exercises provide overall balancing and help get rid of fatigue and tension. By stimulating the circulation of the cerebro-spinal fluid, these exercises increase our mental and physical awareness. Since most of us work at sedate jobs where we experience compression on the spine, we need quick exercises during the day to renew our energy, increase our blood and oxygen circulation, and keep us grounded so that we can focus on the tasks at hand. As the day progresses tension increases in our neck and shoulders and the muscles begin to tighten creating headaches and back problems. Stopping work for five minutes to do some simple techniques and exercises will definitely increase your energy, productivity and creativity.

How To Charge Yourself Up Energetically

Neurolinguistic programming teaches us that which we store in various emotional states in our bodies. We can learn how to automatically place powerful emotional feelings at certain areas of our body. When we want to feel that same emotional response, we tap or touch that same place to recall the emotional feeling.

Technique: The area we call the Third Eye is the location of the sixth chakra and the place we connect with the Mind of God. The Third Eye is located in the middle of your forehead, between your eyebrows and above the bridge of your nose. The next time your feel your highest energy, connected, on a high, and tremendously happy, tap your Third Eye for around 10 seconds. This will set this positive emotional feeling and you can access it whenever you desire.

Relaxation Techniques

First Technique

- Stand with your feet close together, arms loose at your side, and eyes closed.
- Relax your head and face muscles so that even your hair feels relaxed.
- Relax your shoulders by releasing all collected tension.
- Breathe naturally to relax your chest.
- Feel all the tightness released from the muscles in your back.
- Relax your arms beginning at the shoulders down to the fingertips.

- Relax your legs down to the bottoms of your feet. Release the tension out of your soles.
- Empty your mind of all thoughts.

Second Technique

- Pull the nose downward or move it in a circular motion.

Third Technique

- To create poise and tranquility use your index finger to massage on the other hand. Massage deeply under the wrinkle where the thumb connects to the hand.

If you go to a massage therapist he/she will probably do the next three techniques on you. You need to do them on yourself between visits.

Do the **Lung Press**, also called the "Metatarsal Kneading," by putting your left foot on your right knee and then wrap your left hand around the foot just below the base of the toes. See the illustration. After making a fist with your right hand, press the fingers into the fleshy part of the foot. You are going to rotate and knead both hands several times. Then squeeze with the hand that is supporting the foot and relax somewhat the hand formed into a fist. Repeat these actions with both feet.

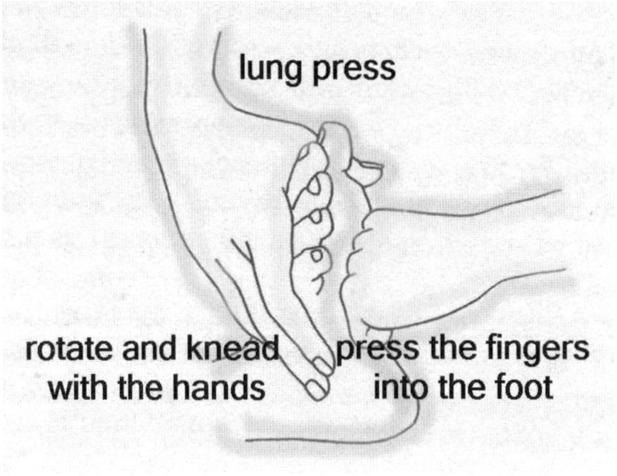

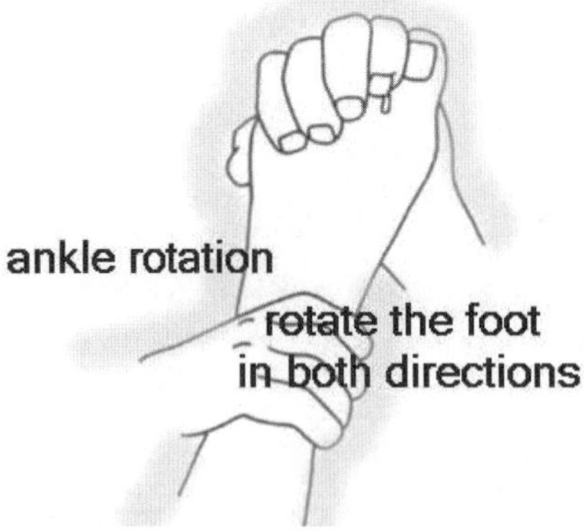

Place your hand as in the illustration with the webbing of the thumb and fingers over the ankle. Grasp the foot with the other hand and rotate in both directions. Do both feet and remember that blocked energy likes to gather in joints. So do this exercise often.

Sit anyway that is comfortable for you to be able to reach your toes. Use the thumb and index finger to grasp each toe near the base. Lift or pull each toe slightly, gently stretching and rotating it in one direction and then another. Look at the reflexology chart at the end of the book and you will see why this exercise is affecting you all the way to your head. This is a great exercise if you have sinus problems.

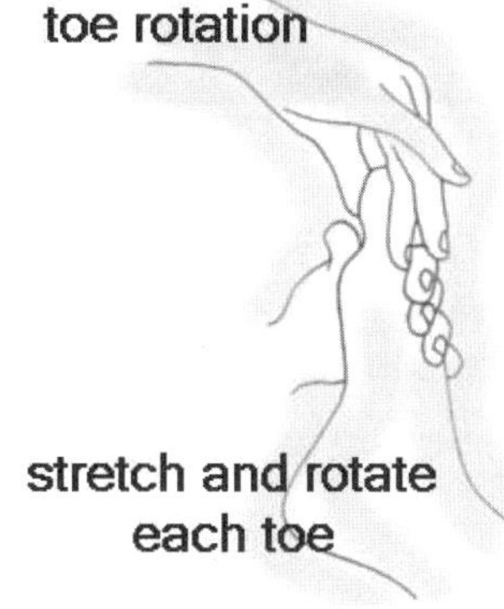

Toe Rotation
Begin with either foot. Balance your foot on your knee. Use your thumb and index finger to hold your foot below the big toe as illustrated. Grasp the big toe near the base with your other hand. Stretch each toe and rotate them by lifting slightly and pulling in one direction for several times, then in the opposite direction for several times. You move your hand over as you move to the next toe.

Exercises To Do On The Floor

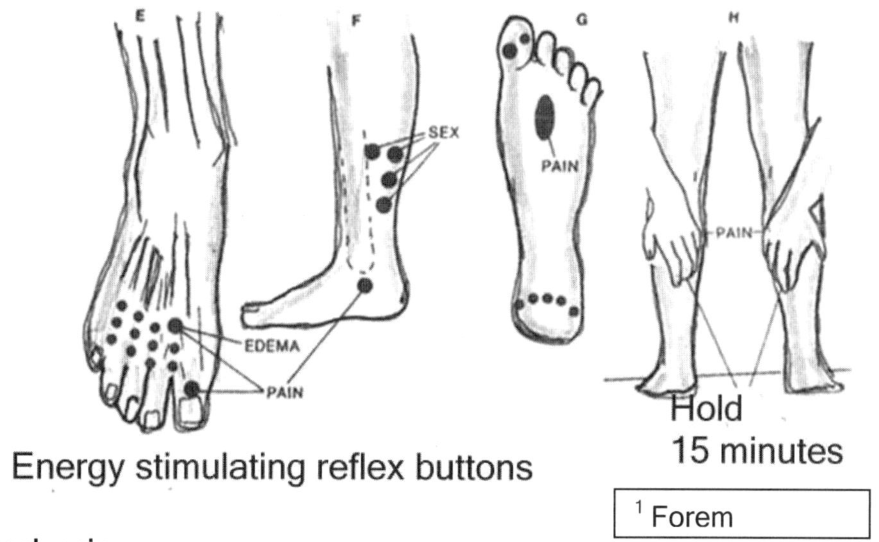

Energy stimulating reflex buttons

[1] Forem

Back pain

While lying on the floor with your legs straight, slowly move your right heel toward the chest so that the knee bends. Your fingers are together holding below the knees. Slowly raise the right knee close to the chest. Breathe in and then as you exhale, push the knee into the hands. There won't be movement. Inhale, relaxing the knee so that it drops to the chest. Repeat twice. Repeat with left leg and then both legs.

Posture

The pelvic area is the recipient area of the first and second chakras energy. You can look at a person's pelvic posture and know their sense of power and courage. If they are holding onto emotional traumas, old memories and unexpressed and unprocessed feelings, the pelvic area will be tightened and tilted. The following pelvic exercises will make your chiropractic adjustments last longer.

Pelvic Lift

While lying on the floor with the knees bent, lift the buttocks by pushing down with the feet. Move your various lower back muscles to strengthen the pelvic area. Lower one vertebra at a time until the back is on the floor.

Pelvic Area Exercises

Sit on the floor with the knees bent and the soles of the feet touching. Place your hands on the insides of the knees, inhale and, as you exhale with pursed lips, push the legs into the hands with gentle force. When you inhale, the legs will automatically lower. Do the exercise at least three more times and then allow the body to rest.

Daily Energy Management

How To Protect Yourself From The Energy You Are Releasing

Energy has all the attributes discussed in Chapter One. It is real though you can't see it; and though it is neither good nor bad, it can have a low frequency. You don't want that energy released on to you. Here are different ways you can protect yourself.

Remember the medically documented cases of adults and children who have healed themselves of cancer with the power of visualization. In the same way, you can visualize a protective shield placed around your body and auric field that released energy cannot penetrate. You direct white light, containing all the colors, or different colors (energy) to fill the shield. Another visualization is to imagine a white plastic bag surrounding your body to protect you. You can't suffocate in this kind of bag! It is also wise to visualize a clear ball of protection all around your house.

Red Morris teaches the following technique in her workshops to prevent taking toxins and negative energy into your body. When you are pulling energy out of a body caused by a trauma, you can visualize PVC pipe going through your body from one hand to the other and the energy, which appears visually in different colors, probably black, brown, or gray, moving through that PVC pipe and not entering your body. You may feel the energy as being prickly, slimy, slow moving, or any number of descriptions. Some people will even be able to smell the energy.

Energizing Techniques

Daily Energizing Plan

- Sitting on too soft a seat or chair weakens our muscles causing our minds to be less alert and aware.
- Stay away from energy draining people (drama queens)
- Protect yourself from sending and receiving negative thoughts
- Do not listen to loud and inharmonious music
- Certain colors: Don't sleep on black, brown, or gray sheets because they will absorb the energy you are trying to regain during sleep. Also dry your sheets in the sunshine to receive energy while you are sleeping.
- Massage and pinch the skin that is the web between the thumb and the forefinger, called the Adjoining Valley Acupressure Point. If there is soreness, continue until it is gone. This will activate your life force energy.

What to do daily

- Use a body brush to daily scrub your skin to remove old dead skin cells.
- Purchase a special razor at beauty supply stores to scrap the dead calluses off the feet. Massage your feet every night to heal the body's organs, activate your nerves, relieve tension, and open the channels of energy.
- Due to the changes in the earth atmosphere we need to know how to protect ourselves from harmful UV rays.

Dr. Charles McWilliams in his book, *Photobiotic,* recommends the following filters to protect the eyes–gray tones for partial sunlight subdued by cloud cover, frost white/opaque filters for full sunlight. Sun gazing, he says, is preferable during sunrise or sunset for no more than one minute through a chromoviewer.

Massaging The Head Area

- Lightly tap your head with a wire brush.
- Use the handle of a clean spoon to press on the top of both sides of the tongue.
- Increase energy by pressing the lymph nodes under the chin with the thumbs. This also prevents wrinkles by increasing hormones.
- Massage the thyroid gland. Directions two pages further.
- Begin at the bottom of your ear and pull lightly along the edge. Roll the edge between your thumb and index finger. When you get to the ridge directly above the ear canal, lift up firmly.

Releasing Anger Held In The Jaw

We hold anger in our jaws that stops the flow of energy. Where the jaw hinges to the skull is the reflex point for the pelvic area, a major place in the body where we store emotional traumas, old memories and unexpressed and unprocessed feelings. Rub out tension with gentle circular motions as you open and close your mouth. You can increase your energy by yawning or making the "a-h-h-h" sound. You can see many people automatically pull down on their facial tissue. Any stroking in this area from the lower lip or following the jaw line going on down to the Adam's apple will release blocked, negative energy.

Etheric Vitality

The etheric level of the body is the first subtle (physical) body. It is located just a few inches beyond the skin so you can feel if there is a disturbance or free flowing of the energy field. The person who is going to move the energy should scan the body of the person with the blocked energy. You will probably be intuitively lead about which way to move your hands. Run your hands over the meridians to see if they are blocked. Feel if there are any cords or strands of energy leaving the etheric body. You can use your pendulum and ask that it swing "yes" when you have located a cord or strand. Also check out the chakras. You can ask the pendulum if the chakras are in alignment and to what degree they are open or closed.

Make a tape of the following meditation so that you are not interrupted by reading. If someone is sending you energy, they should place their hands on your head. At the end of the meditation both of you will feel centered and connected to the Universal energy.
Ideally, the person receiving the energy is lying on a massage table or bed without a headboard with a pillow underneath the knees. The meditation can be done sitting in a chair.

1. The energy sender should place the palm of their hands on the crown chakra of the energy receiver for around seven minutes. As you become more sensitive to energy you will know when the body is energetically open.
2. With your eyes closed or opened, repeat to yourself, "I focus all of my attention on the soles of my feet, nothing else but the soles of my feet. I hold my full attention on the soles of my feet."
3. "Now I move the energy upward. I feel the movement to the ankles. I am aware of only the soles of my feet and my ankles, nothing else. I hold my attention on my ankles and feet"
4. "Now I move the energy upward from my ankles to my knees. I feel the energy moving upward as I inhale and become aware of my knees, ankles, and feet. I hold in my awareness only the feeling of my knees, ankles, and feet. Nothing else enters my mind."

5. "I again breathe the energy from the knees into the hips and feel the energy move into the hips and pelvis. I focus my attention on my legs, hips, and pelvis. Now I breathe the light energy outward and surround my entire legs in glowing white light. I feel the healing white light all around both legs and my pelvis."
6. "I now breathe the energy into the abdomen and imagine a nebula of blue-white light rotating clockwise in my stomach."
7. "I breathe the energy into my heart and imagine a nebula of rose-white light, swirling clockwise in my heart. I focus entirely on the nebula of rose-white light watching it as it swirls within my heart."
8. "I breathe the energy into my throat and imagine a nebula of orange-white light within my throat area. I watch intensely the nebular of orange-white light within my throat as it swirls clockwise. Then I watch this nebula of intense light separate and move to each shoulder then down my arms into my palms, activating my healing hands to do the work I am about to do. I imagine the white light surrounding my arms and hands."

Physical Activities To Increase Energy

- Walk backwards to unscramble energies.
- Release neck and shoulder tension by doing shoulder lifting and head rolls.

Energy Principle: The level of your breathing determines your life energy.

Correct Breathing Techniques

- Breathe consciously to get centered.
- Breathe deeply to aid emotional release due to fear.

Benefits of abdominal breathing: calmness and relaxation, increased circulation of the blood, relief of abdominal tension, strengthens abdominal muscles Learn to breathe with the whole body.

The Importance And Benefits Of Good And Proper Posture

Negative emotional states, depression, sadness, indifference, fear, withdrawal, and pride create poor posture.
Do exercises to stretch and lift the spine upward.
Misalignment creates compression of organs decreases power of mind, body, and emotions.

Hypertension

Hypertension is usually caused by a blocked first (root) chakra. Use the chakra clearing techniques.

Ulcers And Stomach Problems

- Press on the stomach reflex with one finger

- While lying on your back, if you feel a pulse when you press on your naval with several fingers, you have stomach problems. Stimulate the area with pressure until the pain is relieved.
- The medulla oblongata is located where the base of your skull and your neck meet. Find the hollow spot in the middle. Pressing and massaging it will give you stress relief and unlimited energy.

- Place your hands across each other in the middle of your head about two inches your hairline. Gently use your fingers to massage all the way to the back of the head.

Headaches

The June/July edition of Massage & Bodywork Magazine had an interesting five-page article on headaches. It said that fifty million Americans have chronic headaches. Twenty-eight million of them, mostly women, get debilitating migraines that cause incalculable pain, suffering, and financial problems. Employers and employees spend more than a billion dollars each on medical treatment for chronic headaches. An estimated $13 billion is lost in productivity due to inefficient and missed work. The author, Jan Mundo has been helping with people with headaches since 1970 and has created the Mundo program in which 97% of the people taking the six-week course said, "They felt more in control and had greater understanding of their headache pattern." Tension headaches, she says, can be relieved by exercise, hot/cold pack application, meditation, breathing, qi gong, yoga, stretching, massage, and bodywork. You can reach Jan at www.headachehealing.com. Medications to treat headaches often cause dizziness, loss of appetite, nausea, vomiting, diarrhea or constipation, gastric bleeding, and sedation, not to mention an increased risk of stroke.

Tension Headaches And Jaw Tension

When the body is in a state of tension, movement, breathing, and feeling are constricted. Each part of the body constricts in different ways. For instance, people who are neurotic have tense scalps and foreheads that lead to headaches. People who chronically raise their eyebrows and contract the muscles in the forehead create deep wrinkles and severe headaches. Tension in the back of the neck tightens the muscles below the occipital bones.

Look at the GDV camera images and you will see that most of the examples have pink emotional energy at the back of the head. Our history of thinking and reacting reflects in our faces. People create tight jaws showing anger, down turned mouths showing despair, weak chins showing weakness, and stiff upper lips showing compulsiveness.

Massage the traditional headache points: crown pull, forehead pull
Hold the head using one hand on the front and one hand on the back of the head to relieve headaches
Use the visualization techniques in the book to increase blood flow

Do Exercises For Relaxation
The Inner Smile: Smiling has a powerful effect on the body's organs because it helps the body release mood altering hormones. It really does work! Sitting on the edge of a chair with your hands clasped and eyes closed, permits you to go within. Begin by picturing a smiling face in front of you that is sending you radiant energy to the middle of your eyebrows and your eyes. The middle of the head contains the hypothalamus, pineal, and pituitary glands, all part of the endocrine system that produce melatonin, seratonin, and ACTH. Also smile at your brain and then down your spinal column.

As your own face smiles, you can direct the spiraling warm energy in through your mid-eyebrow. Now smile at the thymus gland, located above the heart, where important chemicals and hormones are produced to affect our immune system, and the heart. Smile at all the organs: lungs, liver, pancreas, spleen, kidneys, and sexual organs. Draw in more smiling energy through your eyes and send it down the esophagus, stomach, small intestine, large intestine, bladder, and urethra. Lastly, bring your attention to your eyes, again seeing the smiling face sending your energy. Smile down your whole body.

The Importance of Massage And Self-Massage For Good Health And Energy
Boosts your immune system
Increases the circulation of lymph throughout your body to fight infection and unhealthy organisms
Releases body stiffness, repairs and rejuvenates your body

Rid Yourself Of Energy Depleters

- Stop people who are "energy vampires" Stop mental negativity that creates stagnate body toxins.
- States of fear, guilt self-doubt and worry deplete your energy.
- Get rid of old baggage that is weighing you down.
- Quit paying the "energy price" of placing judgments on people and events.
- Stop mental and emotional anxiety that keeps you on the bottom.
- Learn what the "twins" anger and revenge cost you in "green" energy (money), mentally, physically, emotionally, and spiritually.

Personal Revitalizing Techniques

- Take personal responsibility for your life.
- Become "whole-seeing".
- State positive affirmations.

- Find out what Aromatherapy fragrances replenish your energy.
- Use full spectrum lighting.
- Decide which colors in your environment and your clothes will give your energy.

Do Meditation To Release Unwanted Energy

1. Sit so that your spine is straight.
2. Tilt your head slightly.
3. Place your palms on your knees or in front of you on your legs.
4. You can also have one palm on top of the other with the thumbs slightly touching.
5. Gently close your eyes and clear your mind of all thoughts.
6. Breathe naturally and then forget about your breathing.
7. Keep your mind empty.
8. If a thought enters your mind, gently release it.
9. Begin with about 5 minutes and increase to 15 minutes.

Meditation Posture

Do meditation to keep major organs and endocrine glands healthy
Stop patterned, judgmental, linear, and past thinking with meditation

Watch your breath: This technique brings relaxation through contemplation. Find a comfortable position and close the eyes. Concentrate on the breath without any intention of changing it in any way. "Watch" what it does. It will adjust without conscious effort.

Alternate Nostril Breathing- This is a yogic breathing exercise that facilitates balance of the right and left nostrils, brain hemispheres and sympathetic and parasympathetic nervous systems. During the day we normally switch breathing for time periods (when healthy, every 2 hours), so that one nostril and then the other predominates. The right (Yang, male side) nostril is activating in its effect and the left (Yin, feminine side) nostril is relaxing. Breathe and "watch" the breath. Determine which nostril you are currently using. Next, purposefully alternate nostrils by using the thumb and forefinger to close off one nostril and then the other by pressing just above the flared portion of the nostril. Close off the right nostril with the thumb. Inhale and then exhale through the left nostril. Switch so the forefinger is closing off the left nostril. Inhale and exhale through the right nostril. Continue this process and notice the effects.

Benefits

- Re-establishes balanced breathing, concentrates attention

Balancing Postures To Increase Concentration And Focus

You probably already do postures naturally that help your concentration. Some examples are: resting of the forehead on the thumb and forefinger in deep thought, placing the hands behind the skull when lying on the back, and crossing ankles while sitting. Here are some new ones.

Sensory Balance Posture

In this posture the body is comfortably arranged to resemble the shape of the Yin evolutionary energy. This can be done when sitting in a chair, either by bringing the legs up, or by extending them out crossing at the ankles, with hands lightly clasped in front. This posture is associated with cultivating receptivity, and is sometimes used as a meditation position. Because the arms and ankles are "crossed over", a connection is made of transverse (side-to side) currents which inhibits further incoming stimulation from the outside.
Sit cross-legged and rest the hands on the front of the opposite side calf area. Close the eyes and relax. At first, breathe consciously, with a deep inhale and exhale; then forget the breathing and rest quietly. Allow the internal energy currents to come to balance.

Benefits

- Soothing, relaxing
- Rejuvenating for the senses, especially when "overloaded." The posture integrates sensory input with mental absorption.
- Useful for meditative practices, or "getting away from it all." Helps bring the attention inward. [2] Stone

Cook's Hook-ups

This posture comes from Education Kinesiology. It restores balance to disturbed energy circuits. Sit comfortably with the legs crossed at the ankles. Cross the arms over the chest with hands under the armpits, thumbs out and up. Hold this position until you "feel complete." Some people can feel the

actual balancing taking place as tingles, shudders, throbs or other sensation or movements happen. Stay in part one until you feel this energy release.
[3] Walther.

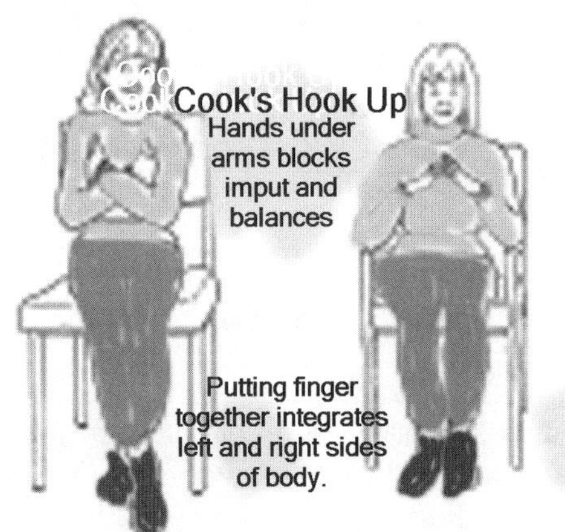

For part two, uncross the legs and arms and place the fingertips together in a "rainbow arch." Many people feel the tingling of energy crossing the fingers and balancing.

A variation is to "double cross" the arms and turn them under or "leg cross" while seated, with one leg over the other sides' knee. Hold the ankle with one hand then the ball of the foot with the other hand, so that the forearms are crossed. It connects the upper and lower bodies.

In the double cross (2) you cross the wrists and turn the palms facing each other and then clasp the fingers. Next, turn the hands under until they rest on the chest.

Benefits

- General relaxation and concentration, release of tension, removes distractions and allows integration of mind and emotions Walther

Buttons

Learn and use the next five exercises when you want to re-energize, and have feelings of clarity, balance and peak performance on all levels. The exercises require holding acupuncture points; some call the "buttons," on different meridians. The meridians relate to specific organs that were listed in the chapters on meridians. When we are tired, confused, or performing poorly, the meridians are out of balance. Hold the points only briefly with light pressure.

Earth Buttons

Feel more stable, practical and grounded

Benefits

- Good for precise activities like mathematical calculations or balancing a check book

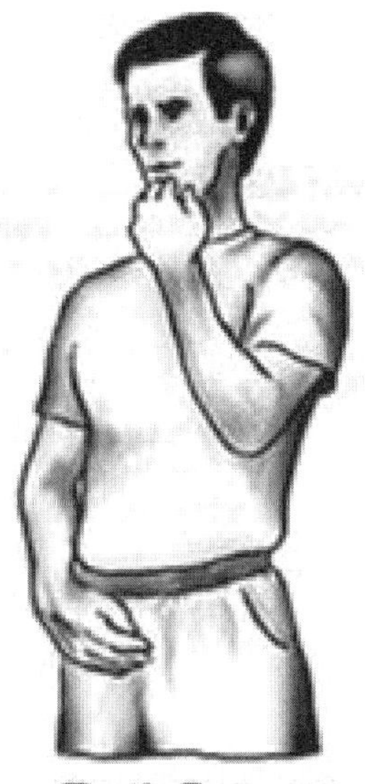
Earth Buttons

Place two fingers of one hand directly above the pubic bone and two fingers of the other hand just below the lower lip. Stimulate with the two upper fingers and then gently hold both contacts. Breathe deeply, visualizing the movement of energy up the center of the body. Add looking up and down with your eyes (without moving the head) to assist the top-bottom connection. When "complete" remove the hands from their contacts. Repeat with the opposite hand holding the points. Finish by looking all around in a downward direction: downward eye placement activates the brain's top/bottom dimension. This emphasizes the feeling of stability and anchors in a feeling of being grounded. [4] Stone

- Helps restore proper energy flow to the Governing meridian that comes up the center of the body from the tailbone over the head to directly above the upper lip.
- Helps with back-front brain integration, controlling such activities as quick decision making.

Space Buttons: Energy movement and balance

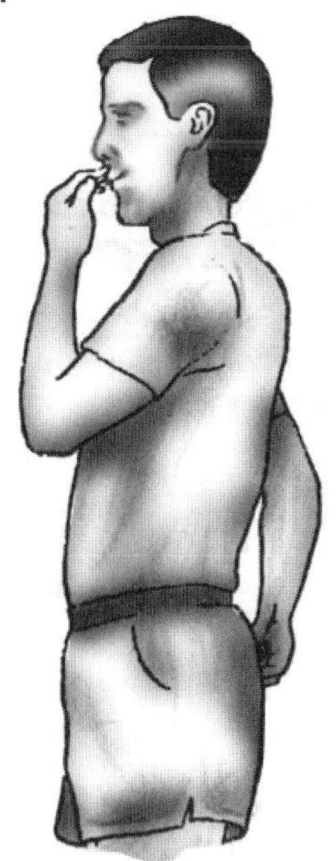
Space Buttons

At the very base of the lower back and spine put two fingers of one hand on the hard bony area where the coccyx and the sacrum join. Then place two fingers of the other hand between the upper lip and nose. Stimulate with two upper fingers and then hold. Breathe deeply, and visualize a movement of energy up the back and over the top of the head and to the lip area. Repeat with the opposite hand holding the points. Remember how eye movement shows what you are thinking. Finish by looking all around in an upward direction. This emphasizes the upward direction and anchors a feeling of the expansiveness of space. [5] Stone

Brain Buttons

Because the navel is a linking point for all the acupuncture meridians, this exercise like many others, has you place one hand so that it covers it. With the other hand, touch on either side of the breastbone just under the clavicle (collar bone.) In acupuncture these points are called K27 and are the top of the kidney meridian. Use two fingers to contact one side and the thumb to contact the other. Rub with the upper hand to stimulate then stop and hold. Most of the time you will find this area is painful when stimulated because it holds blocked energy.

Benefits

- Integrates left and right brains.
- Restores energy flow in the kidney meridian.
- Facilitates activities that require total brain function such as reading or using eyes in concentrated study.
- Open the mental perspective when you feel overly focused on detail or "one sided" on an issue.

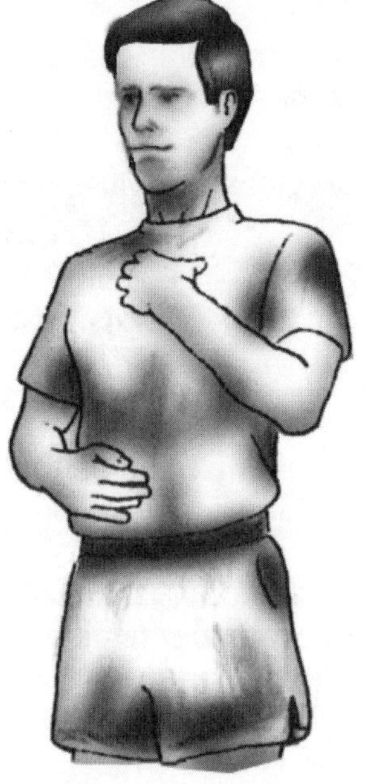

Brain Buttons

This is a three-part posture that does meridian balance. In all three parts, hold one hand so that the fingertips surround the navel. For right/left balance, stimulate and hold the same acupuncture points as brain buttons, on each side of the sternum. For top/bottom balance, stimulate and hold with the thumb below the lower lip and two fingers above the upper lip. For back/front balance, stimulate and hold directly behind the navel on the back.

Benefits

- Balance of the top-bottom, left-right, back-front dimensions of energy flow and brain function.

Balance Buttons

As you did with other exercises, place one hand with the fingertips covering the navel. Move the two fingers of the other hand about one inch behind the bottom of the ear where the base of the skull indents. As you breathe deeply, visualize the energy moving up from the navel to the head, holding for a minute or so. Do one side, then switch hands and do the other. Sense the effect on the body and stop when you feel complete. You will be amazed at the effect.

Benefits

- Links the navel with points affecting balance, creating a state of relaxed body, alert mind.
- A good stress release break for computer workers

Positive Points

Contact the forehead lightly on both sides, just above the eyebrow and midway between the hairline and brow. Use either, both hands, two fingers on each side, or one hand, thumb one side and two fingers on the other. A slight bulge, the frontal eminence, is the exact location. Holding this area of the forehead helps to process emotional stress from past and present. These are reflex points for emotional centers of the brain.

Benefits

- Ability to approach goals with less worry and emotion. Makes it easier to face situations that have been upsetting
- Defuses emotional tension

Releasing Nervous And Emotional Tension In The Head and Shoulders

The neck is affected by experiences relating to self-expression and making choices. When a person holds back speaking their truth, the energy of the neck is blocked. When the person is very angry their neck stays red. Negative emotions such as pride and shame will create constriction. The throat chakra is where we express the Will of God so our spiritual motives are manifest here. Because the throat is an instrument of sound, this area greatly benefits from sound healing.

Most of us carry tension in our shoulders because we carry our experiences relating to desire, hope, and ambition in this area. We become frustrated by our unfulfilled desires and unfilled expectations of ourselves and others.

Foot Reflexology For Neck And Shoulders

This is a good warm-up exercise for the exercises that follow. Reflexes to the neck are located in the “neck” of each toe, especially the big toe. When you massage these areas and the areas all over the foot, feel for tender spots that are sore. To release energy gently push in and hold for a count of eight, with full breathing. Put your fingers between the toes as the illustration shows and pull and stretch the toes as close to the leg as possible. Also press the areas at the bases of the toes.

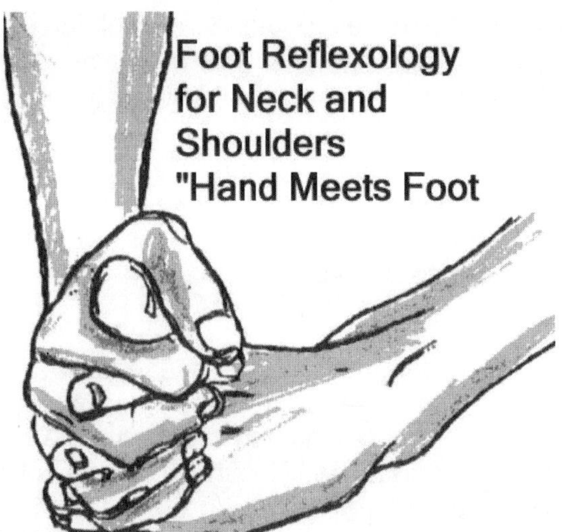

Second exercise: You may have to pull the toes apart to make space for the fingers which should be close to the base of the toes. (Check out illustration). Breathe consciously for a minute before you stretch the toes backward and forward and then rotating.

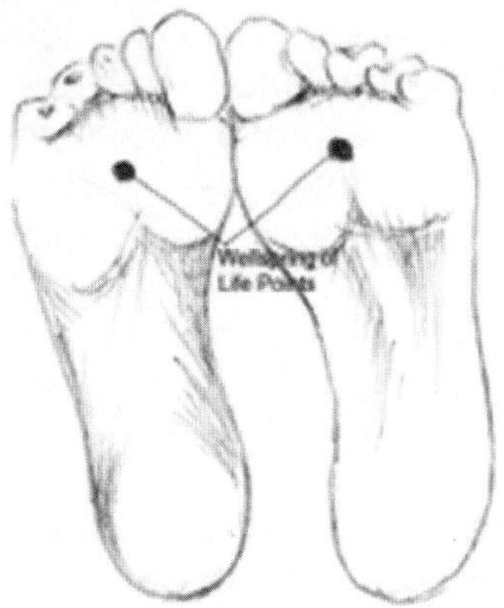

Massage the Wellspring of Life Points to renew energy all over the body.
Bridge Reflex

These points relate to the junction of neck and shoulders. When this area of the body is blocked, the brachial nerve plexus is inhibited and breathing and relaxation suffer. These points are also used to release eye tension.

Take a position in which the head can rest on the hands: squatting is best or seated at a table. Place the curled fist of one hand inside the other, leaving the thumbs extending out and next to each other. Use these two thumbs to contact the area just to the side of where the bridge of the nose and the ridge above the eyes meet.

Benefits

- Helps restore balance in breathing and movement of gas
- Good to counteract dizziness after exercise
- Release shoulder-neck tension and allows the circulation to balance between the head and the rest of the body.

Another good exercise is to use your thumbs and make small circular movements where the eyebrow meets the bridge of the nose. You may feel some tender spots on either side of the nose that need further attention.

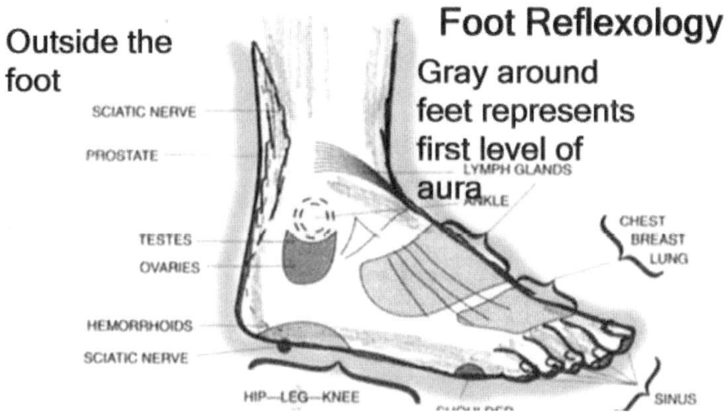

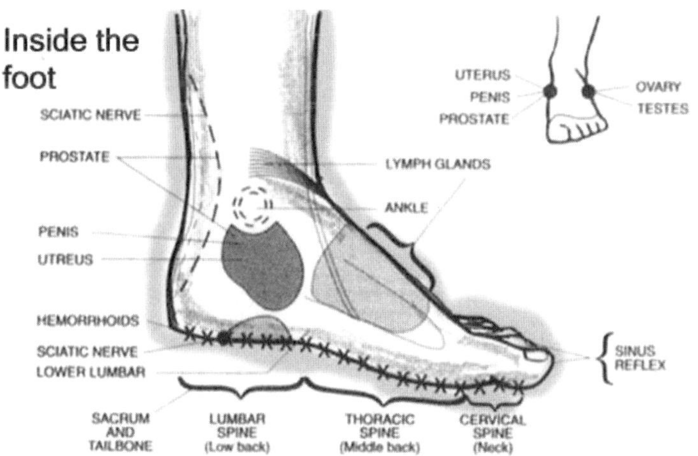

Hand Reflexology: You can activate energy in the body at specific points by massaging with your thumb. Activate energy all over the body by massaging all the areas.

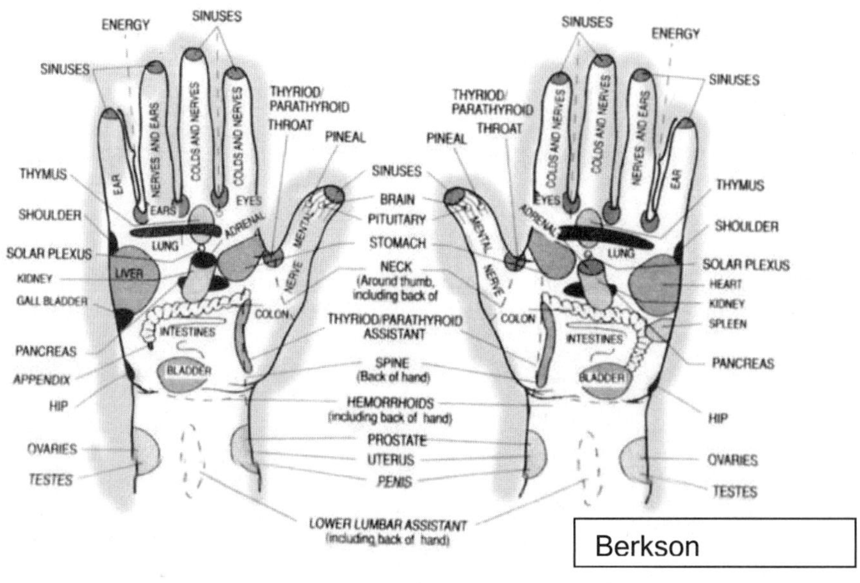

Berkson

Ridge Meets Bridge

The eyebrow line is a reflex to the shoulders. Gently use your thumbs to press with small circular movements. If you find a tender spot, concentrate on those areas.

Neck And Shoulder Tapping
For shoulders, tap with the fingertips in the hollow of the shoulder. For the neck, tap an acupuncture point in the stomach midway between the navel and the xiphoid process (the cartilage tip at the bottom of the sternum). These points are on the appropriate acupuncture meridians. When finished, take a quiet moment to feel the results on neck and shoulder area.

The Owl
The exercise releases the shoulder and neck area, especially the trapezius and brachial plexus. Grab the fleshy part on top of your shoulder and maintain a firm yet sensitive grip. Inhale and turn your head toward that shoulder until you can look back over it. Exhale and turn you head toward the other shoulder. Repeat this several times and then return the head to the middle. Now inhale and life your chin up. Exhale and lower the chin toward your chest. After doing this several times, return the head to the middle, relax your grip and feel the change in the shoulder area. Then, repeat the sequence with the other shoulder.
Variations
Grab the shoulder and again rotate the head toward the shoulder you are gripping. Continuing this firm grasp, lift the arm out on that side with the thumb up and move the arm back behind you. Then turn the head back the other way.

Channeling
Place one hand on someone's body, the other preferably on the ground but a floor will do. Imagine the energy in the core of the energy flowing through the hand on the ground or floor. Just as there is an abundant blue sky, there is energy everywhere in the sky. Visualize a funnel above your head with lots of energy flowing through it. Visualize that energy as different colors or the white light because it contains all the colors. You can regulate the amount of energy you want to flow through your body to the person you are touching. Be sure to mentally close off the connection between you and the other person before you remove your hands. Always wash your hands in cold running water after any energy work.

Neck and Shoulder Tension Relief
Position yourself as shown in the illustration. Rock back and forth thrusting your chest forward and arching back. On the inhale rock back and round the shoulders so that there is a lengthening across the shoulders. You chest will be expanded with a full breath. As you rock forward you will exhale and pull your shoulders back. Keep your chin tucked in. You will feel the tension released from the shoulders, neck and upper back. This exercise is good for people with bronchial and asthmatic conditions.

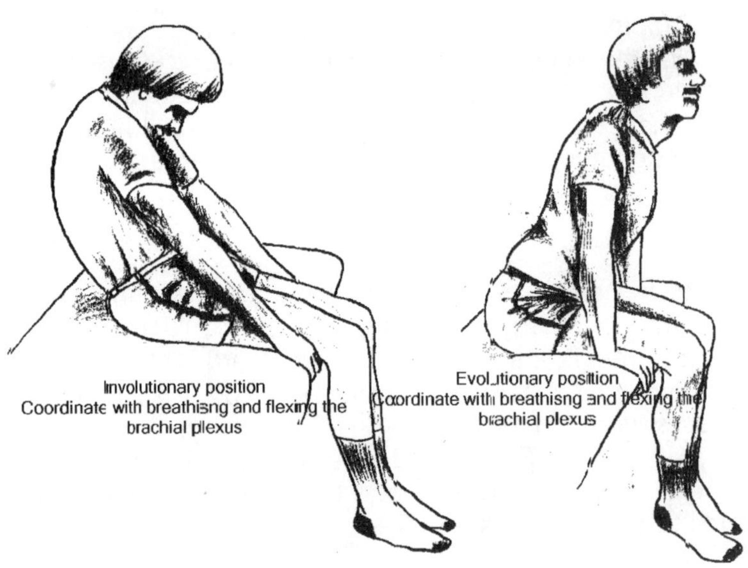

How To Drain Pain

Ask the person you are working on where the pain is or you can use your pendulum. Place your left hand where you find pain or blocked energy. Hold your right hand away from your body and downward so when you pull out the energy, the earth will absorb it. Visualize the PVC pipe going through your arms and the energy flowing through it. Hold the position until the sensation of pulling energy stops and you don't feel pressure.

When you pull out energy, you must replace it with new energy. Reverse the hand positions but this time hold the left hand upward to bring in the healing energy from the Universal Energy. You can use your pendulum to ask which colors you need to send in.

Using Your Hands To Energize

Make fists with your hands; relax your wrists. Use your hands to gently tap all over your head for thirty seconds.

Buff your fingernails.

Massaging The Stomach Area

Press on the navel with any finger for seven seconds.

Press on 4th toe for pelvic area tension

Thymus Gland

The thymus gland is located in the middle of the chest above the heart, two inches below the K-27 points, and it guards against infection and cancer growth. If you ignore your body's needs, the thymus becomes sluggish and is thrown into disarray.

Thymus Thump

Thump lightly and quickly on the thymus 20 times everyday to produce cancer-killing cells and help it monitor and regulate the body's energy flow. Tapping the area over your thymus gland is a simple technique that will stimulate all of your energies, boost your immune system and increase your strength and vitality. This technique can help you if you are feeling bombarded by negative energies, catching a cold, fighting an infection, or if your immune system is otherwise challenged. **The first two dots are the K-27 points, the next dot is the thymus gland, and the two dots below the breast are the spleen neurolymphatic points.**

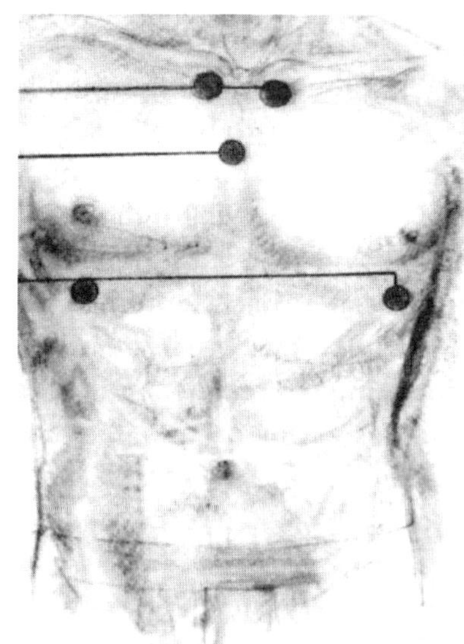

K-27

Thymus Point

Spleen Neural
Lymphatic
Points

Take the tip of your tongue and press it in the roof your mouth above your teeth to activate the thymus reflex point. Smile to activate the thymus gland. After tapping the K-27 points, move your fingers down a couple of inches and into the center of your sternum. As you breathe deeply, firmly tap your thymus point with the four fingers of each hand for about 20 seconds.

Heart

Because the heart controls the mind, our energy and health are determined by the attitudes and actions of the heart.

Massage the muscles on the left arm each day because this is a major source of blood to the heart. Begin at the wrist and release the tension in the muscles that are squeezing your arteries. Press the muscles from side to side with the tips of your fingers

Place the fingers in the center of the body above your breasts and loosen the tight muscles. Especially spend time on the muscles and lymph glands under your arms.
Place both hands on your shoulders by your neck on the front of your body and massage out tightness.
You can prevent a heart attack until the paramedics arrive by pinching on either the left little finger or the left little toe of a person with a malfunctioning heart.

Foot Massage
Big toe: This is where the hallucis tendon originates. It is connected to the pelvic area where we store emotions and unexpressed feelings. Use your fingers to find the thick tendon running up the inside of the leg just behind the ankle. Push your fingers in to find it and continue pushing steadily to get the energy flowing. If you seek balance in your body, push lightly; if you seek change, push moderately.
Press on the tendons on to of the foot. Massage around the ball of your foot. **Each tendon corresponds to an energy center in the body.** Use your thumb to find the tendon in each toe and then use pressure to move the tendon. You've probably had massage therapists bend your toes back. You need to do it for yourself between visits. Bend each toe back as far as it feels comfortable and then inhale and relax. On the exhale push the toe into the fingers. Inhale and relax and gently repeat the process except bend the toe further. (Check the illustration on Foot Reflexology)
Energizing And Healing Techniques
Allergies: Adjoining Valley
Arthritis: Adjoining Valley
Blocked Meridians
Trace the meridians every day
Governing meridian: restore proper energy flow
Space buttons: Moves energy that comes up the center of the body from the tailbone over the head to directly above the upper lip.
Kidney meridian: Brain buttons
Carpal Tunnel Syndrome: Repetitive strain injuries such as carpal tunnel may be caused by problems in the wrist, elbow, shoulder, neck, knee, foot, or lower back.
Directions

1. Send energy into the wrists.
1. Send energy to the seventh cervical and the first thoracic vertebra
2. Send energy in the lower back.
3. The sinuses are located at the ends of the toes in foot reflexology. Put lotion on your feet and toes and rub them each night.

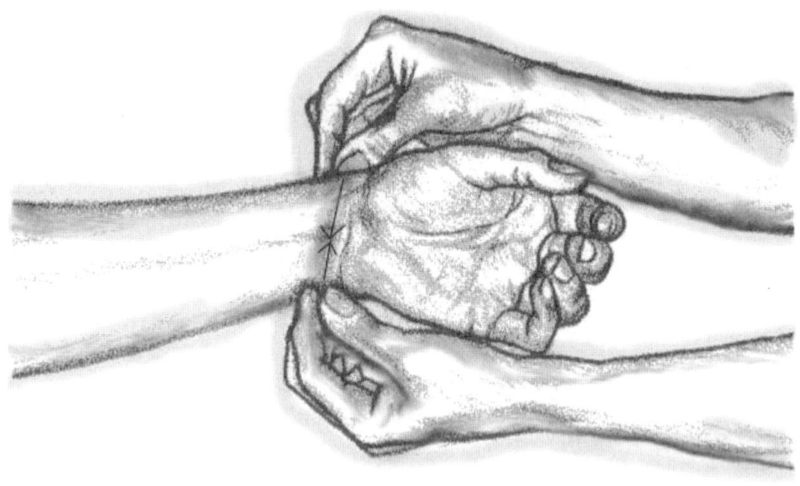

Constipation: Adjoining Valley
Coughing: Press the top of the mouth with a clean thumb to stop coughing.
Eyes: Move your index and middle fingers slowly across the muscles located on the bony ridge below the eyes until there is no tightness or pain.
Cross the fingers of each hand over each other. Put the palms over the eyes and hold them for a few seconds. Do this several times a day, especially if you work on a computer.
Place your hands gently over the eyes and send in the energy.
Gallbladder: Use your third, fourth and fifth fingers to flatten your ears forward. Use your index finger five times to create a tapping sound.
Headache: Find where the skull meets the neck at the back of the head. Place your index and middle fingers in the indented spaces about two inches from the middle of the neck and massage. This will warm and energize your body. This is a pressure point
Indigestion: Gently pull your hair. Place your fingers two inches above the eyebrows, vertically in the middle of your forehead and slowly pull across the forehead.
Insomnia: Back Curl– This exercise is to help you relax. Lie on the bed or floor with the legs out straight. Keep you feet on the floor while you slowly slide the heels and bend the knees. Bring the knees close to the chest and hold them with the arms. Rock from side to side, occasionally stopping to relax.
Pain relief: Renew energy by removing pain– We tend to do what's called "Double Hand Balancing" naturally when we are in pain. The left hand is placed over the right hand where there is pain or where you want to energize and balance major or minor chakras.
Magnetic pain drain: Useful for acute pain and congestion in the energy field.

Shoulders: Place your hand under the armpit and send energy into the shoulder. Send energy to the sutures, the occipital ridge, neck, lower back, and hips.
Sinus: Place your fingertips above the eyebrows (some people may have a ridge in their forehead,) and the thumbs on either side of the nose, above the nostrils. Massage where the toes join the foot.
Do adjoining Valley Pressure Point or Welcome Fragrance
TMJ: The Temporal-Mandibular Joint is where the jawbone connects to the skull. Problems occur when it comes it comes out of alignment. You can hear popping when you move your jaw from side to side. The energy sender should place their thumb, index, and middle finger in a tripod position on both sides of the face and send in energy.
The Pyramid: Stand with your feet wider apart than the width of your shoulders. Position your feet at 90-degree angles.
Lean forward in a beginning crouching position, putting the palms of the hands just above the knees. Place the fingers on the outside and thumbs on the inside. Make your shoulders hold the weight of the body with your back and arms straight. Move your body from side to side of up and down lightly.

How To Stay High Energy Even If You Are Working At A Computer All Day

You can look at your face, neck, and shoulder area to see the effects of working at a computer or doing a desk job all day. The eyes show your tiredness. The stress of the day's challenges shows all over your face, in the raised shoulders, and in the tense, tightened muscles at the back of your neck. Here's some things you can do during the day so that you have energy when you go home at night.

1. Gently massage your head and neck area. It feels especially good to massage the head with your fingertips. Your can rub and massage the shoulder area more firmly. Do the neck and shoulder tapping exercise. Do the hand under the armpit exercise on the preceding page.
2. Massage both hands one at a time using the opposite hand beginning with the fingers and moving up the arm. I have used my GDV camera several times so show the benefits of a few minutes massage to get the energy flowing again.
3. To relieve a headache, neck stiffness and pain caused by eyestrain, emotional stress and tension or poor posture do the Wind Pool Gb 20 pressure point.

Deep Breathing

Deep breathing increases your oxygen, blood flow, and your chi (energy). Long and deep breaths increase your oxygen and releases pain and tension. You may have heard the saying "breathe into the pain". Remember, your body is always trying to communicate with you, and you will know what the message is if you are open and conscious. You know how you get information in the shower or riding down the road? Well, a message will come to you about why you feel the weight of the world on your back, why there is tension at the back of your neck, or a sick feeling in your stomach.

The Effect of Stress On Your Energy Levels
Stress suppresses the thymus gland and as a result, the body's defenses are impaired. However, two people can experience the exact same stress and their health be affected entirely differently. Our perception of the stress in addition to our belief systems and attitudes determines how the stress will affect us. We have a tendency to respond to all the events that happen in our lives in characteristic patterns. When our consciousness is presented with an idea or a group of thoughts, our attitudes of our sense of power or weakness determine what emotions we will feel. For instance, when some people are told they can't achieve their dreams, they give up and accept whatever comes to them, while others being told the same information will fight harder for their dreams.

All attitudes, thoughts, and beliefs are connected with the meridians of energy discussed in Chapter 9. Through kinesiologic testing, it can be demonstrated that specific acupuncture points are linked with specific attitudes, and the meridian, in turn serves as the energy channel to specific muscles and body organs.

Chapter 2 discussed the different attributes of energy. While there is an invisible universe of thoughts and attitudes, they become visible in our bodies. Look again at the GDV image of Dan and you can see the how rapidly the body can change as result of prevailing thought patterns. If we consider the millions of thoughts that go through the mind continually, it isn't surprising that the body's condition could radically change to reflect prevailing thought patterns, as modified by genetic and environmental factors. Redington, D., and Reidbond, S. Interestingly, David Hawkins, M.D., PhD. In *Power vs. Force* says that all illness should be reversible by changing thought patterns and habitual responses. Furthermore, he notes, that spontaneous recoveries from every disease known to man have been recorded throughout history.

Here's what happens in the body when it is faced with acute stress. The pea sized hypothalamus and the pituitary glands located in the brain create steroid hormones (glucocortocoids) that are sent to the adrenal glands. The hypothalamus, pituitary, and the pineal gland, the body's light meter, are embedded in the head and protected by the skull. Their sphere of influence of operation in the body is immeasurable. The primary stress hormone, cortisol is a hormone that quickly goes throughout the heart, lungs, circulation, metabolism, and immune system. It also exists through the skin and this is why we can smell fear.

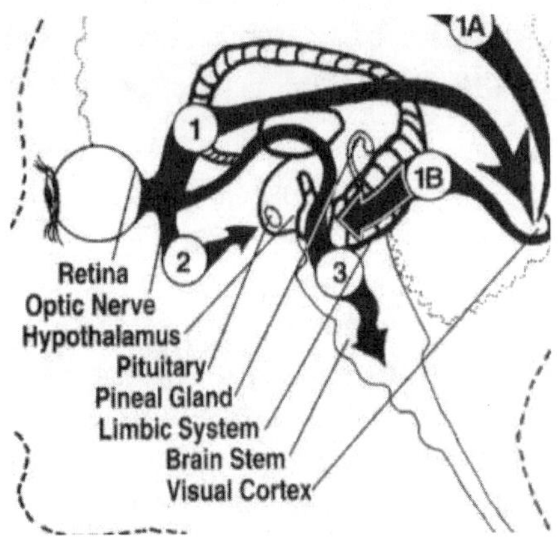

When a person has Chronic Fatigue Syndrome, the way that their muscle cells burn oxygen and other nutrients is abnormal and it is called “oxidative muscle metabolism”. ATP (adenosine triphosphate) is the chemical intermediate through which at least half of the energy of cells is released during the breakdown of carbohydrates, fats, and proteins. Half of the energy produced goes to the cell and the other half is released as heat energy. Creatine phosphate, which produces a phosphorus molecule, has to be around for the ATP to work and produce energy.

> “I breathe the light into my head and imagine a nebula of gold-white light inside my head and expanding outward, surround my head and expanding outward, surrounding my head until a shimmering gold-white light is all around my entire body. I remain in the shimmering gold-white light as I do the healing work.” K. Markikdes

Massaging The Throat Area

To stimulate the thyroid and other hormone-producing glands, place the hands under the neck with the thumb and fingers of one hand on opposite sides of the throat. Use the fingers to create a soft rolling motion. Stay gentle as you move down to the collarbone. Work your way back up to the jawbone. Change your hands and repeat slowly.

Exercises To Balance Your Energies

You probably already do some of the following natural activities to balance your body, which in turn, balances your energies.

When you are in deep thought, you rest your forehead on your thumb and forefinger, you place your hands behind your head when you are sitting or lying on the floor, you intertwine your fingers together over your stomach, or you cross your ankles. All of these activities help you get centered, balanced, and achieve stillness.

Hand Roll

Put your left hand on your forehead and place your right thumb above your naval with your fingers below it. Move your hand from right to left, either

quickly to stimulate or slowly to soothe. Keep your hand on the naval after you stop to feel the energy continue to move.
Use the hand roll to soothe an upset stomach, balance digestion functions, relieve confusion, fatigue, and poor performance.

The Jelly Roll works in the areas of digestion, for instance, soothing an upset stomach, circulation, action and confidence as it balances the Yang functions. In Martial Arts, the body's center of gravity and one of the major sources of outgoing force is called the hara. This is a good exercise to do before active movement. It can be done singly or in pairs.
Method
Place the left hand on the forehead and the right hand on the navel while you either lie, sit, or stand comfortably. The navel should be between the thumb and forefinger which enables you to rock the lower hand from side to side For stimulation, rock fast and firm and for a more soothing feeling, rock slow and soft After you stop you can feel the energy moving as a surge, tingling or other sensation if your hand remains in contact.

Before You Go To Bed
Do self-massage techniques to relax muscles, release mental and physical toxins, and promote health.
If you have some questions or challenges, ask the Creator to give you the answers the next morning. It works!
Meditation before bed helps relax your body to get a good night's sleep.
Deep breathing stimulates the lower abdominal area.
Relaxation exercises rid the body of throbs and pulsations.
Do neck pats.
Write all your thoughts and worries on an imaginary blackboard and then. erase them to release your thoughts so your mind doesn't rehash them all night.
Mental exercises to release worries, fears, anger, and doubts
Use sleep affirmations, releasing self-judgment and judgment of others to aid sleep.
Listen to meditative music or sounds of nature to put yourself to sleep.
Set your mind to dream.
Don't eat stimulants like sugar, chocolate or drink coffee or coke before sleep.
If you awaken during the night don't get in the habit of watching TV; do something you don't like to do so your mind will want to turn off.

Techniques Before You Get Out Of Bed To Start Every Day At Peak Performance

Pay attention to your thoughts when you first start to awaken.

Decide where to focus your energy and attention this day.

Clear out yesterday's thoughts so you have room for new ones.

Direct your energy toward today's goals.

Cross your arms and legs with deep breathing to increase your energy flow.

Tug on your ears to activate energy.

Making Your Shower More Healthy

Affirm your gratitude for everything you have, especially your body.

Sing.

Express self-love and unconditional love to others.

Early Morning One Minute Techniques

Do energy crossover technique with the legs to get the energy flowing.

Lightly hit your shoulder with a hairbrush to remove stagnate energy.

Do the energy fluff and energy weave described in the book.

Detoxify your dry cleaning by hanging it outside before you wear it.

Massage your navel clockwise with all your fingers and then use the palm of your hand over the whole abdominal area. Then massage counterclockwise.

What You Can Do While You Are Driving Your Car

Do the circulation meridian.

Do the Auric facelift. Start at the chine and move your hand up to the top of the head.

Zip up the central meridian.

Sing to raise your energy level.

Mind/Body Relaxation During the Day

Do deep breathing when you feel like you are "going to lose it".

Learn how to reprogram your autonomic nervous system.

Stop the committee of idiots by bringing in new thoughts.

Keeping the energy flowing through expressing time, money, connection, and love.

Be in the moment.

Do spontaneous actions to produce superior results.

Increase focused attention and concentration to decrease mistakes and accidents by doing the Thymus Thump, Cross Crawl, and Seated Crossover.

Do the Separating Heaven and Earth Exercise

Take a break from your work and do an energy exercise that activates your respiratory system. Separating Heaven and Earth pulls in extra oxygen, releases carbon dioxide, stretches the body so energy can more readily flow through it, and opens the joints, releasing trapped energy. It also opens the meridians while getting rid of toxic energies. Like any kind of movement, it stimulates energy to flow through the joints, muscles, and organs. If you feel that you have picked up unwanted energy from another person, do this exercise to release it.

Dirctions

1. Stand up. Spread you fingers and place your hands on your thighs.
2. As you do a deep inhalation through your nose, move your arms so they make a circle. Bring your hands to your chest as pictured. Exhale through your mouth.
3. Do another inhalation through your nose as you separate your arms. Flatten both of your hands. Stretch one arm above your head and push your hand upward. Then stretch your other arm down as if pushing something down. Stop when you feel like it.
4. Exhale through your mouth as you return your hands to the prayer position.
5. Repeat the exercise using the other hand. Do several sets.
6. Each time you bring your arm down bend your body at the waist. Bend your knees slightly as you take two deep breaths.
7. As you stand up, roll your shoulders backward.

Weaving The Aura

1.Place your open hands, spread fingers, on your thighs to ground yourself. Be aware of the energy traveling down your legs.
2.Rub your hands together to generate energy.
3. Lift your hands six inches away from your ears for about ten seconds.
4. Breathe in deeply as you bring your elbows together.
5. Cross your forearms and hands in front of your face as you exhale.
6. Allow your arms to swing naturally in front of you and cross one another as you inhale.
7. Bend at the waist, exhale as your swing your arms out.
8. Cross your arms at your ankles as you inhale.
9. Stay bent over, exhale, and swing your arms out.
10. Turn your hand frontward as you swing your arms behind you. Your knees are slightly bent as you bring the energy over your head while standing up. Visualize energy flowing all around your body.

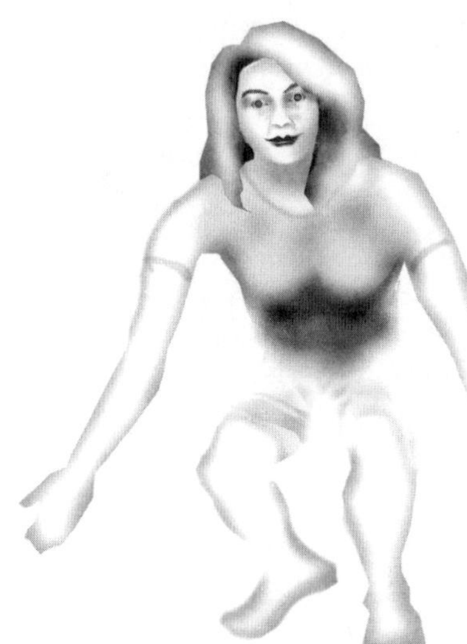

Cross Crawl

When the energy from either side of your body is not able to cross over, your energy will slow down dramatically. While the energy may move up and down the body, it does not move from one side to the other. Stagnant energy keeps your body from healing.

This technique facilitates the crossover energy between the brain's right and left hemispheres. It will help you think more clearly, feel more balanced by harmonizing your energies, and improve your coordination. If you are feeling physically or mentally exhausted, feeling worse after you exercise, or are feeling lethargic and unmotivated you need to take a few minutes for the cross crawl.

1. While standing, lift your left arm and right leg simultaneously. 2. As you let them down, raise your right arm and left leg. 3. Repeat, but this time exaggerate the lift of your leg and the swing of your arm across the midline to the opposite side of your body. 4. Continue this march for at least a minute, again breathing deeply in through your nose and out your mouth. John Philip Sousa music would be excellent here!

When I speak at conferences I ask a woman to walk around the room carrying her purse on one shoulder. When she is finished I do muscle testing to show the audience how the purse's strap has cut off her energy.
Cross your arms if you feel that you need to be in a defensive mode because someone is sending out negative energy. Crossing your arms and feet will help reconnect your energies.

Illness Prevention And Body Rejuvenation

Techniques to increase vitality and strength: Separating Heaven and Earth, thymus thumps, K-27 points, and spinal flush.
Trace the meridians each day:.
Techniques to boost your immune system: Spinal flush, neurolymphatic reflex points.
Learn how to control your body's blood pressure, heartbeat, brain waves and muscle contraction using meditation.

Pain

Did you know that you can feel pain in a person as far as twenty feet away? Pain can feel warm, even hot and more than likely congested. It has a tension or vibration so you can also locate it with your pendulum in the person's energetic field. Ask the pendulum to swing clockwise or back and forth toward you to signify the pain location. Remember that pain is energy and has all the attributes of energy–it is moveable and transferable so it can be smoothed out. Begin at the farthest point you sense the pain and take several minutes to smooth out the pain while you are moving closer and closer to the body.
This technique can be used with migraine headaches, TMJ, trigeminal neuralgia, and fractured bones.

Ultrasound can be used on muscles and joints where pain is experienced. Often pain comes from a spinal area; for example, the hip joint may hurt from an energy block in the back. To find the pain, ask the person, use a pendulum or do muscle testing to show you the exact location of the pain. Place your hands above the location, set your intention to remove the pain, and then direct energy to the painful location with your thoughts.

Cliff Hanger

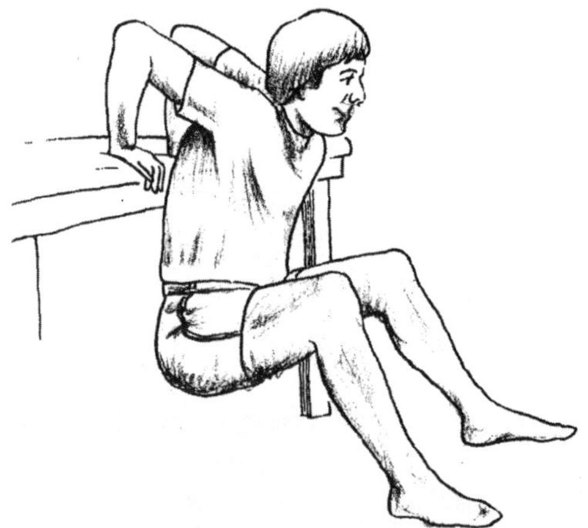

Before you do this exercise be sure that you do some warm up exercises like yoga, reflexology and lengthening. Dr. Stone, the creator of this exercise, said in *Health For Building,* the shoulder level base and the hip base must be engaged simultaneously in one stretching posture to move the gross energy blocks by means of the subtle energy in the united actions on both levels.

Technique: Stand with your sacrum and heels of the hands resting on the edge of the table. Your feet are shoulder-width or maybe slightly further apart. Your back will have slight contact with the table as you drop down.

You will feel most of the weight on your hands. The pelvis will feel like it is hanging from the spine. Do not tighten your buttocks or stomach muscles. Feel relaxed, breathe easily, and hold your head down.

The benefits of this exercise are that you will feel a release of tension in the chest, neck, shoulders, diaphragm and pelvic areas. It is a preventative for chronic heart conditions. By breathing deeply, you will be more aware of the world around you. For those who feel pushed back by life and have a concave chest, this exercise will increase use of unused lung areas.

Neck Pain

If you have pain in the lower part of the back, it is usually necessary to have someone send energy to the neck also. And vice versa. The energy sender should use a lighter touch when working on the neck than on the back. You need to look at the spine as one unit so you need to have an energy practioner work on the whole spine.

To relieve neck pain, have an energy practioner place their fingertips on the occipital ridge, where the skull and neck meet, for two minutes and then down the vertebrae in the neck. They should hold their fingers longer in the pain and tightness locations. Then they should send energy in the lower back, and the front and back of the hips.

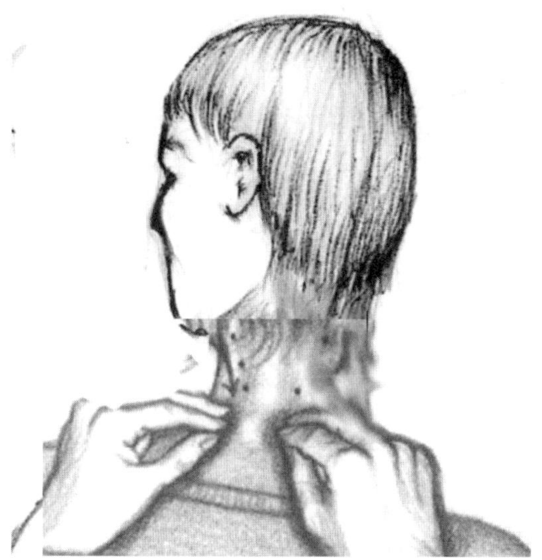

Back Pain And Stiffness

Most back problems are caused by a person's belief that they are burdened. Edgar Cayce, known as "America's Sleeping Prophet," received information from his readings that the adrenals glands, situated on top astride and back of the kidneys, are the storehouse of one's emotional ***karma*** in the body. I recommend that you read Cayce's books and *The Healing Secrets of the Ages* by Catherine Ponder, a pioneer of positive thinking.

Back pain is caused by the accumulation of toxins and tension in the stomach that then press against the nerves, muscles, and tendons causing the nerves to stop communicating. Consequently the muscles do not receive the message to relax.

Lower back pain: massage the Achilles tendon to relieve tightness

Note that the inside edge of the foot looks and corresponds to the back. Massage this area of the foot to relieve back pain.

Work on both sides of the spine to alleviate neck or back pain. Place your hand or fingers on the back at the ends of each vertebra. Use the thumb, index, and middle fingers of each hand at the location of the pain. The energy that resonates between your fingers will cause the vertebrae to quickly move back into correct alignment.

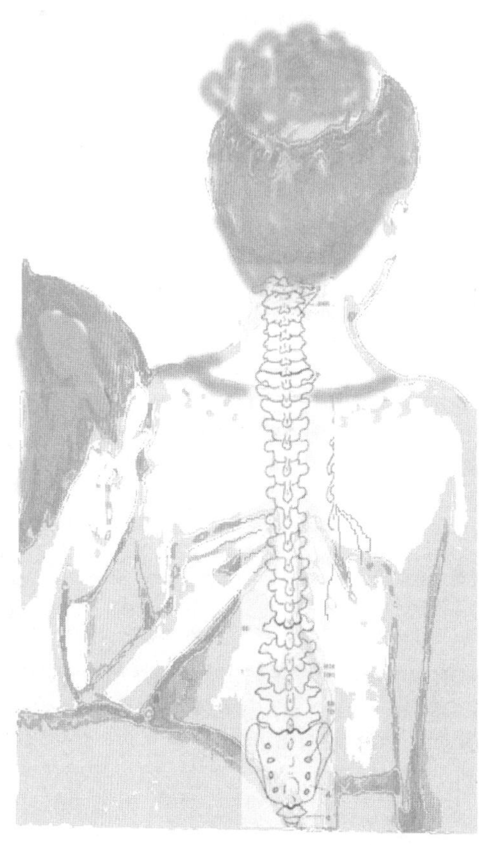

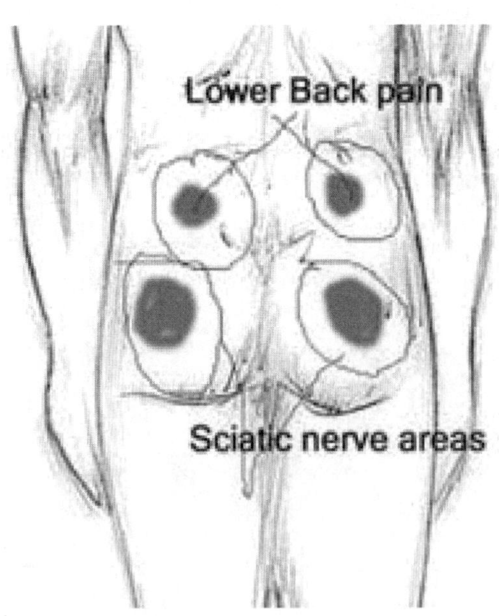
Lower Back pain
Sciatic nerve areas

Oh My Sciatica!
Look at the picture on the preceding page to fine the sciatic nerves and have the energy sender place their thumbs there, holding longer on the side with the most pain. Soon the pain will move down the legs or to the foot. The energy sender should continue to send energy to these painful places.

Computer And Desk Exercises
Sit with your ankles and legs out to the sides as far as you can comfortably. Keep you arms straight and place the palms of the hands on the knees, fingers on the outside, thumbs on the inside. Let your shoulders bear the torso's weight. Push outward to open the pelvic area. Stretch slowly to elongate the spine. Gently rocking forward and backward or side-to-side will release the neck and shoulder tension acquired from mental concentration and non-movement.

How To Stay Energized While Traveling
Wonder why travel takes so much energy out of you? You may find that you are so tired that you can't sleep or you need a huge amount of sleep to finally feel rested. When you try to work you are unable to focus or concentrate. You may find yourself just trying to get through the day, maybe a little short tempered, your whole body, even your eyes are sore. When you fly you receive excessive exposure to Electromagnetic fields and Cosmic Radiation. Staying indoors in buildings, airplanes and cars causes you to be sun light deprived. Both heat and air conditioning cause you to be dehydrated.

Riding in a car for several hours is exhausting because your body is bombarded by the car's vibration that is out of sync with your own vibration. Bucket car seats and small airline seats force you to remain stationary, preventing body movement. Want to arrive at your destination energized? Here are some suggestions.

- ✓ Don't drink coffee, tea or soft drinks several hours prior to travel because they all contain caffeine that dehydrates your body.
- ✓ Drink plenty of water, lay off the salt on your food, especially the salty pretzels and nuts the airlines give you; instead, eat foods rich in water such as fruit.
- ✓ If you are driving, make stops every few hours and walk around briskly.
- ✓ Move around on the plane as much as you can.
- ✓ While you are traveling either in a car or plane, use your mind to send electrical energy through your muscles. Far fetched as it may sound, you can actually build muscles without exercising by thinking and then choosing to send energy through your muscles. That's how your muscles perform all their activities anyhow. You can actually build up your muscles using your mind energy!

Pete had his GDV images (Figure 10) done the day after he had just spent two weeks in London going to a workshop, gotten up at 5 A.M and flown for eight hours on an airplane. You could look at his body, especially his eyes and face, and see that all his energies were drained. His images in the colored illustrations give you good insight in to why you feel so tired after your trips.

Products to avoid

Deodorants with aluminum salts, benzene in colognes and perfumes, propyl alcohol in shampoos, soaps made from animal fats, lye, synthetic smelling agents, formaldehyde (also called formalin).

References

Berkson, The Foot Book: Healing the Body through Foot Reflexology, 1992, p. 46-53

Forem, Jack, Steve Shimer *Healing with Pressure Point Therapy* published by Prentice Hall, 1999, 17.

Markides, K, (1987) Homage to the sun (p,8), New York: Arkana Books, Penguin Group, p. 12.

Redington, D., and Reidbond,S., Journal of Nervous and Mental Disease. No. 180, pgs. 649-665; No.181, pgs 428-435. 1993.

Stone, Health Building, p.180.

Stone, Polarity Therapy, Vol. I, Book 2, p. 11, 37,40, 44, 80.

Stone, Polarity Therapy Vol. II, p. 105 ff, pp.183-184.

Walther, D., *Applied Kinesiology,* Pueblo, Colorado: Systems DC. 1976, p. 124.

Conclusion

I have become impatient with many things, two of which are: the media describing people as "ordinary" and "average". We are fabulous works of individual and extraordinary creation. I hope you marvel at all the activities going on in your body every microsecond. All of these activities join together to create your aura. I also have a problem with people who hold ignorant beliefs in things that they have not studied or are not open to learning about. Access to information is so easy today we have no excuses not to understand how subtle energy works.

Finishing this book was such a relief I told my friends it would be a long time before I wrote another one! I hope that I succeeded in laying the groundwork proving that there is subtle energy and explaining its properties. The more that you understand how subtle energy works, the more powerful you will become.

Admittedly though, I realized that I had only scratched the surface on the topic of energy. I was beginning to formulate in my mind what I would write about in the next book and the ones to follow. Knowledge and the speed of the planet have dramatically increased. My job is to educate people about energy and share the increased use of vibrational medicine so that people are empowered to be responsible for their health. We are still in physical body form so it is our responsibility to be proactive concerning health. I also want to show people the power of connection on all levels, and to present more techniques to access the wisdom of Universal Mind. Most people are afraid of the power they possess.

Here is a list of things to do to transform your life:

1. Learn how to break the contracts you have made with people in this lifetime and past lifetimes who are holding you back from achieving your purpose in life.
2. Carefully guard your energy field and remove all energy vampires.
3. Remove all negative thought forms from your environment: mind, furniture, and space.
4. Seek help from your angels and guides.
5. Learn to trust the information you receive from your body.
6. Always commit to "do no harm".
7. Do not "Neglect your soul or you will forfeit your happiness."

Appendix

Pendulum

The pendulum is an extension of our higher self and it depends upon our awareness. Our thoughts are able make connection with objects almost instantaneously.

History

Feng shui masters used pendulums over 5,000 ago to ensure that buildings were constructed in earthquake free, healthy areas.

Egyptians tombs contain pendulums and other dowsing instruments.

Early Celts dowsed for water, minerals, and items in the soil.

Abbé Mermet was a French priest who practiced dowsing with a pendulum (also called radiesthesia) for over forty years throughout Europe and at the Vatican. He was able to pinpoint water sources, monitor train traffic from a distance, solve crimes, treasure hunt, find missing people, analyze illnesses, and select proper remedies.

How the pendulum works

The body has thirty-seven miles of nervous system that tunes into subtle vibrations. The body contains 99% of the subtle energy in the body. We are able to receive information from Universal Mind via the Universal Energy Field.

How to use a pendulum

Clear your mind of all extraneous thoughts. Hold the string or chain of the pendulum between your thumb and index finger.

Make an agreement with your pendulum about which direction indicates "yes" and which direction indicate "no". My agreement is that the pendulum will swing clockwise for flowing energy and in body and counterclockwise for blocked energy. It moves back and forth toward me for a yes answer to a question and from side to side for a no answer.

If you have not asked the questions properly or it is not a question that you should have asked the pendulum will move diagonally.

Get a book on pendulums for more details

Glossary

Applied Kinesiology or Muscle Testing: Two things to remember: the body does not lie, and it will tell you everything you need to know about your health. Applied Kinesiology or muscle testing is a balancing technique that evaluates the function and effectiveness of muscles. When you restore a muscle by restoring the energy flow, you also restore the energy to the organ that is sharing that system.
ATP: Adenosine triphosphate, a tiny molecule made from the food and sunlight we take in every day. At least 2 million ATP molecules vibrate every one ten-thousandth of a second in each of our 75 trillion cells to serve as a powerful info-energetic source.
Aura: also called Human Energy Field or bioplasmic body, a light or radiance emanating from the body
Amorphous: having no definite form, shapeless, an amorphous cloud
Balance: describes reducing surplus or increasing deficiency to achieve an equality of force.
Biomagnetic: the study of magnetic fields produced by living things
Bioenergetics: the study of energy transformation in living systems
Bioplasmic Body: aura or Human energy field
Bodywork: energy-balancing contact.
Breathing: refers to conscious inhalation and exhalation, often timed with specific movements, sometimes combined with sound. Breathing contributes physical, emotional and esoteric benefits.
Consciousness: the totality of the impressions, thoughts and feelings of an individual; the output expressions from the manifested in-dwelling spirit of an individual
Crystallization: derived from the Greek "congealed by cold," are solids that have long-range order and regular periodicity in their structures.
Cytoskeletal: the nervous system of the cell
Emergent properties: one example is consciousness
Entrainment: When two similarly tuned systems align their movement and energy so that they match in rhythm and phase. For instance, two grandfather clocks mounted in the same wall with their pendulums wining out of phase to one another, will come into phase with one another because of the energy transfer through the wall.
Ether: from the Sanskrit *aksash.* Parahahansa Yogananda spoke of ether as the background on which God projects the cosmic motion picture of creation. Space gives dimension to object, ether separates the images.
Gamma ray: A beam of high-energy photons of the type emitted in some nuclear or subatomic particle decays. Gamma rays are similar to X rays in much of their behavior.
Higher self: soul
Homeopathy:
Vibrational essences can include energies from a whole host of natural phenomenon including gems, flowers, trees, music, butterflies, sounds, thunderstorms and energy from different Earth and spiritual sources. Each remedy contains a unique high-frequency energy and its use will transfer the essence vibration into our own physical and energetic bodies, so that areas of imbalance are adjusted.
Human Energy Field: see aura
Intentionality: the quality of one's conscious purpose, often thought of as self-directed mind.
Ions: Ions are an electrically charged atom or molecule. They are created when atoms and molecules exchange tiny negatively charged articles called electrons.

Kirlian Photography- Discovered by Semyon Davidovich Kirlian in 1939 in Krasnodar, near the Black Sea in Russia. Semyon an electrician, and his wife, Valentina Kirlian, a teacher and journalist, became fascinated by the sight of a tiny flash of light which occurred between the electrodes of an electrotherapy machine and the skin of a patient. Other Russian scientists had also noted this energy, but ignored it. The equipment and procedures they finally developed were to record on film this luminous energy emanating from the physical body-the HEF. They invented a new type of photography, and had more than fourteen patents. The original system photographed static images of fingers or leaves. Next, they developed a special optical instrument to observe the motion of this luminous phenomenon. Now they saw the hand as either flashing, sparkling, steadily glowing, or as diminishing particles of light. They also showed the difference in the HEF of a human being harboring a disease that had not as of yet manifested symptoms in the human body!

Light: Light is color, vibratory wave bands of photons. Color is light at various frequencies. When pure light intermingles and integrates with the atoms of matter, colors, hues, and intensities are created.

Living matrix: The connective tissue of the body.

Magnetbiology: the study of the effects of magnetic fields on living systems

Microtubules: Hollow tubes in every cell in the body latticed with kernel-like hexagons that contain and convey intracellular information.

Movement: increases circulation, fires neurons, exercises muscles.

Non-Linear: situation where the response is not simply proportional to the stimulus.

Nonlocality: Principle that states distance and barriers of time and space are illusions.

Polarization: the shifting away from neutral balance. In dielectrics, it is associated with the displacement of positive and negative electric charges.

Reciprocal Determinism: The theory that individuals can be self-directive and exercise some control over their thoughts, feelings, and actions through conscious decision.

Resonance: When sound waves from one instrument transfer acoustical energy to another tuned instrument and they play the same note. All object have a certain natural or resonant frequency caused by either striking it, bumping it, pluck it, or heating it.

Shiatsu: Therapists uses his or her palms, knuckles, elbows, fists, or feet to apply pressure in the optimum ways for the points and meridians being treated. Probably brought to Japan in the 6th century by Buddhist monks.

Spectroscope: a device that uses a prism to separate light into its many component colors, each of which corresponds to a wave of a definite wavelength.

Subtle energies: all those energies existing in the universe beyond the four known: weak and strong nuclear, electrical, magnetic, and chemical.

Systems Theory: The concept that all people, places, things, and forces in the universe are integrated into a hierarch of mutually influential matter and energy.

Volume Conduction: Concept that says that the electrical potential generated by the heart and as measured by an electrocardiograph can be recorded from any side on the body. The entire body is a moment-to-moment expression of the info-energy of its heart. The heart sends out energy at the speed of light to connect with other energy systems.

Wave/Particle Duality: Everything in the cosmos is both “matter” and “energy.” All particles are waves and vice versa, whether the particle or wave nature of something is observed is determined by what is being looked for and when.

Suggested Reading

Achterberg, J. Imagery and Healing: Shamanism & Modern Medicine. New Science Library: Boston, MA 1985.
Bailey, Alice A. Esoteric Healing. Lucis Trust Publishing Co.: Albany, NY. 1984
Bailey, Alice, A. Serving Humanity, Lucis Publishing Co.: Albany NY. 1993.
Becker, Robert O., et al. The Body Electric: Electromagnetism and the Foundation of Life. New York: William Morrow and Company, 1987
Benford, Sue, et al. "Exploring the Concept of Energy in Touch-Based Healing" in Clinician's Complete Reference to Complementary and Alternative Medicine, ed.
Benor, Daniel Healing Research: Holistic Energy Medicine and Spirituality, Helix Editions: United Kingdom, 1992.
Benor, Daniel, *Spiritual Healing: Scientific Validation of a Healing Revolution,* Visions Publications, 2001
Borysenko, Joan. Minding the Body, Mending the Mind. Reading, Addison-Wesley Publishing Company, Inc.: Reading, MA. 1987
Brennen, Barbara, Light Emerging, New York, NY: Bantam Books, 1993
Brennen, Barbara, Hands of Light: A Guide to Healing Through the Human Energy Field. New York, NY: Bantam Books, 1998
Breilling, Brian, Light Years Ahead, The Illustrated Guide to Full Spectrum and Colored Light in Mindbody Healing, Celestial Arts, Berkeley, California
Bridges: Quarterly magazine of the International Society for the Study of Subtle Energies and Energy Medicine. Boulder CO.
Brodie, Renee, Crystal Bowl Therapy and Holographic Sound Healing!
Brodie, Renee The Healing Tones of Crystal Bowls
Bruyere, Rosalyn. Wheels of Light. Simon & Schuster: NY, NY. 1990.
Capra, Fritjof. The Turning point: Science, Society, and the Rising Culture. Simon & Schuster: NY, NY, 1990.
Carter, Mildred, Body Reflexology, Prentice Hall, Paramus, NJ 1994
Chia, Mantak & Maneewan. Chi Nei Tsang: Internal Organs Chi Massage. Healing Toa Books.: Huntington, NY. 1990
Chopra, Deepak, Quantum Healing. Bantam Books: NY,NY. 1989.
Collinge, William, PhD. Subtle Energy: Awakening to the Unseen Forces in Our Lives. New York: Warner Books, Inc. 1998
Dossey, Larry, M.D. Reinventing Medicine: Beyond Mind-Body to a New Ear of Healing. New York: Warner Books, Inc., 1998
Dossey, Larry. M.D. Healing Beyond the Body: Medicine and the Infinite Reach of the Mind. Shambhala Publications. Boston, MA. 2001
Dossey, Larry. Reinventing Medicine. HarperSan Francisco: San Francisco, CA. 1999.
Eisenberg, David. Encounters with Qi Exploring Chinese Medicine. W.W. Norton & Co: NY, NY. 1985.
Ferguson. M. "Kirlian Photos Forecast Illness," Brain/Mind Bulletin, Los Angeles: CA, May 7, 1984.
Forem, Jack, Shimer, Steve, Healing With Pressure Point Therapy, Prentice Hall, Paramus, NJ
Gerber, Richard, Vibrational Medicine, Inner Traditions International, Limited 2001
Gerber, Richard, Vibrational Medicine for the 21st Century: The Complete Guide to Energy Healing and Spiritual Transformations. Harper\Collins Publishers: NY, NY. 2000.

Gordon, Richard, Quantum Touch, North Atlantic Books, Berkeley, California, 2002.
Hay, Louis. You Can Heal Your Life. The Hay House, Inc. Carlsbad, CA. 1984.
Hunt, Valerie V., Infinite Mind: Science of Human Vibrations of Consciousn*ess,* Malibu Publishing Company, 1996
Joy, Brugh, Joy's Way. Jeremy P. Tarcher: NY, NY. 1979.
Krippner, Stanley, Villoldo, Alberto. The Realms of Healing. Celestial Arts: Millbrae, CA. 1976.
Meek, G. Healers and the Healing Process. Theosophical Publishing House: London, England. 1977.
Ornish, Dean. Love & Survival: The Scientific Basis for the Healing Power of Intimacy, HarperCollins Publishers: NY, NY. 1998.
Oschman, James L., Energy Medicine: The Scientific Basis, Churchill Livingstone, Inc., 2000
Oschman, James L Energy Medicine in Therapeutics and Human Performance. Butterworth Heinemann, Boston 2003.
Redpath,l W.M. Trauma Energetics: A Study of Held-Energy Systems. Barberry Press: Lesington, MA. 1994.
Rubik, Beverly. Life at the Edge of Science. Institute of Frontier Science. Oakland, CA, 1996.
Russek, L.G. and Schwartz, G. Energy cardiology: A Dynamical Energy Systems Approach for Integrating Conventional and Alternative Medicine. Advances. 12 (4), 4-24. 1996.
Sherwood, Keith, The Art of Spiritual Healing. Llewellyn: St. Paul, MN. 1985.
Slate, Joe, Aura Energy, Llewellyn Worldwide, 2000 (Contact information: Joe H. Slate, % Llewellyn Worldwide, P.O. Box 64383, Dept. K637-8, St. Paul, MN, 55164-0383, U.S.A.)
Tiller, William, 1997. Science and Human Transformation: Subtle Energies. Intentionality and Consciousness. Pavior Publishing: Walnut Creek, CA. 1997.

Other Suggested Readings
AquaTerra, Jacqueline Froelich
Geopathic Stress–How Earth Energies Affect Our Lives, Jane Thurnell-Read
Living Energies, Callum Coats
Living Water, Olaf Alexanderson
The Water Wizard, Callum Coats

Institutes

The School of Syntonic Optometry, a non-profit corporation dedicated to research in photoretinology, the therapeutic application of light to the visual system.
Dr. Samuel Pesner, Journal Editor, 133 Second Street Los Altos, CA 94002, 415-948-3700
Society for Light Treatment and Biological Rhythms, P.O. Box 47, Wilsonville, OR 97070, 503-694-2404
Light Therapy Information Service, New York Psychiatric Institute, 212-960-5714
A referral source for information on light therapy for seasonal affective disorder, sleep disorders, jet lag, shift work adjustment, chronobiology, and biological rhythms.
The International Society for the Study of Subtle Energies and Energy Medicine
5800 West 6th, Topeka, KS 66606, 913-273-7500
The Fetzer Institute, Dr. Arthur Zajonc, President, Kalamazoo, MI 49009, 616-345-8387 This non-profit is dedicated to mindbody approaches to health and healing. It

supports research on the bio-electromagnetic and subtle energetic nature of the human body.
The Qi Gong Institute East-West Academy of Healing Arts, Kenneth M. Sanciker, Ph.D. 450 Sutter Street. #2104. Sam Francisco. CA 94108. 415-788-2227. 415-3123-1221
Institute for Frontier Science. 6114 LaSalle Ave. Oakland, CA 94611. 610-5231-5767. e-mail brubik@compuserve.com htt//www.healthy.net/frontierscience/

Organizations
Barbara Brennan School Of Healing, P.O. Box 2005, East Hampton, NY 11937. 516-329-0951 Fax 516-324-9745. e-mail:bbshoffice@barbarabrennan.com
Healing Light Center Church 261 E Alegna Ave. #12. Sierra Madre, CA 91024 626-306-2170 Fax: 626-355-0996.
International Society for the Study of Subtle Energies and Energy Medicine (ISSEEM). 356 Goldco Circle. Golden, CO 80401 303-27-226

I recommend the Nova series on PBS called *Our Elegant World.* It is most informative, enlightening, and masterfully presented. The series informs you about the String Theory which contends that everything in the universe of made of strings of energy.

Index

Abundant splendor 150
Acupressure Points Chapter 9 126, 134
Acupuncture 24,25,56, 65, 84, 91, 103, 105, 135, 137,155, 162, 169, 170, 192, 197
Adjoining valley 147, 201, 219, 220, 224
Aura, 4, 14, 37-39, 55, 59, 71, 88, 109, Chapter 8, 182
Balance buttons 211
Basset, Andrew 44, 50-51
Baule, G.M. 25, 74
Bigger rushing 148
Black light 40, 61
Bodies of the aura, 5
Brain energy balance 96
Brain buttons 2101
Brennen, Barbara 65, 181
Brodie, Renee 168-170
Bubbling springs 146
Chakras24, 33, 60-61, 65, 163, 165, 169, 170,186, 299
Chi 46,47
Chi Net Tsand 181
Cliff hanger 229
Collinge 107
Consciousness 157, 162, 222
Cook's hook-ups 207-208
Conklin, Patti 164-165
Connective tissue 44, 175, 176
Cross crawl 225, 227
Crystalline 47, 50, 52, 165
Crystals 54, 171, 193
Defensive mode 31,184, 228,
Distant healing 29
Dowsing 4, 35
Dubin, Bob 108
Earth buttons 209
Einstein 3, 8, 9, 39, 107, 166
Electrical 10, 15. 21, 24-29, 39, 43, 45
Electrocardiogram 19
Electromagnetic fields 19-20, 40, 49-53, 59, 63,69-70
Electromagnetic energy 16, 20-21, 32, 40, 93, 175
Emotional energy 12, 71, 195-196, 204,99
Emotional Freedom Technique 24, 30, 75, 103, 87, 89, 103, 87, 101
Energy Age 13
Energy clusters 118
Energy healers 24, 156, 190
Energy leaks 1o8, 116,117
Energy release, channel 151
Energy streams 117
Energy vampires 113, 190
Energy wells 189
Focal center 143-144

Floyd, Keith 17
Foot reflexology 212-214
Forem, Jack 150-172
Gas Discharge Camera 24, 29, 32, 79, 88, 81, 116, 158, 197
Gerber, Richard M.D. 87, 106, 155, 161
Gimbel, Theo 163
Green, Elmer 26
Hand roll 223
Hand reflexology 214
Hawkin, Stephen 14
Hawkins, David, Dr. 87, 195, 222
Headaches 145, 147, 150, 228
Healing channel 152
Hippocrates, 81
Human Energy Field 2, 9, 15, 18, 28, 37, 81
Hunt, Valorie 37
Hypothalamus 43, 69, 76, 189
Imagery 90, 94, 168
Inyushin, Victor 2
Johnson, J. F. 52
Julie 71, 113. 114, 117-118, 196
Kargagulla, S. 70
LeDoux, Joseph 90-91
Lieberman, Jacob 106
Lifting the sky 145-146
Lipton, Bruce 15, 46-48, 160
Lord's Prayer 60
Lung press 198
Magnetic 16, 24-27, 30, 36, 41, 53-54, 56
Magnetic Resonance Imaging MRI 25, 55, 164
Magnetic ruffle 19, 188
Magnetocardiogram 19, 54, 70
Maman, Fabien 169
Mandel, Peter 104
Marshall, 104
Marciniak, Barbara 169
Masochistic Defense 183,
Mc Williams, Charles 62, 103. 201
Melody, 44
Medical Intuitives 50, 109, 159
Meditation 60, 167, 189, 202, 206
Meridians Chapter 9
Mesmer 84
Miksell, Norm 53, 65
Motoyama, Hiroshi 25
Motz, J 28
Muscular armor 98
Myss, Carolyn 159
Nadis 65-66, 105
Non-local (energy) 27,55, 73

Oschman, James 162
Occipital bone 94, 204, 229
Oster, G 57
Owl 216
Paracelsus 83-84
Pearsall, Paul 31. 33
Pendulum 50, 195, 202, 217, 228,
Physical energy 3, 6-7, 54, 69, 71, 74, 106, 107
Pool at the crook 147
Posture 161, 163, 175
Psychological energy 99, 103
Piezoelectricity 44, 50, 51
Points of light 118
Polarity Therapy 16, 155, 170
Ponder, Katherine 193
Powell, A.E. 112
Prana 56, 65, 66, 81, 82, 83, 168
Pranic healing 83, 164
Psychometry 4
Pulsed electromagnetic field 49, 162
Qigong 35, 83
Quantum physics 9, 25, 30, 38, 104
Rapp. P.R. 47
Reflex points, 52, 143, 211, 228
Reflexology 171-172
Rein, Glen 78
Relativity (energy) 23
Resonance 15, 38, 51, 77
Rigid Defense 186
Rhythmic pulse 14
Rolf, Ida 120
Rubik, Beverly 84
Russek, Linda 19
Schizoid character 182
Separating Heaven and Earth 228
Sherwood, Keith, 65
Shiatsu points 143
Slate, Joe 18, 108, 119
Schwartz, Gary 19, 22, 58
Sea of blood 149
Sound Therapy Healing 167-170
Space buttons 209, 215
SQUID Superconducting Quantum Interference Device 25, 70
Stars 18-19
Star Powered Healing 163
States of mind 116
Stone, Randolph 15-16, 171
Stress relief 9, 119, 204
Subtle energy, 2-4, 6-7, 17-18 Chap. 2, Chap. 3, 53-54 ,65-69, 73. 5-6
Supreme Stream 148

Synapses 50, 90-91,189
Tansley, David 65
Thought Field Therapy 24, 103
Three mile foot 148
Thought forms 35, 53, 71
Thymus Thump 218, 225
Tiller, William, 2, 35, 79
Three yin meeting 147
Tsong, 46
Universal Energy Field, UEF 1,9, 11. 23, 27, 39, 59, 66, 74,85, 105, 118, 179
Universal Mind 1, 4, 12, 18, 27, 38, 85, 113, 163
Vibrational 10. 15, 19, 36, 43, 46, 50, 53, 56, 79, 87, 105, 116, 155, 162
Visualization 17, 24,29, 31,61, 74, 76, 78, 191, 200, 205
Yang 26, 27, 69, 72, 81, 145, 170
Yin 26, 27, 69, 72, 81, 84, 145, 170
Water, structured 64
Weaving the aura 227
White, John 83
White light 156, 191, 200, 203, 216, 223
Wind pool 150, 221
Zinn, Jon Kabat 8
Zukav, Gary 6, 59,

Biography

Barbara Gray is the author of Life's Instruction Books for Women, Volumes I, II, and III, Come Grow With Me, Success Through Spirituality for Women, The Christmas Angels, Energy Management, How To Increase Your Positive Energy Levels, and Secrets Of Energy.

"Three experiences with one of the rarest forms of cancer, myoleiosarcoma, forced me to do some serious reflection and inspired me to become an expert in using my God-given Internal Resources–the power of my mind to control my thoughts and emotions and to receive intuitive information."

ENERGY MANAGMENT™ grew from studying Tai Chi, Energy Medicine, Ki, Progressive Relaxation, Matrix Integration Healing, Prana Healing, Chi Nei Tsang (internal organ massage), Foot, Hand, and Body Reflexology, and Quantum Healing. Attendees to Gray's workshops and seminars learn how the body's energy flow determines health, the body's energy pathways-meridians, the body's acupuncture strengthening and sedating points. She helps people remove energy blocks using the Emotional Freedom Technique.

A visionary and intuitive, Barbara sees and feels energy emanating in the electro-magnetic fields of people, businesses, and in objects. She is in private practice as an Energy Psychology Practioner and has the ability to help people heal physically and emotionally. Barbara was publisher of the Metro-Atlanta Health and Wellness Directory.

She teaches classes and speaks on developing internal resources, creativity and intuition, communication, self-reflection, meditation, healing, and success to associations, government agencies, hospitals and healthcare employees, businesses and corporations, and churches.

Energy Management Seminars

Barbara Gray, **America's "Energy Expert,"** is the creator of the world's most innovative and transformative **Employee Productive System**. ENERGY MANAGEMENT™ is a system teaching and a catalyst for: **Thinking, Acting,**

and Producing at the **Highest Level**, and **Focusing** and **Directing Energies** for **company profitability**.

ENERGY MANAGEMENT™ is filled with so many fresh ideas it is literally in a class by itself. Barbara transmits her energy to audiences and businesses teaching people how to expand their sphere of influence beyond their dreams. She has the stage presence necessary to communicate with large audiences connecting with every member of the audience so that they feel that she is talking just to them, despite the hundreds of other people in the room.

Barbara Gray electrifies audiences with her magical personal energy by talking about new concepts and ideas that are absolutely necessary for **productivity** and **peak performance** in today's fast-paced and every-changing market. ENERGY MANAGEMENT™ provides companies the creative and provocative thinking to establish staying power. **Barbara connects with virtually every group in every industry celebrating the diversity of people who are specialists in considerably different fields.**

Who doesn't need more energy and want to know the most effective ways to use it? Her approaches to sales and marketing, leadership, and management are drawn from timeless wisdom, not just quick-fix fads. Her client focus is organizational.

Audiences will hear innovative, successful ideas that highly successful companies can use to motivate their people. Barbara is sensitive to the individual needs of her clients. She is an interesting, caring professional interested in building productive workplaces plus high performance individuals and teams. *She never tells an audience what to do without telling them how to do it.* ***Furthermore, she motivates people to want to do it! Managers and supervisors will discover how to inspire employees to*** *DESIRE* ***to give their best.*** *They will learn to transform employees who just show up for work into enthusiastic producers.*

Gray has spent the last twelve years studying energy and researching with the Gas Discharge Visualization Camera. The GDV camera shows a person's mental, physical, emotional energy levels. The camera is also being researched by the National Institute of Health.

"The most important thing to do to be successful is to decide how you choose to use your energy and where you want to direct it." Barbara Gray

Contact Information:

Starlight Productions 770-971-0179
399 Old Canton Road, Marietta, Georgia 3006
barbaragray399@Comcast.net
www.energiesmanagement.net